THE COMPLETE ACTIVITY GUIDE

The Complete
ACTIVITY GUIDE

Angela Hollest & Penelope Gaine

PIATKUS

To David, Edward and Clare
and Michael, David and Daniel

First published in
Great Britain in 1987 by
Judy Piatkus (Publishers) Limited
5 Windmill Street, London W1P 1HF

British Library Cataloguing in Publication Data

Hollest, Angela
  The complete activity guide.
  1. Games 2. Amusements
  I. Title II. Gaine, Penelope
  790.1'922   GV1203

  ISBN 0-86188-617-8
  ISBN 0-86188-622-4 Pbk

Edited by Clare Bond
Illustrated by Julian Sharp
Designed by Paul Saunders

Phototypeset in 10/12pt VIP Times by
D P Media Ltd, Hitchin
Printed & bound in Great Britain by
Mackays of Chatham Ltd

CONTENTS

Acknowledgements

We should like to thank all the organisations and individuals who have been so helpful in supplying us with information, in particular the Anglia Holiday Club, Ann Sachs, Claudette Bush, Peter de Voile, Pam Gale, Didi Helme, Sue Martineau, Basil Morgan, Maggie Shepherd, Marion Swetenham, Rosie Tinny, Cherry Vernon Harcourt. We should also like to thank Jean Shave for her hard work in typing the manuscript; Tom Serby for allowing us to use extracts from his experiences abroad, our editor Gill Cormode for her constant kindness and patience, and finally Judy Piatkus for her support and encouragement.

The authors and publisher have made every effort to ensure that all the information in this book is accurate at the time of going to press. However, no guide book can ever be completely up to date. Any correspondence in connection with *The Complete Activity Guide* should be addressed to Angela Hollest and Penelope Gaine, c/o Piatkus Books, 5 Windmill Street, London W1P 1HF.

Please note that in the few places where phone numbers are not included, this is because the people or group concerned would prefer you to write in to them rather than telephone.

INTRODUCTION

'I'm bored' – You won't be after flicking through this book! There is something here for everyone whether aged 8 or 18. At the outset we had not realised what we were letting ourselves in for! It is quite staggering how many opportunities there are available for the young of today, if you know where and how to get going. We have sifted through mountains of information to channel you in the right direction. The details we give are designed to help you and your parents see what's on offer. Much of the material will be invaluable for holiday activities, but term-time, indeed, lifelong interests may well follow from them.

In the first chapter we cover sport, and what a choice there is here! Try some of the new ones like street or roller hockey, bicycle polo, American football or cyclo-cross. Whatever your inclinations are there is something for the least gamesy amongst you. Remember that joining in a sport will also mean that you will meet many new friends. So, keep fit and have fun all at the same time!

Next we give you all the relevant details for taking up one or more of a kaleidoscope of activities, from dog training or the under-17s car club, to archaeology and wildlife conservation. There are addresses and telephone numbers of main contacts, so look through and choose the most interesting to you. We follow with a chapter on all the clubs and organisations you could wish to join.

Chapter 4 covers sports, activities and holidays for young people with a handicap. Today we are at last beginning to appreciate that a disability does not bar anyone from participating in most interests. Have a good look here to see how to get in touch with relevant organisations to get you started.

Most of us are living in such a privileged society in the UK and it is often you, the young, who prick the consciences of us oldies to think more about the less fortunate. We have included lots of ideas for you to actually raise money yourselves for whatever is your pet cause. Alternatively we recognise that you may need to finance your own projects, whether it's a BMX fund or a trip abroad, and you could use the suggestions for these too.

We all count the weeks till the holidays, but how often are they a bit of an anti-climax? For the children, the constant companionship of school or college friends contrasts to the life with just the family. Frustrated parents find their patience waning too, and scratch their heads about what to do with everyone. Now you can have a look through here and find masses of ways of occupying one and all. Maybe you can join together to set up a holiday club, take a residential or day adventure holiday, go skiing, or join in a foreign exchange. You could go with friends down a coalmine or try your hand at engraving glass; on a holiday, try abseiling or learn to survive on a desert island! It's all here. This chapter is packed with ideas of what to do and where to go whether as a family group or on your own.

Make the most of your holiday time before you start work or further education. Today it is so easy to get abroad and it really helps to have that experience. We felt it was important to include a chapter to give details of how to do this. You may want to go grape picking in France, trek in Tibet, or undertake voluntary service. There's plenty of practical help such as what to take, whether you need a visa, how to get cheap travel and lots more. You don't have to go that far afield though – there's masses to do here too. Think about using spare time to obtain job experience which might lead you to find a career. See here where you should apply and what sort of thing is available.

It's hard enough for mums at home to keep children occupied, working mothers face even more problems, especially in the holidays trying to make sure their brood is safe and happy. There is an appendix with information to help solve this growing worry.

Whether you want to undertake specialist interests or just try something new for a day we hope you can find the info to get going! You will find everyone very supportive and we hope you will be as inspired by their enthusiastic help as we have been. Our one regret is that we are not 8 or 18!

1.

SPORTS

We have always been a sports-mad nation, indeed we gave the world football, cricket, golf and various others, and led the way in them for many years, but while there is still strong support for the traditional games, although sometimes played in modern ways, there is now also a tremendous enthusiasm for a wider variety of different sports. Part of this is no doubt due to television – we see something new and exciting, such as American football, and want to have a go ourselves. Much of it, though, is because of enormously improved facilities around the United Kingdom. Most of us now have a leisure centre within easy reach where we can swim, trampoline, play squash, badminton, tennis, handball and many other sports; and new swimming pools, ice or roller skating rinks are springing up all the time. A great motivating force has been the Sports Council, who are vigorously pursuing the idea of more sport for everyone with their Ten Year Strategy and their schemes of 'Action Sport Project' and 'Ever Thought of Sport' (full details of these are on page 44 in this book). These encourage us all to enjoy sport, even if we aren't budding Olympic champions!

There is no need to emphasise nowadays the physical benefits of sport – you only have to think how marvellous you feel after a good swim or an energetic game of tennis to know how much good it must be doing! Perhaps more importantly, sport can provide hours of absorbing and challenging entertainment. You can have great fun with your friends learning how to sail, go-kart, fence, moto-cross, etc, or having an exciting game of water polo or football. So don't dismiss all sport just because you don't shine at school games – you may discover you have a natural aptitude for other activities such as skiing, hang-gliding or trampolining. Remember, also, that many sports clubs and centres have a well organised social life, and so are good places to make new friends. You could even go on a sporting holiday (see PGL on page 198).

You will find the sports in this section arranged in alphabetical order. Any more information you need can be obtained from the addresses we give you (remember to enclose a stamped addressed envelope). Your nearest leisure centre will also be able to help with information on many sports concerning local clubs, coaching classes, team fixtures and so on. As with our activity section, we should like to say how enthusiastic and helpful we found almost everyone we approached, so don't be shy about contacting them.

Sports Sponsorship One final point, taking up a sport seriously does cost money, and it is a great pity if some people with talent but without enough money should be prevented from developing their potential to the full. On page 46 we give details of the **Sports Aid Trust** which has been set up precisely with the aim of helping talented young people to excel in their chosen sport by providing the financial backing they need.

• American Football
Junior American Football Association, 8 Quorn Close, Wellingborough, Northants (0933 229580)

As anyone who has ever watched Channel 4 television will know, American football is now catching on in a big way in England. In spite of its rather formidable appearance, it is a game that can be played by boys, and from the age of 7 upwards. There are three kinds of junior football, as follows: Flag football which is the safest for young children, followed by Double Touch and Limited Contact. None of these require any protective hood or body gear, and in fact the kit would not be needed until a player reaches the age of 17, when he would start to play with adult clubs. It is easy to set up a team yourself as the only gear younger players need is a ball and a tracksuit and trainers, and a football or rugger pitch to play on. At the moment there are about 140 junior clubs around the country. Write to the address above to find your nearest or ask the Association's help in starting your own – they are very friendly and will do all they can for you.

• Archery

The Grand National Archery Society, 7th Street, National Agricultural Centre, Stoneleigh, Kenilworth, Warwickshire CV8 2LG (0203 23907)

The Society will send details of your local club, of which there are about 800 throughout the country, if you write to them. They have junior sections up to the age of 16, but in general, for safety reasons, will only accept juniors if a parent is a shooting member. The Archery Centre, Highgate, Hewkhurst, Kent (05805 2808), is very helpful and informative, and has lists of clubs in the south and east regions.

The Association for Archery in Schools, Bloxham School, Banbury, Oxon OX15 4PE (0295 720443), is self-explanatory. It encourages junior archers (under-15s and under-18s) to improve their bowmanship by coaching and by participating in national tournaments. Archery need not be an expensive sport – club subscriptions are modest and a bow, in kit form, can cost as little as £25. Coaching will normally include the use of club bows and arrows.

• Athletics

Amateur Athletic Association, Francis House, Francis Street, London SW1P 1DL

You will almost certainly have the opportunity to take part in athletics at school, and your school probably takes part in the 5-Star Award Scheme which issues certificates for merit in athletic performance (one and a half million certificates are awarded each year!). Outside school there are over a thousand athletics clubs and most of these accept young people from the age of 10 years upwards. Boys can compete in the Young Athletics League in which clubs join on a nationwide competitive basis.

Athletics is not an expensive sport – your own kit is really the only item that you will need to spend money on; for instance good running shoes (which are essential) cost about £30. If you are a member of a club you will find that the club will buy the equipment that you will need for training.

• Badminton

The Badminton Association of England, National Badminton Centre, Bradwell Road, Loughton Lodge, Milton Keynes MK8 9LA (0908 568822)

Badminton must be one of the most popular indoor sports in the country, and you will find there are plenty of opportunities to take it up. Most school gymnasiums have a badminton court marked out (if yours hasn't then persuade them to get on with it), and the English Schools Badminton Association organises tournaments for the under-14s and under-16s. There is really no minimum age for playing however, because even very young children can handle the light racket and shuttlecock, and the cost of taking up the game is very low. Leisure centres have badminton courts (but book well in advance) or you can join one of 6,000 local clubs, all of which encourage juniors with reduced fees and subscriptions. The clubs are joined into local leagues, which are part of county associations; and tournaments are organised at all levels up to international events, so with plenty of hard work you may have a chance to shine!

• Baseball

British Amateur Baseball and Softball Federation, 197 Newbridge Road, Hull, North Humberside HU9 2LR (0482 76169)

The American game of baseball is now gaining ground over here – witness the recent Channel 4 series on it – and it is easy to see why. It is a versatile game, very exciting, but easy to learn and costs are minimal. Comparing baseball to rounders is not well received by baseball enthusiasts, but there is no doubt that it had its origins in rounders, even if it is now a faster, more 'masculine' game. Players can start around the age of 10, and the six leagues that have been set up in this country all have junior programmes for 10 to 16-year-olds. After 16 you become a senior player. It is possible to play all the year round as the game can be played indoors in the winter using a soft ball. Equipment is simple – players wear jeans, T shirts and trainers – and the glove, bat and ball cost around £10 altogether, but in any case these would be supplied by your team to start with. If you are interested in the game you can always start up your own team either at school or with a group of friends – the Federation will give you all the help and advice it can.

• Basketball

English Basketball Association, Calomax House, Lupton Avenue, Leeds LS9 7EE (0532 496044)

Basketball is a five-a-side game (a cousin to netball), normally played in an indoor court, but the Association is keen to encourage outdoor basketball as well. This is played as a fun game, with small groups of players and you don't even need a court, just a single backboard and ring fitted on to the wall of a building. There is no lower age limit to basketball as there is an English Mini Basketball Association for the under-12s, as well as an English Schools Basketball Association. If your school doesn't play basketball there

I'm delighted to hear you're training for the Olympics, but would you mind training somewhere else?

Jules

are lots of local clubs all round the country. The Association will let you have addresses of these and of your local area association. The clubs all admit juniors – the under-19s – and again there is no minimum age limit. The clubs compete in a league programme culminating with the National Championship. And, who knows, you might end up playing Olympic basketball!

• BMX (Bicycle Moto-Cross)

National BMX Association, 13 Chelford Avenue, Louton, near Warrington, WA3 2RU
UK BMX Association, 5 Church Hill, Staplehurst, Tunbridge, Kent TN12 0AY

There are a large number of local BMX clubs throughout the country for this rapidly growing sport, and either of the above two associations will let you have details if you contact them – there is probably one in your area or you could set up your own! They also organise tournaments nationwide (sometimes between the two organisations). Clubs will ideally hold their races on a special BMX race track with steeply banked corners and bumps across the track. Anyone aged 5 to 16 can compete in races without being a club member, but the advantages of club membership (for an average fee of £3 a year) are a regular newsletter and reduced entrance fees for races, because your racing licence will cover the cost of insurance. Equipment, apart from the bike, includes helmet, knee and elbow pads and BMX gloves, all of which, brand new, will set you back about £40.

• Bicycle Polo

Bicycle Polo Association of Great Britain, 5 Puffin Gardens, Peel Common, Gosport, Hampshire PO13 0RF (0329 285967)

Bicycle polo is not unlike the polo played with horses except that it has been described as a rather more robust game, in that players can ride across in front of each other and shoulder charges are permitted! It can be played by young people from the age of 14 onwards and is becoming popular with cycling clubs as a winter game.

You need a grass pitch the size of a football pitch (in fact football pitches are often used) and bicycles which conform to special safety standards (ie: low gears, short handlebars, no brakes). A bike will cost about £150 – or you can build your own – and other equipment such as mallet and ball will cost about £15 and £5 respectively. You will also need shin and knee pads and headgear, but most teams have a pool of such items which you will be able to borrow.

Contact the address above to see if there is a club near you – or have a go at setting up your own.

• Bridge
The English Bridge Union, 15b High Street, Thame, Oxon OX9 2BZ (084 421 2221)

Many children start learning bridge in school from as young as 8 years old, if one of the teachers is a bridge enthusiast. If your school has no such teacher, then you can approach your local authority which will tell you if they run evening classes for bridge in your area, or contact the English Bridge Union, who will give you the name of your nearest club and/or teacher. There are at least 600 teachers throughout the country who would be able to give you coaching. Why not organise a group of four, so that you can learn and practise together?

• Canoeing
British Canoe Union, Flexel House, 45–47 High Street, Addlestone, Weybridge KT15 1JV (0932 41341)

There are several hundred canoeing centres throughout the country – write to the above address for a list – which cater largely for young people in the 13 to 16 age range, but a number of the centres also run special courses for younger age groups. There are also 600 clubs, most of which offer introductory courses, but some of these do not accept under-16s on their own, preferring a family membership. Canoeing need not be expensive to start with – clubs and centres will loan canoes or kayaks, and your own clothes plus a waterproof anorak are all you will need. Later, when you are hooked, you will want special clothing (wet suits etc), a buoyancy aid (£18), a paddle (£12) and your own kayak or canoe, which (secondhand) can cost from £50 to £150. Subscriptions to clubs vary from £5 to £50. Membership of the BCU is £4 for the first year to people under 16. This provides you with a licence to canoe on all British Waterways Board rivers and canals, and with all 2,000 miles of these open to you, canoeing is certainly an absorbing and exciting sport.

• Chess

British Chess Federation, 9a Grand Parade, St Leonards on Sea, East Sussex TN38 0DD (0424 442500)

Once you have discovered chess, you are hooked for life. If you don't play at school, the Federation will send you the address of your nearest club on request. Some of these have junior sections, others will accept you (but probably not below the age of 10 or 11). There are chess championships (organised by the Federation) for the under-9s, -11s, -12s up to under-21s. The English Primary Schools Chess Association, 162 Waddens Brook, Wednesfield, Wolverhampton co-ordinates chess in primary schools, leagues and other associations and organises four major competitions for children from the age of 5 upwards. Write to the Association for full details of their activities.

• Clay Pigeon Shooting

Clay Pigeon Shooting Association, 107 Epping New Road, Buck-hurst Hill, Essex IG9 5TQ (01-505 6221)

The Association will send you a list of local clubs, most of whom run shooting schools for coaching young people. Shooting competitions include junior categories for members up to the age of 18. You will be able to use club guns, at least to begin with. Cartridges cost from £5.50 for 50.

• Climbing

British Mountaineering Council, Crawford House, Precinct Centre, Booth Street East, Manchester M13 9RZ (061-273 5839)

The British Mountaineering Council offers novice courses for young people under the age of 16 (minimum age is 9). Write to the Training Administrator at the above address for details. They also have a booklet *Outdoor Pursuit Courses* which they will send on request, and which gives details of adventure courses including climbing, canoeing, caving, sailing and orienteering in various adventure centres throughout the country, especially in Scotland, Wales and the Lake District. These are for adults and young people as individuals, or in groups, and could make a very reasonably priced holiday for all the family.

See also **Outward Bound** for details on snow and ice climbing and

winter mountaineering courses for experienced climbers; and pp. 232–233 for **British Schools Exploring Society**.

● Cricket

Get in touch with your County Club (see Yellow Pages). It will probably have an indoor cricket school and coaching, and will run holiday courses. Some of these run every day for a week, some for an hour or evening once a week. Boys (and girls) can join in from the age of 8. Private clubs are usually allowed to hire the nets.

The week-long courses are really for the enthusiasts – some cricket schools, eg the MCC at Lord's, ask a games master to verify that a child is good enough to be likely to benefit from the experience. This does not mean on the other hand that someone has to be a child prodigy before they can participate, but it is hard work and obviously a certain standard is required or everyone would be held up. You have to pay for the course, and you will need all the equipment. Sometimes you are asked if you want to do wicket-keeping practice too, in which case you will need wicket keepers' gloves. However, if you haven't your own personal tackle we are sure your school would lend some to a promising youngster.

The most popular courses are in the spring holidays; you will need to contact the school early in the Christmas holiday to get on the list as they are usually heavily over-subscribed. The classes are divided up into age groups and normally you will be involved either in a morning or an afternoon session, depending on your age. If you have to travel some distance it would be worth arranging to do the course with a friend from your area so a 'run' can be organised for the journeys. We think it is more fun to do it with a friend anyway, especially if you are in the younger group. You should be armed with some sustenance and a drink (or have some money to buy something after the sessions) as it is hard work. The courses are very beneficial, particularly as a warm up before the summer term.

• Croquet

The Croquet Association, Hurlingham Club, Ranelagh Gardens, London SW6 3PR (01-736 3148)

Croquet is a fascinating and skilful game, and you can play short croquet in your own garden – you don't need a large lawn, but you do need a flat one!

You will need mallets, hoops and balls to play croquet, but these can often be bought secondhand, and if you join a club they will loan you a mallet to start off with. It is one of the fastest-growing games in the country and new clubs are starting up everywhere. Most clubs now have children's sections with reduced subscriptions. Croquet is an ideal game for children, who can start playing as young as 7.

The Association is very keen to encourage children to take up croquet and an Inter-Schools tournament and National Junior Championships have been set up. They have also introduced short croquet, which is played with the same number of hoops, but on a half-sized lawn.

Why not find out too about alternative croquet games, such as golf croquet, Pirates and others?

• Curling

Royal Caledonian Curling Club, 2 Coates Crescent, Edinburgh EH3 7AN

English Curling Association, 66 Preston Old Road, Freckleton, Preston PR4 1PD

Curling is mainly a Scottish game, played on ice, with a puck (a curling stone). Schools in Scotland have curling as an extra activity and there are Scottish School Championships. You would need to be about 12 before playing in curling at competition level as the curling stone weighs between 40 and 44 lb and is not an easy object to lift. (In Canada younger children can play, as special lightweight stones have been made.) Costs are not high – you will need ice skates of course – but a game at an ice rink will cost approximately £1. There are a number of young curling clubs in Scotland where young people between the age of 12 and 21 play regularly, and there is a World Junior Curling Championship open to contestants of 21 and under.

• Cycle Speedway Racing
The Cycle Speedway Council, 9 Meadow Close, Hethersett, Norwich NR9 3DZ (0603 811304)

Children as young as 7 years old can take up the challenge of cycle speedway, and the Council organises competitions for under-12s, under-15s and under-18s, on a national scale. There are cycle speedway clubs throughout the UK and 200 permanent racing tracks. The Speedway Council will give you the addresses of the clubs if you write to them. Competitions take place during the summer, with August Bank Holiday providing the grand climax. The cost of taking part in cycle speedway ranges from nothing, as most clubs allow newcomers to race on club machines, to several hundred pounds for a top class machine, but beginners of course can get hold of a secondhand adapted road bike for a few pounds. Don't forget you will need safety gear, eg helmet, which you will probably be able to buy secondhand.

• Cycling
RoSPA (Royal Society for the Prevention of Accidents), Cannon House, The Priory, Queensway, Birmingham B4 6BS (021-233 2461)

RoSPA organises the National Cycling Proficiency Scheme for 8 to 12-year-olds. The courses are usually organised through schools, so if yours does not have one, contact your local police station for the address of your local Road Safety Officer or write to RoSPA at the address above. 'Cycleway' is a longer school course, including classroom projects and practical cycling activities, spread over a whole school year.

The National Bike Club (address as above) provides a starter pack of badge, poster and information as soon as you join, as well as a quarterly *Newsbrief* and Third Party Insurance. They provide a free advice service and special offers on cycling accessories, publications and holidays. Individual membership is £3.75 per year, or £6 for a family membership. Write to RoSPA at the address above for an application form.

See also **BMX, Bicycle Polo, Cyclo-Cross,** and **Cycle Speedway Racing.**

• Cyclo-Cross

British Cyclo-Cross Association, 59 Jordan Road, Four Oaks, Sutton Coldfield, West Midlands B75 5AE

Cyclo-cross is an exciting cross-country race on bicycles over a course which might include steep hills, zig-zag bends, streams to cross or banks to climb. There are 300 clubs around the country (details from the address above) and about 200 races in a National League Competition. They run a Juvenile Award Scheme for 12 to 16s. All promotions should hold an under-12s event, with no entry fee required. Club membership is about £6 per annum, so cyclo-cross is not an expensive sport.

You will need a bike – your own will do, but it should be as light and as strong as possible. Take off lamps, mudguards, bells, etc, to reduce weight. Wear tough, comfortable clothes, with tight-fitting shoes, long-sleeved jersey and gloves.

The Association is keen for new organisers to set up cyclo-cross courses because so many young people want to take part. Write to them for help and information on your nearest cyclo-cross course, even if you would prefer to be just a spectator. They publish an annual handbook which will tell you everything you need to know.

• Fencing

Amateur Fencing Association. The de Beaumont Centre, 83 Perham Road, London W14 9SP (01-385 7442)

Junior membership of the AFA is £3 per year. Their magazine *The Sword* is issued four times a year, for a cost of £5. People can start fencing as young as 7 or 8, although not all clubs will accept members under the age of 14.

The Schools Fencing Union (address as above) promotes under-18 fencing in Britain. There are now some 200 school clubs, most of which are well-equipped with blades and protective clothing, so that you would not have to buy your own equipment, which can be expensive. The SFU organises National Age Group competitions each year, ranging from under-14 to under-18. If your school does not have and cannot be persuaded to start a fencing club, write to the AFA for the address of your nearest local club. They all admit juniors (ie the under-18s) but some will have a minimum age limit. There are various fencing courses run throughout the year – details from the AFA.

• Fishing

Fishing is Britain's largest outdoor participant sport, and one of the least expensive. Some schools run angling clubs, and if yours doesn't, why not help to organise one within the school? The National Anglers Council, 11 Cowgate, Peterborough PE1 1LZ (0733 54084), runs a bronze, silver and gold proficiency awards scheme for clubs and groups (not for individuals), so it is well worth joining a club. Find out the name of your local club from the nearest fishing tackle dealer (look him up in Yellow Pages) – he will be a useful friend and adviser over the years. If you live near the sea, you will be able to take up sea fishing. Inland, there is coarse angling in rivers or game fishing (fly fishing) for trout in reservoirs. Contact your local water authority for information on local rivers and reservoirs, on obtaining a rod licence and on the cost of a day's fishing.

• Football

Most schools will allow their pitches to be used for practice in the holidays – or why not try and organise your own matches with a group of friends? The Football Association, 22 Lancaster Gardens, London W2 (01-262 4542), will give you the address of your County Football Association who will give you the names of your local league clubs. Most league clubs accept boys from 8 years upwards.

For summer holiday courses write to McVities United Soccer Schools, Bedford House, 68 Bedford Road, London E17 4TX (01-520 2900). They run five-day non-residential football courses for 8 to 16-year-olds (divided into age groups) in most major cities in the UK. They use sports centres, schools or university playing fields, etc. You can win awards or badges at the end of the course.

Don't forget that you don't have to necessarily be a brilliant sportsman to enjoy your football. You can also go and watch matches, for although football has such a bad name at the moment there are ways of avoiding trouble, for example, some clubs have areas reserved for family groups. Contact your club and they can give you a fixture list and suggest which matches are most suitable for you to attend. Try to avoid local derbys – and book seats rather than stand on the terraces. It is actually very exciting to watch a match, but do remember that it does get cold even under the stands, so go prepared if it is a chilly day.

● Gliding

The British Gliding Association Ltd, 47 Vaughan Way, Leicester (0553 531051)

If you write to the above address they will send you an information pack containing a club list, a sales list of publications and details on gliding courses and certificates. Costs do vary, but gliding is not a particularly cheap sport. Most clubs do not allow you to fly solo until you are 16, but you can start a gliding course under that age and go up in a glider with an adult. You can then progress to hiring a solo glider (by the hour) and, eventually, you may decide to buy a share in a syndicate-owned machine. Most clubs run one- or two-week training courses and, of course, they all have weekend training.

See also the **Air Training Corps** (page 74) for gliding as well as flying.

● Golf

The Golf Foundation Limited, 78 Third Avenue, Bush Hill Park, Enfield, Middlesex EN1 1BX (01-363 1245)

The Foundation exists to promote golf among young people by

subsidising coaching, paying for instruction for young handicapped people, organising school competitive golf and so on. Get in touch with them for advice on junior membership of clubs and information on reduced subscriptions and coaching during the holidays. They will send you, free of charge, the booklet, *A Brief Guide to the Rules of Golf*. They recommend that you have at least one golf club to start off with, but others can, of course, be hired or borrowed. There is virtually no lower age limit for junior golfers – 6 to 7 year olds can play with special small clubs. The Gold Foundation organises a Schools Golf Team Championship and sponsors an under-15 Tournament. It also runs a Merit Award Scheme, under which successful candidates will have identity cards which should make it easier for them to join clubs and allow them to play for a nominal green fee at off-peak times.

• Gymnastics
British Amateur Gymnastics Association, 2 Buckingham Avenue East, Slough, Berks SL1 3EA
Gymnastics is one of the fastest growing sports in the UK for young people – 10,000 gymnastic clubs and 27,000 schools teaching gymnastics give some idea of its popularity. It is possible to begin gym at the age of two, but the BAGA emphasises, however, that people can take up gymnastics at almost any age, and still go on to win medals, if they try hard! The usual age, though, for children to start is about 6 or 7, and this is the sort of age at which they might join a gymnastics club. Ask for details at your local leisure centre. The British School of Gymnastics organises competitions starting with under-11s and under-13s, and Junior Olympic training begins at about 15. There are various competitions open to young people, with badge awards to work for. It is important that you are taught by a qualified BAGA coach, but with a reputable club (or school!) you should have no problem about this. The costs of gymnastics are minimal – leotards etc, are only a few pounds, and gym sessions at a club or leisure centre usually cost about 50 pence.

• Handball
British Handball Association, 32 Grove Place, Bedford MK40 3JJ (0234 213597)
Handball is a fast, exciting game played indoors or outdoors, with a leather ball which is thrown into a defended goal, about the same

size as a hockey goal. It is very easy to learn, and can be enjoyed at all levels of skill, from beginners to Olympic standard. Handball is ideal for schools – it can be played summer and winter, and costs very little to set up, as even equipment such as goals can be improvised from jump posts, or by marking tape on walls. It is a game which caters particularly for children: mini-handball, with a small-sized court and a soft ball, is for 5 to 9-year-olds, and junior handball, the halfway stage, is for 10 to 14-year-olds. Fourteen-year-olds and over play the full version, which is an Olympic sport.

There are a number of clubs around the country which are affiliated to the Association, and which have the opportunity to take part in inter regional championships, the British League, and the European cup.

• Hockey

The Hockey Association, 16 Upper Woburn Place, London WC1H 0QD (01-387 9315)

Hockey is an exciting, skilful game played extensively in both boys' and girls' schools, but if your school does not play hockey or if you want to take it a stage further, you can join one of the hockey clubs which exist throughout the country. Write to the Association for the address of your nearest club.

The cost of playing hockey is not especially high – club subscriptions for juniors vary but might be around £15 a year, and the basic kit, ie stick and boots, should cost under £50, particularly if you buy a secondhand stick; do always get help to ensure you have a correct-sized stick.

The English Schoolboys' Hockey Association (which caters for boys only!) has about 550 schools affiliated with it, but you can also join as an individual. Contact the Association (via the above address) and they will give you the name of the County Secretary.

See also **Ice Hockey**, **Roller Hockey**, **Street Hockey**.

• Hovering

The Hoverclub of Great Britain Limited, 10 Long Acre, Bingham, Notts (0949 37291)

The club brings together people of all ages who are interested in building and operating a light hovercraft. Junior membership of the club is £7 a year. For those who are not familiar with the look of the hovercraft used in the sport of hovering, the best description of them would be that when the skirt is inflated, they look a little like a small one-man rubber dinghy with a motor on top. They function in the same way as the big hovercraft which take us across the Channel.

A smaller lighter hovercraft called Formula Junior has now been introduced to cater for younger drivers aged 12 to 16, and the popularity of junior racing has rapidly increased. Schools are now taking part in hovering and building their own hovercraft. The Hoverclub will help in providing plans and the cost of building a hovercraft is from about £150 upwards, National races are held all over Great Britain, on rivers or lakes, and international meetings are now being held in France, Germany, Belgium and Sweden. But racing is not the Hoverclub's only activity – they also arrange 'hover-ins' and 'hover-hols' and they will appear at exhibitions and fêtes. They are very helpful, and will be able to give you lots of help and advice if you contact them at the address above.

● Ice Hockey

The British Ice Hockey Association, 48 Barmouth Road, Shirley, Croydon C10 5EQ (01-654 6851)

There is no minimum age limit to ice hockey – it is possible to start playing as young as 7, and most clubs have a 'Pee-Wee' section for players up to 13 years, as well as a 'Junior' section for those up to 16 years. Write to the above address to see if there is a club near you – they exist in Scotland, England and Wales – and new ice rinks are

opening all the time. It is not a cheap sport to take up – to kit out a player with new skates and protective equipment can cost £200 to £400, but clubs will have a 'pool' of equipment which juniors can draw on and pass on when outgrown, and this will be very much less expensive. You will know from television coverage that this is a fast-moving, physical sport, so be prepared for a few crashes and spills on the ice!

● Judo

The British Judo Association, 16 Upper Woburn Place, London WC1H 0QH (01-387 9340)

This Association will send you a brochure and information pack telling you all you want to know about Judo. There are about 1,200 local clubs, and the Association will put you in touch with your nearest. Try joining Judo as soon as you can (minimum age 8), as most kids love it. The training hall is called a 'dojo', where you will be able to give vent to all your aggressions, hopefully in a controlled manner! You will need an outfit called a 'Judogi', consisting of a reinforced jacket, trousers and a belt which will cost between £10 and £20, and club fees for juniors are very reasonable. Judokas (those who practice Judo) consider that Judo is more than just a sport, it can include a philosophy for life itself.

● Karate

The British Amateur Karate Association, 120 Cromer Street, London WC1 (01-837 4406)

Karate is a fascinating sport, with about 50 different styles of teaching and techniques, such as Kung Fu etc, all grouped under the heading 'Martial Arts'. There are about 500 clubs throughout the country and the Karate Association will give you the address of the club nearest to you which is suitable for your age group. You can start learning Karate in a track-suit but when you want to buy the outfit, you can buy it wholesale through the Association, and it will cost about £10. Once you have joined, try to resist chopping Dad's bookshelves in half – he won't appreciate it!

● Karting

RAC Motor Sports Association, 31 Belgrave Square, London SW1X 8QH (01-235 8601)

This is an exciting sport that you can now take part in from the age of 10 upwards. For those who have never seen a kart, it has a low-slung metal chassis, four wheels, steering wheel, single seat and a rear engine. Cadets and other junior class karts (for the 10 to 13-year-olds) have 100cc engines and no gearbox. Larger machines get more powerful and more complicated, to put it in an untechnical way. There are about 40 kart racing clubs and circuits distributed around the UK (including two in the Channel Islands). Some clubs have permanent circuits with year-round racing and practice sessions, others have summer circuits only. Write to the address above for your nearest club, as well as essential information on licences, safety equipment (especially crash helmets) and so on. Karting is not one of the cheaper sports – club membership will be around £20 per year, although this entitles you to reduced racing fees. A secondhand kart would cost about £150, and a brand new one around £600. An expert tells us that the best course is to join a club first, and then get help and advice on choosing the right type of kart for the appropriate class. The same expert also told us that karting had changed the course of his life, and that he and his son have now become permanently addicted, so you have been warned!

• Lacrosse

The All England Women's Lacrosse Association, 16 Upper Woburn Place, London WC1H 0QJ (01-387 4430)

You will have the opportunity to play lacrosse either at school, college, or one of the clubs throughout the country. If your school does not offer lacrosse as a sport at the moment, try to persuade them to borrow a hire kit from the Association. These kits contain everything you need for the game – sticks, ball, goalpads and a rule book – and are designed to encourage schools to take up the game. Costs of buying equipment are not high – from £16 to £35 for a stick or try and find a secondhand one – although you have to pay to enter club tournaments etc.

The Association encourages Junior Lacrosse and teams of under-13s, -14s and -15s can now join the tournaments. Mini-Lacrosse, played with a light plastic stick and a soft ball, either indoors or outdoors, is designed for younger girls (and boys) and is getting more popular every year.

• Land Yachting

British Federation of Sand and Yacht Clubs, 23 Piper Drive, Long

Whatton, Loughborough, Leicestershire LE12 5DF (0509 842292)

Land Yachting or land sailing is an exhilarating sport, reaching sailing speeds of up to 70 mph, and is practised on various beaches or airfields around the country. Club sailing is recommended because it provides training for beginners, competitions, insurance and safety advice etc. There are a number of clubs around the country – write to the address above for your nearest. There are some club sailors of about 10 to 11 years old, but major competitions are open to 14-year-olds upwards. A secondhand yacht would cost from about £200, but many people make their own – this could be an ideal school or youth club project.

• Life Saving

The Royal Life Saving Society, Mountbatten House, Studley, Warwickshire B80 7NN (052 785 3943)

It's a very good idea to undertake a life saving course, especially if you are involved in any water sports. The RLSS has developed a complete new life saving system, which it calls 'Aquapack', combining water safety, safe swimming and rescue skills. There are two levels of Aquapack and as people gain skills they will achieve awards at each level. There are also Teachers' Aquapack kits to meet the needs of schools and clubs. If your school does not already teach Aquapack, why not persuade them, or else ask at your local swimming pool.

• Moto-cross

Motor Cycle Association of Great Britain Ltd, Starley House, Eaton Road, Coventry CV1 2FH (0203 27427)

Moto-cross (once upon a time known as motor cycle scrambling) is a race in which up to 40 riders compete on a special circuit with a given number of laps. As you can imagine it is fast, noisy and very exciting, but not dangerous if all the safety regulations are followed. The minimum age to start moto-cross is 6(!) and racing is divided into the age groups 7 to 9, 10 to 14 and 14 to 16-year-olds. Write to whichever of the addresses below is nearest to you and they will give you details of clubs in your area, and also of how to obtain a competition licence and race entry.

Amateur Motor Cycle Association, Darlaston Road, Walsall, Staffs WS2 9XL (0922 39517).

Auto Cycle Union, Milbuck House, Corporation Street, Rugby, Warwickshire CV21 2DN (0788 70332).

Auto Cycle Union (Youth Division), Milbuck House, Corporation Street, Rugby, Warwickshire CV21 2DN (0788 70322).

British Schoolboy Motor Cycle Association, 18 Glenpark Crescent, Kingscourt, Stroud, Glos (045 366516).

Motor Cycle Union of Ireland, 10 Windamere Drive, Bangor BT20 4QF (0232 703004).

Scottish Auto Cycle Union, 'Kippilaw', Longridge Road, Whitburn, West Lothian EH47 0LG (0501 42663).

Youth Motor Cycle Sport Association, 20 Kensington Gardens, Ilkeston, Derbyshire (0602 328989).

In addition to moto-cross there are also two other types of 'off road' motor cycle sports that might appeal to you; these are 'Trials' and 'Enduro'. A trial is not a race, but it is a test of skill and control on a closed circuit, in which points are lost if the rider touches the ground with his feet. Youth trials are open to 6-year-olds and upwards, and are graded according to levels of skill and age. 'Enduro' also takes place on a closed circuit which varied in length from 2 miles to 20 miles, and which has to be negotiated within a certain time limit.

You will of course need special equipment to take part in any of these motor cycle sports. The first essential is of course a bike, and the costs of these can vary from £100 to £1,000. Go and watch some moto-cross first to decide what kind of bike you will need. You will probably be offered one or two secondhand machines straight away. Then you will need a helmet, boots, special trousers and gloves – these are essential for safety – so it is not a particularly cheap sport to get involved in, but it is a very exciting one that could keep you absorbed for years. *Dirt Bike Rider* is the magazine for the moto-cross enthusiast.

Why not increase your skills by a training course in moto-cross? Kawasaki run and subsidise the Team Green Training School in Chippenham where a day course will cost between £10 and £15 (but you must bring your own bike). Contact 0753 38255 and ask for details of the next training course, but be prepared to book well in advance as the courses fill up very quickly.

• Netball

All England Netball Association Limited, Francis House, Francis Street, London SW1P 1DE (01-828 2176)

You will probably be able to play netball at school, but if not, or if you would like to take it up more seriously, then there are plenty of clubs which have junior sections and junior netball leagues – contact AENA headquarters (address as above) for details of a club in your area. The cost of taking up netball is low – you will simply need good shoes and your own kit.

• Pentathlon

The Modern Pentathlon Association of Great Britain, 1a Godstone Road, Purley, Surrey CR2 2DH (01-668 7855)

If you get bored concentrating on just one sport, Modern Pentathlon might well appeal to you. It consists of five sports, ie: riding, shooting, fencing, swimming and cross-country running, and it is of course an Olympic event. There is a junior (under-21) group, but younger people can now take part in Biathlon and Triathlon and compete for badges in both. Biathlon consists of swimming and running. Triathlon also includes air-pistol shooting, and both sports award badges for under-13s and under-15s. Most probably your school or sports club will be affiliated to the Association, but you can also join as an individual member for an annual subscription of £7.50.

• Polo

It is not very likely that many of us will ever play polo ourselves, but it is a fascinating sport to watch. And even if you are not interested in watching the game, a polo ground is the fashionable place to be seen nowadays!

The Pony Club (see **Riding**) runs a Polo Tournament for its members. It is played on a shortened pitch, with a soft ball, and the matches are played between the various Pony Club branches.

The Polo Association, Cowdray Estate Office, Midhurst, West Sussex, will send you a fixture list of official tournaments and also the name(s) of clubs in your area.

● Riding

The Pony Club, The British Horse Society, British Equestrian Centre, Stoneleigh, Kenilworth, Warwickshire CV8 2LR

Riding is one of the most popular and varied sports in the country, and whether you want just to have a quiet hack round the country lanes or go in for the more demanding activities such as show jumping or hunting, riding can cater for every need. Find a good local riding school which specialises in teaching children to start you off – riders can start as young as 4 years old. The only equipment you will need at first is a Pony Club approved hat (and no good school will let you ride without one) plus low-heeled leather shoes and tough jeans. Later of course, when you are sure you like riding, can come the jodhpurs, hacking jacket, gloves and so on.

The next step for keen riders is to join the Pony Club. There are over 360 branches around the country, but if you don't know your local one, write to the address above for information. The Pony Club is the largest association of riders in the world and is open to anyone under 21 years of age. Membership is £9.50 per year. The backbone of the Club is the Working Rally, which is usually arranged during the school holidays. Members are given lessons in riding and pony management and take part in mounted games and sports. You don't need to own a pony to join the Pony Club, although they do not provide them for you, but often riding schools will agree to lend a pony for a Rally or a summer camp.

In addition to Rallies the Club arranges visits to kennels, stud farms, horse shows, etc, and organises its own Horse Trials Championships, Polo Tournaments, Show Jumping Championships, and other events. They award Efficiency Certificates to their members and everyone is expected to try for these.

British Riding Clubs are another way to participate in riding events. There will probably be one in your area that you can join, attached to a riding school or riding centre. Many of them are affiliated to the British Horse Society at the address above. Write to the Riding Clubs Office and ask for the name of one in your area. Most of the clubs have a junior section for riders up to the age of 16, and they organise national inter-club junior events such as dressage and show jumping. They also run four riding tests at different levels, starting with one for beginners.

See also page 203, **Riding Holidays**, and page 177 for horse shows and events that you can visit.

• Roller Hockey
National Roller Hockey Association of Great Britain, 528 Loose Road, Maidstone, Kent ME15 9UF (0622 43155)

Roller hockey (hockey played on roller skates) is one of the world's fastest growing sports – it is skilful, exciting, full of thrills and can be played at any age. You should be able to skate quite well before trying to play roller hockey, but 8 to 9-year-olds upwards can learn the game and play very well. There are clubs around the country (write to the above address for the nearest), and although in some areas venues are few and far between, the gaps are being filled quite quickly. It is a competitive sport, obviously, and runs nation-wide schoolboy leagues and championships. You will need boots – you can start with disco-type roller boots, which cost about £20, and a stick as well as shin pads and knee protectors. Other equipment will be provided by the club. Finally, if there is no club in your area, why not start one up yourself (with teachers or parents to help)? The Roller Hockey Association will be very pleased to give you all the help they can.

• Rounders
National Rounders Association, c/o Sports Council, 16 Upper Woburn Place, London WC1H 0QP (01-388 1277)

There is plenty of opportunity to play rounders at school or in youth clubs. It is also an easy game to organise with a group of friends and great fun to play. If you are interested in rounders in a more dedicated way, and aged 15 to 16, then you can play at county level in a ladies' or mixed club – get details of your nearest one from the address above. The club will provide the equipment, although as this need consist only of a bat and ball, it will not be expensive in any case.

● Rowing

The Amateur Rowing Association, 6 Lower Mall, London W6 9DJ (01-748 3632)

If rowing is not an activity in your school, then you can join a local club. Write to the Rowing Association for the address of your nearest club. There are about 400 of these, and most of them have junior sections, with reduced membership fees. The minimum age is about 12, but both boys and girls can join. You can find yourself rowing on rivers, lakes and any open stretch of water. Sea rowing is also very popular. In general, the clubs will supply boats and equipment and provide coaching so that it is not an expensive sport.

'Sea rowing is also very popular'

● Rugby Football/League

Rugby Football Union, Whitton Road, Twickenham, Middlesex (01-892 8161)

Boys aged from 8 to 12 can join their local club as juniors and start off by playing mini-rugby, which is nine-a-side and played on an abbreviated pitch. If you do not know where your nearest club is, write to the Football Union at Twickenham. They have a handbook with a complete list of all clubs. Once you are older you will move into full-scale rugger.

Fathers get very involved with mini-rugger – normally coaching takes place on Sunday mornings. There are plenty of organised matches and even inter-area tournaments for more experienced players – you will find the whole family gets addicted and trundles off to them for a day out with a picnic – which no doubt will have to be eaten inside the car!

• Sailing

Royal Yachting Association, Training Division, Victoria Way, Woking, Surrey GU21 1EO (048 625022)

Write to this address for their booklet *Learn to Sail*. Whether you want to learn to sail a dinghy, or family-size cruiser or in the Tall Ships, the booklet give you the chance to learn from the experts. It lists types of courses and sailing clubs and schools all round the country; you can sail inland on lakes and reservoirs as well as the open sea. Sailing is one of the most enjoyable of all activities whether you like to race or, like Water Rat, simply mess about in boats. There is really no minimum age but, of course, all ages must observe stringent safety precautions such as the wearing of life jackets.

Club subscriptions are reasonable and it is possible to hire boats, but there is little to beat the joy of owning your own dinghy. You can get good secondhand boats, which have been overhauled, for a reasonable price. The following is a rough guide, but you could of course pay much less if you were willing to do some work on the boat yourself.

Mirror dinghy or Laser: £300–400.
Hornet or 505 (racing dinghies): £700.

• Shooting

This one word covers such a wide field and involves so many different organisations that you could really write an entire book on the subject! Perhaps the most suitable kind of gun for young novices is an air pistol or air rifle. These are dealt with by the National Small-bore Rifle Association, Lord Roberts House, Bisley Camp, Brookwood, Woking, Surrey GU24 0ND (04867 6969). Many schools are affiliated to the Association, which organises junior team shoots and junior championships for the under-16s and under-18s, and there are also 2,500 clubs around the country, catering for air guns, small-bore rifles and pistols. The Association will send you the name of your nearest club if you write to them (for reasons of security they do not issue lists of clubs). The minimum age for joining a club will not usually be below 8. There are laws governing the age at which you are allowed to own a gun of any kind – 14 for an air gun – but you will be allowed to use a club gun as a member below that age.

B-B (ball-bearing) shooting using a small air rifle is now becoming popular in the Midlands, mainly for the 11 to 15 age group, and this is also organised by the Small-bore Rifle Association).

The National Rifle Association (at the address above) is the governing body of full-bore rifle shooting and you will have opportunities for shooting with a full-bore rifle, either at school, in a cadet force, or at various clubs throughout the country – again, write to the Association for your nearest one, as they do not issue lists of clubs, for security reasons.

If you are interested in shooting, it is really important to join a club. They can teach you so much about using guns, most especially the importance of absolute safety in handling a gun. The cost of buying an air gun is not excessive – air pistols from £32 and air rifles from £60 – but you must check up on the laws governing the purchase of guns, and also gun licences.

See also **Clay Pigeon Shooting**; **Army Cadet Force Association**.

• Skateboarding

English Skateboard Association, Maryland, Mareham on the Hill, Horncastle, Lincs (0658 26012)

There has been a few years' lull in the skateboarding craze, but now, with a new generation of young skateboarders, the enthusiasm is once again on the up and up. Any young person can buy a skateboard of course, but the problem is where to practise – you are not always welcome on the pavements of your local streets! Write to the above address and they will send you details of 'skateplaces' around the United Kingdom – the list is constantly being added to, and they try to keep it up to date. You can join the ESA for £3 a year, which entitles you to a monthly news sheet and reductions on competition entrance fees. Competitions are divided into three groupings: A, B and C, which depend entirely on ability – there is no minimum age limit or segregation. The most expensive piece of equipment is obviously the skateboard. These range in price from about £14 to £75 plus, but you can get a very good basic plastic skateboard for about £16. Apart from the board you will need knee pads, elbow pads and helmet – this safety gear is very important and costs about £40 new, but you can easily get good secondhand equipment.

• Skating (Ice and Roller Skating)

National Skating Association of Great Britain, 15–27 Gee Street, London EC1V 3RE (01-253 3824)

The Association is the governing body for both ice and roller skating. It arranges proficiency tests ranging from beginner's level to the most advanced, as well as national championship and competitions which can eventually lead to World Olympic class skating. There are five branches of skating, ie: ice figure skating, ice dance, ice speed skating, roller skating and artistic roller skating. The last of these has a national centre and national coach at Rollerbury, Bury St Edmunds. The Association can supply information sheets and manuals on all these five disciplines, and, if you do not know of an ice or roller skating rink near you, they will be able to let you have a list of rinks as well as local clubs. You can hire boots at ice rinks, but if you are a keen skater you will eventually want to buy your own – your own club at the ice rink will be able to advise you.

• Skiing

The Ski Club of Great Britain, 118 Eaton Square, London SW1W 9AF (01-245 1033)

If you have been lucky enough to go skiing on school trips or with your parents, you will know what an exhilarating experience this is, even when you can barely stand upright on your skis! It is an expensive sport, but junior membership of the Ski Club (which costs approximately £7 per year) entitles you to discounts on dry ski slopes, skiing holidays and lots of shops and services. The Club will send you a list of dry ski slopes on request. They will also send you a *Ski-Fit* booklet with useful hints for getting fit before your holiday and suggestions for beginners to get started in skiing (where to learn, clothes to wear, hire or buy boots and so on). They also organise skiing parties for groups aged 9 to 15, 12 to 15 and 16 to 18. These are for beginners, intermediates and advanced and are

accompanied by highly trained leaders. Although they are not cheap they provide concentrated skiing tuition as well as other activities such as swimming when skiing is over for the day. They can arrange for ski and boot hire.

Cross Country Skiing, although less fast and exciting than downhill skiing, has a lot to offer and is a wonderful way of seeing the countryside. It is possible to ski-trek in Scotland and Snowdonia during the winter.

Grass skiing is another spin off from snow skiing, and is now recognised by the National Ski Federation of Great Britain as a separate sport. You use very short skis which have rollers or a caterpillar track attached underneath; it is possible to reach speeds of 50 mph with grass skis.

See also our section on skiing holidays on pages 206–210 for more information.

● Snooker
The Billiard and Snooker Control Council, Coronet House, Queen Street, Leeds LS1 2TN (0532 440586)

Perhaps you have watched and been fascinated by The World Snooker Championships on television, so why don't you have a go yourself – waistcoat and bow tie are not compulsory! The Council runs a Junior Membership Scheme for people under the age of 18 for an annual fee of £1.15, which entitles each member to a copy of the twice-yearly newsletter. The Billiards and Snooker Foundation (address as above) was set up to teach young people under the age of 18. It provides coaches throughout the country, so that pupils can be taught in their own area, and it awards trophies for the best pupils of the preceding year. Contact them for the address of your County Association or nearest club.

• Snorkelling

National Snorkellers' Club, 13 Langham Gardens, Wembley, Middlesex HA0 3RG (01-904 7850)

There is a network of about 400 branches of the Snorkellers Club – get the name of the nearest branch from the address above. They cater for young people from 8 to 18. The basic equipment required is a mask, fins and a snorkel which will cost about £20. Branches run weekend and holiday courses away from home, as well as local tuition. The main branch organises an annual snorkelling trip to Yugoslavia at Easter for about 100 young people, which is always heavily over-subscribed.

See also **Sub-aqua**.

• Squash

The Squash Racquets Association, Francis House, Francis Street, London SW1 (01-828 3064)

Squash is played throughout the country in schools, clubs, leisure centres and even some companies which have their own courts and a family membership scheme. Boys and girls can play squash together but the Women's Squash Racquets Association, 345 Upper Richmond Road, West Sheen, London, also has junior membership for girls. Boys and girls as young as 8 can start playing with a junior racket. Write to the Association for your nearest club, of which there are thousands throughout the country. They all have Junior membership, mostly with half price membership fees, and will often let juniors play for free or reduced charge at non-peak hours. It is not an expensive sport, court fees are about £1 a session and most clubs will hire equipment to start with, so that newcomers to the game can see how they like it. Once you are hooked on squash, you can become involved in a competitive structure which begins with the under-12s and leads on through inter-club, inter-county and international squash, so that you could end up world champion!

• Street Hockey

British Street Hockey Association, 5N Peabody Building, Duchy Street, London SW1 8DS (01-261 9878)

Street hockey started only a few years ago but is now really taking off. It began in the streets, hence the name, but has since moved indoors to roller skating rinks and sports centres, although a lot of training is still done in the streets. It has more in common with ice hockey than roller hockey (use of short ice hockey stick, etc) but is of course played in roller boots. New leagues, including women's leagues, are springing up around London and in the north in cities such as Warrington, Hull and Liverpool, although the Midlands have yet to be conquered. Players can start around the age of 10 or 12 – although of course you must already be a fast and confident skater – and they usually go on until their early 20s. It is not an expensive game to play – roller boots cost about £20 and protective shin, knee and elbow pads about £10. Top-class players participating in first division matches can of course end up spending much more – up to £250 including special roller boots and shoulder pads.

See also **Ice Hockey** and **Roller Hockey**.

• Sub-Aqua

British Sub-Aqua Club, 16 Upper Woburn Place, London WC1 (01-387 9302)

Many of the sub-aqua branches are attached to the snorkelling branches, but again, the London Office will provide you with the address of the branch nearest to you. No branch will admit anyone under the age of 14 and some prefer 16 as the minimum age, because sub-aqua involves diving below the surface, and therefore requires even greater safety awareness. Basic equipment is again mask, fins and snorkel, as the club will hire aqualung sets and diving suits, etc to beginners. If you are committed to sub-aqua, however, you will eventually need your own equipment, which will cost from about £250, secondhand. Training is carried out at the branches, and weekend or longer breaks by the sea are arranged as part of the training.

See also **Snorkelling**.

• Surfing

British Surfing Association, Room G5, Burrows Chambers, East Burrow Road, Swansea, SA1 1RF (0792 461476)

Surfing is getting very popular in Great Britain and there are now about 40 clubs around the coasts. People as young as 10 can learn to surf, so long as they can swim fairly well and are 'water-confident', but a better starting age is probably around 13, because greater strength to cope with the board will have developed by then. All the clubs encourage juniors, and there are reduced subscriptions for under-18s. Wet suits and boards can usually be hired to start with, but if you are keen you will want your own and prices start at around £35 for a wet suit and £85 for a board, although they can also be bought secondhand. The BSA run courses on the Gower Coast in the summer so if you are an enthusiastic 'gremmie' (surfing slang for a beginner) why not have a go? Once you are hooked on surfing you are in a whole new world.

• Swimming

Amateur Swimming Association, Harold Fern House, Derby Square, Loughborough LE11 0AL (0509 230431)

There is sure to be a club in your area – ask at your local swimming pool. If it is a big club you may be lucky enough to have the opportunity to learn competitive swimming, diving, synchronised swimming, water polo or life saving. Smaller clubs of course will probably be able to offer only one or two of these, but all clubs will cater for you whether you just enjoy swimming and want to develop a certain level of skill or whether you are really dedicated to the pursuit of excellence and international levels.

There are usually special classes for older people who are unable to swim well – so don't be embarrassed about starting at any age.

• Table Tennis

English Table Tennis Association, 21 Claremont, Hastings, East Sussex TN34 1HF (0424 433121)

Table tennis is a game that needs no introduction – everyone thinks they can play – but the better you are the more you enjoy it, and there are now lots of opportunities to improve your game. There is an English Schools' Table Tennis Association which organises local and national competitions for individuals and school teams. Is your school affiliated to the Association? There are also over 300 local tennis table leagues, based in all the major cities (address above for information). Younger people are welcomed into teams whenever possible, and this in fact provides one of the unique aspects of table tennis, in that you can gain, both in table tennis and social skills, by mixing with older players.

In addition, the Dunlop Skills Award Scheme has recently been set up, which appeals especially to people from the age of 8 to 16. Under the scheme you can progress from Grade 1 to the Master Level by improving your basic skills, through hard work and plenty of practice and coaching, to develop a really fast attacking game.

● Tennis

The Lawn Tennis Association, Palliser Road, London W14 9EG (01-385 2366)

You will almost certainly have an opportunity to play tennis at your school, and to go on to join the local club, if you enjoy tennis. If this is not the case, the Lawn Tennis Association has a list of local clubs and also nationwide tournaments, which start with the under-12s.

Many younger children (even as young as 4) are now learning to play tennis by starting with short tennis. This is played on a scaled-down pitch, using plastic rackets (which cost very little) and a soft foam-rubber ball. It is one of the fastest growing games in the country, especially in inner-city areas, and even has its own championship games. If your school is not into short tennis, why not persuade them to make a start? It has already been proved, in Sweden, that it is a wonderful way of producing future champions! Write for help and information to the Short Tennis Department at the address above.

Tennis enthusiasts can go on tennis coaching holidays at various centres throughout the country. Turn to page 204 in this book to see what is on offer.

• Tenpin Bowling

British Tenpin Bowling Association, 19 Canterbury Avenue, Ilford, Essex IG1 3NA

There are more than 60 bowling centres in the country – if you cannot find one in your local telephone directory, contact the address above – and it is a game that can be enjoyed by children from the age of five onwards. Costs are low, on average about £1 per game, with about 25 pence for hire of shoes. Instruction, if you should need it, is normally free.

• Trampolining

British Trampoline Federation, 152a College Road, Harrow, Middlesex HA1 1VH (01-863 7278)

Most trampolining takes place at schools and sports centres who will be affiliated to the Federation. There are local clubs, but nearly all of these use sports centre facilities. Ask at the sports centre and they will give you the names of any clubs that do use their facilities and can give you coaching on the premises. Trampolining must always be supervised to make sure that no one lands badly and hurts themselves.

• Water Skiing

British Water Ski Federation, 390 City Road, London EC1V 2QA (01-833 2855)

This is a non-profit making organisation which is 'devoted to ensuring that efficient growth and enjoyment of water skiing for the family, club and competitive participant through an harmonious association and understanding with the other water users.' This is quoted at length to show that, even though some individual speed boat enthusiasts annoy others by whizzing around with a skier in tow, apparently without a thought for their neighbours in the area, the Association does in fact try very hard to make sure that this does not happen. Reading all their information is fascinating as they are aiming to achieve high levels of tuition and water safety etc. In contrast to your average foreign ski school, the instruction seems very much more thorough and according to their leaflet it is a unique method of learning skiing.

There are 160 affiliated clubs throughout the UK but their numbers are growing all the time. For novice skiers, the clubs with vacancies will provide the equipment, basic instruction and encouragement! The Federation will give details of many courses run under their auspices if you are a complete beginner.

The costs involved vary greatly, according to the club. If eventually you wish to have your own equipment, good sports shops and boat equipment stores stock everything you would need – members of BWSF are given discount at certain stockists and are given the relevant list with club documents.

There are magazines concerned with skiing – *Waterski International*, Kirtons Farm, Water Ski Club, Pingewood, Nr. Reading, Berks, and *Powerboat and Water Skiing Magazine*, Ocean Publications, 22 Buckingham Palace Road, London SW1.

If you want details of BWSF Clubs etc, send an s.a.e. with an 18p stamp – the information they send is excellent.

• Windsurfing

(sometimes known as *Board Sailing*) Royal Yachting Association, Victoria Way, Woking, Surrey GU21 1EQ (048 62 5022)

This is the sport where the skilful speed gracefully across the water with a simple board and sail, and the less skilful spend most of their time actually in the water! It takes time to learn, but once mastered is wonderfully rewarding.

Anyone from the ages of 6 to 7 can take up windsurfing, as special small sails are available for the younger age groups. It is quite expensive to buy the equipment you will need – from £400 for a board and rig, complete, and from £70 for a wet suit (moderately essential in this country!), but if you decide to have lessons from a windsurfing school you will, of course, be able to use their equipment.

There are about 160 schools qualified to teach windsurfing in this country – write to the RYA at the address above for a booklet listing all their addresses – some are on the coast, but a lot of them are on inland lakes and reservoirs. A course of lessons (eight hours) will cost about £30, but is well worthwhile.

You could also write to the International Windsurfer Schools UK, Unit 10, Stort Valley Industrial Park, Bishops Stortford, Herts, and they will send you a list of their schools. A beginner starts on a dry land simulator, ie: a windsurfer mounted on springs, and when he has learnt to balance and to control the board he progresses to free sailing and learns how to tack and gybe and fall gracefully into the water!

Some Useful Addresses

• The Sports Council
16 Upper Woburn Place, London WC1H 0QP (01-388 1277)

The Sports Council provides advice, information, facilities and cash. They have nine regional offices throughout the country as well as six national sports centres listed below. Their Ten-Year Strategy aims to create 5.6 million more sports people by 1992. The cash to help achieve this is provided by government grants which subsidise new schemes such as the Action Sport Project to promote street sport, especially in depressed inner city areas. Another scheme is 'Ever thought of Sport?', a campaign for 13 to 24-year-olds, especially school leavers. Contact the Sports Council at the above address if you have any queries – they will be glad to help. They run an information centre and library at their headquarters.

We haven't room in this book, alas, to include every known sport, but the Sports Council will be able to help you with any that we haven't included. Write to them for information on any of the following: ballooning, bobsleigh, bowls, caving, fives, flying, frisbee discs, hang gliding, microlight flying, parachuting, parascending, petanque, racketball, ski-bob, tchouk-ball, rackets, tug-of-war, volleyball, weight lifting or wrestling. They will send you the address of the national headquarters for each and any of the above, although not all of them cater particularly for young people.

National Sports Centres

Bisham Abbey National Sports Centre
Nr Marlow, Buckinghamshire SL7 1RT (06284 2818/6110/6119).

Crystal Palace National Sports Centre
Norwood, London SE19 (01-778 0131).

Holme Pierrepont National Water Sports Centre
Adbolton Lane, Holme Pierrepont, Nottingham NG12 2LU (0602 821212).

Lilleshall Hall National Sports Centre
Nr Newport, Shropshire TF10 9AT (0952 603003).

National Sailing Centre, Cowes
Arctic Road, Cowes, Isle of Wight (0983 294941/2).

Plas y Brenin National Centre for Mountain Activities
Capel Curig, Gwynedd, North Wales, (069 04 214).

Regional offices

Northern Region
Northumberland, Cumbria, Durham, Cleveland and Tyne and Wear. County Court Building, Hallgarth Street, Durham DH1 3PLB (0385 49595).

North West Region
Lancashire, Cheshire, Greater Manchester and Merseyside. Byrom House, Quay Street, Manchester M3 5FJ (061-834 0338).

Yorkshire and Humberside Region
W Yorkshire, S Yorkshire, N Yorkshire and Humberside. Coronet House, Queen Street, Leeds LS1 4PW (0532 436443/4).

East Midland Region
Derbyshire, Nottinghamshire, Lincolnshire, Leicestershire and Northamptonshire. 26 Musters Road, West Bridgford, Nottingham NG2 7PL (0602 821887 and 822586).

West Midlands Region
Metropolitan County Council of the West Midlands, Hereford & Worcester, Shropshire, Staffordshire and Warwickshire. Metropolitan House, 1 Hagley Road, Five Ways, Birmingham B16 8TT (021-454 3808/9).

Eastern Region
Norfolk, Cambridgeshire, Suffolk, Bedfordshire, Hertfordshire and Essex. 26–28 Bromham Road, Bedford MK40 2QD (0234 45222).

Greater London and South East Region
Greater London, Surrey, Kent and East and West Sussex. PO Box 480, Crystal Palace National Sports Centre, Ledrington Road, London SE19 2BQ (01-778 8600).

Southern Region
Hampshire, Isle of Wight, Berkshire, Buckinghamshire and Oxfordshire. Watlington House, Watlington Street, Reading RG1 4RJ (0734 595616).

South Western Region
Avon, Cornwall, Devon, Dorset, Somerset, Wiltshire and Gloucestershire. Ashlands House, Ashlands, Crewkerne, Somerset TA18 6LQ (0460 73491).

● Sports Aid Trust
16 Upper Woburn Place, London WC1H 0QN (01-387 9380)
The Trust has been set up recently by the Sports Aid foundation with the express intention of helping talented young people achieve their full potential in sport. Students at schools and colleges are eligible for grant aid from the Trust to help them with the specialised training that their parents may not be able to afford. All applications for grants will be considered by a Grant Aid Committee which has wide experience of sport at national and international level. Many great British Olympic Champions (Sebastian Coe, Torvill and Dean, Duncan Goodhew, to name but a few) have been

helped by the Trust, so if you see yourself as a future champion, but need extra financial help, this may be your opportunity.

• The Central Council of Physical Recreation

Francis House, Francis Street, London SW1P 1DE (01-823 3163)

The Council acts as a 'consultative body' to the Sports Council. It exists to provide a central base for sports organisations to come together to improve and develop all different kinds of sport. It has six divisions, covering the various aspects of sport, including water sports, movement and dance and so on. It also runs a charity called Colson Fellowship Fund which provides help for handicapped young people to take part in sport. As with the Sports Council, you can write to the CCPR for help and information on any sport, as just about every sports organisation is a member of the Council.

2.

ACTIVITIES

This chapter is packed with activities and pastimes to help you get the most out of your holidays, especially the long summer break, without having to spend a fortune and of course to provide ideas for year-round interests. It will show you just what there is to do, where to go and how to go about it. Why not go through the ideas and make a short list of your favourites? Even if you already have an absorbing activity, it's great fun to get together with other people who share your interest in it.

We have provided the address and telephone number of the national headquarters of each activity, and if you get in touch with them they will let you have the address of your nearest club or group. Before including each activity in our list, we have checked that it has special facilities for young people, and we have included as much information as we could find room for. Remember always to include a stamped addressed envelope when you write for information. In view of the high cost of postage, all the organisations stressed the importance of this.

If you need more help and information, contact your nearest library, museum, polytechnic and even your local council. People are usually very co-operative when approached for information and will do what they can to advise you.

Finally, last but not least, we should like to mention here how grateful we were to the organisations we contacted for all their kindness and helpfulness. Their enthusiasm was so infectious that we felt we wanted to take up their particular speciality instantly, and we are sure that if and when you contact them you will be greeted with the same warmth and friendliness.

• Archaeology

Young Archaeologists' Club, c/o Dr Kate Pretty, New Hall, Cambridge CB3 0DF

If you are fascinated by the past, and want to know more about prehistoric monuments, Roman villas or castles, then the Young Archaeologists' Club is for you. The Club is a national one for anyone between the ages of 9 to 18 plus. The annual subscription is £2.50 which entitles you to four copies of the magazine *Young Archaeology* each year. The magazine gives details of excavations throughout the country which your membership card will entitle you to visit or to work on. You can join a local branch, go on activity days or field study holidays (for 11 year olds and upwards) in various parts of the country. Schools can join the Club for a subscription of £5, so if several of you are interested ask your school to join and save yourselves money. The Club would prefer you to write to them, which is why we do not give a telephone number.

The Council for British Archaeology, 112 Kensington Road, London SE11 6RE, will send you its monthly newsletter/calendar for £6.50 a year. This lists sites in Britain where volunteer helpers are needed and gives details of training excavations, study tours and courses. Although these are for adults, the sensible younger person would be welcomed.

See page 230 for details of *Archaeology Abroad* and the chance to join foreign excavation sites.

• Astronomy

Junior Astronomical Society, 58 Vaughan Gardens, Ilford, Essex IG1 3PD

The word 'Junior' really refers to knowledge rather than age, since the Junior Astronomical Society appeals to beginners of all ages but, of course, young people are particularly welcome. For an annual subscription of £6.50 members receive four copies of *Popular Astronomy* and about six news circulars. Regular meetings are held in London (a yearly weekend observing course in Shropshire). Your local library will put you in touch with a Society in your area, if there is one. If not, the Society will encourage you and your friends to organise one. They will also answer your queries and advise you in buying your first binoculars or telescope. Did you know you can take an O level in astronomy?

Jodrell Bank (Jodrell Bank Visitor Centre, Macclesfield, Cheshire, 0477 71339). Ring first to find out about opening hours. You will be able to see the Planetarium, learn all about modern radio astronomy and operate the 25-foot radio telescope.

• Backpacking

The Backpackers' Club, 20 St Michaels Road, Tilehurst, Reading RG3 4RP (0734 428754)

This Club exists to promote the interests of walkers and campers. It offers a comprehensive service to help in activities such as cycling, canoeing, pony trekking and motor cycling. The Young Backpackers' membership, up to 18 years, costs £5 per annum. There is no minimum age limit because young children can join in a family membership. If you get in touch with the Club they will tell you if your county has a liaison member who will arrange activities in your area. The Club will also advise on buying equipment, from walking boots to tents and sleeping bags.

The Countryside Commission, Despatch Dept, 19 Albert Road, Manchester M19 2EQ (061-224 6287). Write to them for their book *Long Distance Paths*, which will give you lots of ideas on where to walk, throughout the country.

• Bell Ringing

Go to the belfry of your local parish church (if you know that the church has bells which are rung regularly) to see if the name and address of the local bellringing society is pinned up. If not, ask the vicar or one of the churchwardens. Most change ringing societies are based on local parishes which are grouped into diocesan associations. If you cannot get any information locally contact *Ringing World*, which is the weekly newspaper for bellringers, at Penmark House, Woodbridge Meadow, Guildford, Surrey GU1 1BL (0483 69535). The editor should be able to put you in touch with a society in your area. There is a Central Council of Church Bell Ringers, with members elected from each county, but it exists to set standards and decide on changes, rather than to provide information or promote bellringing.

The ideal age to start bellringing is usually about 12 years old, as we are told that boys or girls who start much younger are too light and run the risk of being lifted off their feet by the bell, which is an alarming experience that might put you off permanently! The costs of bellringing are minimal, as no special equipment is required.

● Birdwatching
Young Ornithologists' Club, The Lodge, Sandy, Bedfordshire SG19 2DL (0767 80551)

Most members of the YOC are between 9 and 14 years old; they can have individual, family (for brothers and sisters) or group membership – the last of which is open to all schools and youth

organisations. Twice a month members receive the very attractive colour magazine *Bird Life* and there is an annual Young Ornithologist of the Year Competition. The YOC runs very popular holiday courses which are based at youth hostels or field centres. In addition, there are many local groups throughout the country which arrange field outings and, during the winter, indoor meetings. When you join the YOC you will be sent a list of these local groups – see if there is one near you.

If you are 17 or over you can apply to one of the bird reserves managed by the **RSPB** (The Royal Society for the Protection of Birds), to spend a working holiday as a temporary warden (see page 230).

The RSPB manages over 100 of these reserves and visitors are allowed to come and birdwatch. On page 172 we list some of them, but write to the address above for the full list.

• Brass Rubbing

The Monumental Brass Society, c/o Society of Antiquaries of London, Burlington House, Piccadilly, London W1V 0HS

The Society organises meetings, lectures and discussion groups. It issues annually a portfolio of illustrated brasses and three bulletins on current activities. It also organises excursions to churches of special interest, and an annual conference at places such as Cambridge and Warwick. You can also buy brass rubbing materials at the meetings. Annual subscription for under-18s is £3. If you intend to do some brass rubbing on your own, then do make sure to get permission in advance and be prepared to pay a fee or make a contribution to church funds. See page 173 for brass rubbing centres around the country.

• Community Service

Contact your nearest Citizens' Advice Bureau who will put you in touch with your Volunteer Bureau. Tell them what kind of work interests you, for instance in a hospital, day care centre and so on and how much time you can give, not necessarily on a regular basis, and they will find plenty for you to do. See also under **First Aid** for details about joining the Red Cross, **St John Ambulance Cadets** and **YMCA**. If you are a member of an organisation such as the Scouts,

Guides, Boys' or Girls' Brigade (see Chapter 3) then they will show you lots of ways you can help. If you are not, you could find ways to help in your own area. You may find that there are children who would love to come to your home for tea, or perhaps you could arrange for several of them to visit your school (with the school's co-operation of course). Perhaps there are elderly people who live alone and would like someone to help around the house, clean the windows, do a little shopping, or even just call in for a chat on a regular basis. Schools can sometimes arrange to give a concert or provide a special tea in an old people's home. These are just a few ideas – once people know you are interested, lots more possibilities will come your way.

The following organisations will offer you plenty of opportunities to help. They do need a degree of commitment and dedication, but if you are helping other people to enjoy a holiday, for instance, you will find that you are enjoying it as well.

Community Service Volunteers, 237 Pentonville Road, London N1 9NJ (01-278 6601). Over 2,500 young people (minimum age 16) become CSVs each year, and receive training in all aspects of the work. They work, either locally or away from home, on a six-week placement with the elderly, mentally or physically disabled or whoever needs their help. CSV also run media projects (such as 'Marcher Action' and 'Contact Wales') to provide information on television and radio or volunteering, community needs, and so on. Your school might be interested in finding out more about this.

International Voluntary Service, Ceresole House, 53 Regent Road, Leicester LE1 6YL (0533 541862). The aims of the IVS are 'to bring together people from different backgrounds, regardless of race, colour, sex or creed, and to create international friendship by co-operating in useful projects to aid peace'. Under-18s can join in a programme of work weekends, workcamps and international volunteer work exchanges. Teenage Projects caters for younger members, and there is no minimum age limit. There are also many projects suitable for those over 18, although that is a matter rather beyond the scope of this book.

National Federation of Gateway Clubs, 117 Golden Lane, London EC1Y 0RT (01-253 9433). The Federation exists to co-ordinate the work of Gateway Clubs in England, Northern Ireland and Wales, in providing opportunities for people with mental handicaps to enjoy leisure in order to help their personal development. They offer support advice and information as well as training opportunities and courses for leaders and helpers. Junior Club membership is open to 7 to 14-year-olds and Senior Club to 14 years upwards. Leaders and helpers are eligible from 14 upwards. There is a total membership at present of 50,000.

PHAB, Tavistock House North, Tavistock Square, London WC1H 9HJ (01-388 1963). PHAB (physically handicapped and able bodied) exists to promote the integration of the physically handicapped into the community by promoting opportunities for physically handicapped and able bodied to come together on equal terms by offering youth clubs for the disabled and able-bodied members, as well as holidays, training resources for other youth organisations to support integration, and international links. There are 450 clubs in the UK and eight other countries, containing equal numbers of PH and AB.

Quaker Workcamps, Friends House, Euston Road, London NW1 2BJ. Volunteers (from 17 upwards) take part in camps which last from one to three weeks. They might be helping to provide a holiday for deprived children, or working with people who have mental or physical handicaps. Some of the camps are abroad. Volunteers pay their own travelling expenses, but food and accommodation (simple) are free.

• Computers
British Computer Society, 13 Mansfield Street, London W1M 0BP (01-637 0471)

If you love messing around with computers and want to develop your skills in programming, etc or just want to meet others with a similar interest, then contact this society. It has recently formed the AYCE (The Association of Young Computer Enthusiasts), and this should spread through the local branches of the Society. AYCE caters for the 13 to 10 year-olds and will provide you with a diary, newsletter and discounts on hard and software.

See also **Computer Holidays** (page 199) for details of courses.

• Conservation

Conservation is a subject that concerns us all. It is very easy to get depressed about the disappearing rain forests or the difficulties of breeding pandas in captivity, but there is not a lot most of us can do about these problems. What we can do is help with projects closer to home. Here are the names of lots of organisations that will be only too pleased to have your help during a working weekend or even a working holiday.

In addition, look around your local area and see all the things that need to be done. Perhaps a pond is choked with weeds and rubbish, or a bus shelter or park could do with cleaning up. You could combine it with a fund-raising function by getting your friends to join in and being sponsored per hour of work or sack load of rubbish you collect. These are just a few suggestions but if you have the enthusiasm you will always find plenty to do. It is immensely rewarding to feel that you have helped to preserve a cathedral, a beautiful building or restore a woodland or wild meadow.

British Trust for Conservation Volunteers, 36 St Mary's Street, Wallingford, Oxon (0491 39766). The British Trust for Conservation Volunteers is all about preserving or recreating woodlands, wild flower meadows, ponds and so on, very often out of old rubbish tips or derelict sites. They need volunteers, from 16 years upwards, either for a day or a week, who need not have special skills, just lots of enthusiasm. There are over 300 local groups, so contact the headquarters (address above) for the address of your regional area office.

Cathedral Camps, Manor House, High Birstwitt, Harrogate, North Yorkshire HG3 2LG. Cathedral Camps are looking for volunteers over 16 to help restore cathedrals. It can be a fascinating experience helping skilled craftsmen such as stonemasons or stained glass window restorers at work, or just joining in with the very necessary tasks of cleaning and painting these historic buildings.

Council for Environmental Education, Youth Unit, Zoological Gardens, Regent's Park, London NW1 4RY (01-240 4936). The CEE Youth Unit is the 'national co-ordinating and promoting body for conservation in England and Wales'. In other words it provides a central reference point for information on all aspects of educating people on the environment. It does this through local authorities, schools, and so on, but does not undertake practical work itself. The Youth Unit works with young people out of school through youth organisations, etc, to teach them about the environment in a way that relates to their own lives. Contact them for advice on training, educational aids, contacts and sources of information.

English Heritage, PO Box 43, Ruislip, Middlesex HA4 0XW. English Heritage was set up in 1984 'to care for England's great inheritance of historic properties – Roman sites, castles, houses and gardens – and to bring them to life again'. The junior membership club for under-16s is called 'Keep' and costs £4, or your family can take out family membership. Write to the above address for application forms. When you have joined you will receive your membership pack giving you full details of your rights as a member, plus a quarterly newsletter, an illustrated guide and a map.

Forest School Camps, Bourne Cottage, Park Lane, Heytesbury, Warminster, Wilts BA12 0HE. FSC run a number of work camps for 17 your olds and over, who help on many diverse projects such as clearing scrub, bricklaying, or helping to build a recreational centre for handicapped children. The camps last either for a full week or just for a weekend, accommodation is in tents and fees are about £2 a day, but you make your own travel arrangements. Write to the above address for the exact dates of the camps, as they change each year.

Friends of the Earth, 377 City Road, London EC1V 1NA (01-837 0731). FoE has become a very successful organisation, and its projects and independent reports concerning conservation matters are now taken very seriously in the political arena. They also run a local group network of over 200 groups which organise members in conservation activities ranging from waste recycling (to produce recycled paper) to tree planting. Student membership is £5 per annum, which entitles you to receive a regular newspaper giving detailed information of current projects. Schools or community groups can apply for special affiliation rates, so why not persuade some of the staff and students in your school to get together and form their own group?

The National Trust, 42 Queen Anne's Gate, London SW1 (01-222 9251). The NT is very much geared to young people. They run Acorn Camps and Young National Trust Groups, PO Box 12, Westbury, Wiltshire. The objects of Acorn Camps are to achieve vital jobs of conservation and to give volunteers a chance to join in a rewarding activity in some of the Trust's most exciting countryside. Volunteers pay part of their costs (£14 a week in 1986) and travelling expenses. The only snag is that they must be aged 16 or over. Write for the annual Acorn Camp programme, which lists projects throughout the country. Young National Trust Groups work in their spare time at local trust properties and organise plenty of social life. New groups are being set up all the time, but if you do not have one in your area, the YNT will do all they can to help you and your friends organise one yourself. Again, minimum age is 16.

The Trust also runs the Young National Trust Theatre which takes school groups to a particular house in their area where they can dress up in the costume of the period and act out its history. If your school does not know about this scheme, then tell them and persuade them to take part. The Theatre's address is 8 Church Street, Lacock, Wiltshire SN15 2LB (024973 569).

The National Trust for Scotland, Youth in Trust, 5 Charlotte Square, Edinburgh EH2 4DU (031-226 5922). Youth in Trust tackles all kinds of tasks (indoor and outdoor) for the National Trust for Scotland – for instance, footpath construction, woodland management, painting, fence-building – all projects which combine exploration, education and entertainment, and which may last for a day or for two weeks. Volunteers may have to pay a small charge for transport and food. The accent is on adventure in Scotland's wild and beautiful countryside.

Youth in Trust also organises Thistle Camps (similar to the Acorn Camps in England), to undertake work, often in remote and beautiful locations in the highlands, which would not otherwise be possible. Volunteers make a contribution of £12 towards expenses, they must be 16 plus, prepared to work hard and live simply. The Camps are for one week, during spring, summer and autumn, except for the Fair Isle Camp which is for two. Write in early, because places are limited and the camps get booked up quite early in the year.

Railways On page 184 we give details of old steam railways that need volunteers to help clear the lines or restore the trains to working order.

Watch (The Watch Trust for Environmental Education Ltd), 22 The Green, Nettleham, Lincoln LN2 2NR. Watch is a club for young people up to the age of 18 who care about wildlife, and their environment in country and town. It has its own magazine *Watchword* and carries out projects such as a butterfly census, tree-planting schemes and a survey of breeding ponds for frogs and toads. Annual subscription is £2 a year, or there is a family membership or a school affiliation scheme. It has hundreds of active local branches throughout the UK and organises many important national projects and competitions for young people under 18. It is sponsored by the Royal Society for Nature Conservation and by the *Sunday Times*.

Working Weekends on Organic Farms, 19 Bradford Road, Lewes, West Sussex BN7 1RB. Anyone over 16 can be a Wwoofer! (someone who enjoys working weekends on organic farms). Work varies from looking after animals to dry stone walling. You will be provided with food, but bring your own sleeping bag.

Young People's Trust for Endangered Species, 19 Quarry Street, Guildford, Surrey GU1 3EH (0483 39600). The aim of the Trust is to encourage young people to become part of the campaign for saving endangered species, and to understand the need for sensible conservation. The Trust works through schools, setting up YPTES support groups (is there one in your school?) providing a free lecture service and a newsletter, *Whale-Tail News*, for members. In addition the Trust has a centre in Dorset which runs five-day junior field study courses for 9 to 13-year-olds as well as summer school programmes for 9 to 16-year-olds. Prices vary but a week will cost under £100. Those taking part will learn about the seashore, woodlands, local geology, etc, but the emphasis is on combining learning and fun, and the centre also offers an outdoor heated swimming pool.

• Country Parks

It would be impossible for us to list here all the Country Parks throughout the UK but write to the Countryside Commission, Despatch Dept, 19 Albert Road, Manchester M19 2EQ (061-224 6287), and they will send you their book called *Country Parks* with information on about 150 of them. Some of the parks offer extra attractions such as rowing, riding, nature trails, adventure playgrounds, birdwatching and so on.

• Dance

There are four bodies to contact if you want to know anything about dance:

The Royal Acadamy of Dancing, 40 Vicarage Crescent, London SW11 3LT (01-223 0091).

The Imperial Society of Teachers of Dancing, Euston Hall, Birkenhead Street, London WC1H 8BE (01-837 9967).

The British Ballet Organisation, Woolborough Houses, 38 Lonsdale Road, London SW3 9JP (01-748 1241).

The International Dance Teachers' Association, 76 Bennett Road, Brighton, Sussex BN2 5JL (0273 685652).

Any of these bodies will supply you with lists of affiliated dance schools in your area, as well as dance centres. They will also have information about vacation ballet schools and courses, for example summer seminars. The monthly magazine, *The Dancing Times*, Clerkenwell House, 45 Clerkenwell Green, London EC1R 0BE is a mine of information on all types of dance. There are advertisements of schools, classes, exams, and dance wear, with articles on dancers and dancing. You can also buy cassettes and videos of graded lessons to use at home.

Ballroom Dancing British Amateur Dancers Association, 14 Oxford Street, London W1N 0HL (01-636 0851). Ballroom dancing, Latin and Old Tyme dancing can be enjoyed by children from a very early age (as young as 5, 6 or 7). There are many schools of dancing all over the country, so write to the address above for one in your area, or look in the Yellow Pages under dancing. Children can then train for competitive work as Juveniles, up to the age of 12, and as Juniors, up to the age of 16, when they enter the adult ranks. Dancing need not be expensive but of course the more lessons and competitions, the greater the costs – although when you are really committed to dancing, you will consider the money well spent!

Disco Dancing Mecca Leisure Ltd, 76 Southwark Street, London SE1 0PP (01-928 2323). Mecca run 50 discothèques around the country and in about 30 of these they organise 'Supertrouper' and 'Boogaloo' dancing sessions, the first of these for children aged 12 to 16, the second for 16 to 20-year-olds, both using the most modern disco lighting and music effects. Supertroupers take place once or twice a week, either in the afternoon or early evening.

Admission varies from 30 pence to £2. If you don't know of a Mecca disco in your area, give the head office (number above) a call, and they will be able to let you know. Sessions are very well run and supervised, so parents are not expected to linger!

Jazz Ballet   This is a form of dance that is full of movement and tremendously energetic. It can complement ballet or it can be an alternative. Those who find ballet's strict discipline difficult or who lack co-ordination will find great freedom and enjoyment in the vigorous music and movement of jazz ballet. Children as young as 6 can begin to learn, and of course there is no upper age limit. A weekly jazz ballet class will typically last 40 minutes, and consist of a warm-up using a fundamental set of exercises followed by a dance routine.

At the moment there are no exams or set standards in jazz ballet, but as it increases in popularity this may well change. If you are interested in taking it up, go to the nearest dance centre in your town, and see what they can offer you. Otherwise look in your local paper and you should find advertisements for different types of dance, including contemporary or jazz ballet.

The style of teaching varies enormously and if you find that the first class doesn't suit you, then just keep looking until you find one that does. A leotard, tights and ballet shoes are all that you need in the way of equipment.

WAC (Weekend Arts College), Interchange, 15 Wilkin Street, London NW5 3NG (01-267 9421). If you live in or near London, WAC might interest you.

Saturday WAC is for 7 to 13-year-olds and consists of classes in ballet, drama and modern movement. It offers technical experience as well as giving you the chance to discover the fun element in the performing arts. Classes run during the school term, from September to June.

Sunday WAC is aimed at young people between the ages of 14 and 21, living in the Greater London area, who have talents in music, drama or dance, and who would perhaps like to make a career out of their talents but lack the training to get into art college or teacher training college. WAC holds classes on Sundays for this age group in ballet, contemporary dance and jazz dance.

WAC also runs a youth company called Fusion, which combines music, dance and drama in witty and lively productions. They will perform around the country in community centres, schools, colleges, etc. If you would like them to come to your school, write to the WAC administrator at the above address for more details.

Friends of Covent Garden, 34 Beckenham Road, Beckenham, Kent BR3 4TU. You can be a Junior Associate Friend if you have not yet reached your 26th birthday for £7 a year. You will receive all the advantages of a full member – that is, priority bookings, 'open' rehearsals, lunch-time introductions to ballets, lectures, concerts, recitals, a free copy of the magazine *About the House* and an invitation to the Christmas party, with a cabaret by artists of the Royal Opera in Covent Garden. In addition to all this, as a Junior Member you receive vouchers to the value of £54 per year, which enables you to buy tickets for yourself and a friend for the opera and ballet at reduced prices.

• Dog and Dog Training

The National Dog Owners' Association, 39–41 North Road, London N7 9DP (01-609 2757)

This Association runs a free advisory service on any question regarding dogs. They receive many letters from children and young people and are always very helpful. They have a list of dog training clubs and will put you in touch with the one nearest to you if you write to them (s.a.e. please).

• Farms

The National Federation of City Farms, The Old Vicarage, 66 Fraser Street, Windmill Hill, Bedminster, Bristol BS3 4LY

These city farms are run by and for the local community on reclaimed waste land, farming both arable crops and livestock. There are now about 30 round the country, and more are being set up. Write to the Bristol address to find out if there is one near you. They encourage volunteers to take an active part in running the farm, and also welcome farm visits.

If you feel you would like to help set up a city farm yourself, get hold of a copy of a book called *City Farming and Community*

Gardening (written by Christopher Wardle and Kay Knight, published by the Inter Change Trust, 15 Wilkin Street, London NW5 3NG at £3.95). The authors use their ten years' experience to provide a guide on finding a suitable site, forming a charity, fund raising, budgeting, and all the other practical essentials.

There are lots of farms around the country which cater specially for young people, where visitors can go in among the animals to stroke them and pick the small ones up, and help with the feeding. We have a list of some of these on page 175, but consult your local tourist board for more in your area.

• First Aid

Youth and Juniors Director, British Red Cross Society, 9 Grosvenor Crescent, London SW1X 7EJ (01-235 5454)

You can join a Red Cross Junior Group from the age of 5 to 11, or a Red Cross Youth Group from 11 to 18. Contact your nearest British Red Cross group (look in your local telephone directory) or contact the headquarters at the address above. The Red Cross will teach you about First Aid and accident prevention, but they are also able to offer far more than this. You can learn about health and hygiene, drill and rescue, fire protection or camping. You can help in hospitals and old people's homes, help take handicapped children on holiday and, because the Red Cross is a worldwide movement, you will have the chance of working with overseas projects and even attending International Study Centres to learn about life in other countries.

See also page 84 for details of the **St John Ambulance Cadets**. In addition to first aid and nursing, cadets are taught many other subjects (eg: animal care, swimming, fire fighting, etc) and they also have the opportunity to attend camps and take part in adventure training.

• Flower Arranging

The National Association of Flower Arrangement Societies of Great Britain, 21a Denbigh Street, London SW1V 2HF (01-828 5145)

They will send you the address of your local club (of which there are 1,365). Some of these have junior flower clubs, but you would be very welcome in any case if you are really interested.

The **Girl Guides** and the **Girls' Venture Corps** also run flower arranging courses.

• Gardening

The Royal Horticultural Society, Vincent Square, London SW1P 2PE (01-834 4333)

The Society accepts junior members, up to the age of 18, for an annual membership fee of £5. This entitles you to a ticket for the flower shows at Vincent Square and the Chelsea Flower Show, free admission to the Royal Horticultural Society Gardens at Wisley and the monthly Royal Horticultural Society magazine.

National Gardens Scheme, 57 Lower Belgrave Street, London SW1 0LR (01-730 0359). Write to them for a copy of their *Yellow Book* (also obtainable from bookshops) for a list of over 1,500 gardens open to the public. Although written for adults, it also lists many gardens with special interest for younger enthusiasts.

The book *City Farming and Community Gardening* (full publishing details under **Farms**) is a practical guide to setting up a community garden on a derelict site in an inner city area. The garden would be run by local people for local people in response to a lack of open spaces in that particular area. The book guides you through finding a site, fund raising, forming a charity and so on.

• Geography

Royal Geographical Society, Kensington Gore, London SW7 2AR (01-589 5466)

You can join the Society as an Associate Member, if you are under 25, for £10. This is one-third the price charged for a Full Fellow, but you receive all the same benefits: the use of the library and map room, and attendance at lectures and social events at the Society headquarters. The Society also runs children's Christmas lectures for members and their children. The age range catered for is from about 5 to 12 years. Admission is free.

• History

One of the most interesting ways to tackle the subject of history is to learn about the place where you live through the local history societies. All towns have at least one of these, and you can get the addresses of those near you by contacting the local library information department, or the County Archivist in the County Hall. Local history societies are not usually aimed at young people, although they are always welcome, and many societies are now thinking of starting a junior section and including activities such as recording farm buildings, town houses and so on, which would appeal to young people. Family history societies also exist in each county – again ask your local library or archivist – and these have been set up to trace family trees and family history. Finding out all about your own family could be a most fascinating project.

See also **Archaeology** and **Young NADFAS** in this chapter.

• Model Making

There are hundreds of clubs throughout the country for model enthusiasts. Your local model shop will be able to advise you on your special interest and any clubs in your area. The monthly magazines *Aero Modeller* and *Radio Controlled Models* will give details of clubs, or write to the editors for help in finding one.

• Model Railways

The Model Railway Club, 4 Calshot Street, London N1 9AT

This Club has an open night every Thursday evening. They will send you a list of local clubs if you write to them (s.a.e. please) but they do not welcome telephone inquiries. You will also find a list of clubs at the back of the monthly magazine *Railway Modeller* which is available at most newsagents. See page 179 for model railways to visit.

• Model Flying

Society of Model Aeronautical Engineers, Kimberley House, Vaughan Way, Leicester LE1 4SE (0533 58500)

The Society is for people involved with today's rapidly developing world of model flying. Junior membership (under 18) is £4. Most of the Society's members are radio control flyers, but some fly engine-assisted planes or gliders. It is a fascinating and absorbing activity for which an Achievement Scheme has been set up to test flying ability and safety and which awards badges and certificates at different levels. If you are interested in model flying, it is a good idea to join the Society as they can be a lot of help to you, providing information, insurance, the use of their handbooks, rule books and so on. Write to the above address for the name of your local club which is affiliated to the Society – there are about 350 of these so there should be one near you.

• Music

If you are interested in music, whether classical, jazz or big band, etc, you should with any luck have the chance of playing at school. We list here some of the ways you can carry your interests further, outside school. There are also several holidays or courses you can attend to increase your musical knowledge where you will get the chance of playing different instruments, attending concerts, and so on, as well as taking part in more conventional holiday activities such as swimming or tennis. We list details of these holidays in Chapter 7.

Concerts   Robert Mayer Concerts, BBC Yalding House, 156 Great Portland Street, London W1N 6AJ (01-927 4523). These concerts are played at the Royal Festival Hall on Saturday mornings from October to March, and are designed for 8 to 13-year-olds, who must behave very well! Booking is in May for the following season, so you must get organised in good time.

Ernest Read Music Association, 9 Cotsford Avenue, New Malden, Surrey KT3 5EU (01-942 0318). The Association organises concerts at the Festival Hall, which run from October to May. They encourage some audience participation in the singing, and the conductors will talk to the audience and explain the instruments and the music that they are playing.

Friends of Covent Garden, 34 Beckenham Road, Kent BR3 4TU. You can be a Junior Associate Friend for £7 a year, and among other benefits you will be able to attend opera rehearsals, as well as getting tickets for opera performances at reduced prices. See under **Dance** on page 61 in this book for more details.

The National Youth Orchestra, 26 Barclay Road, Croydon, Surrey (01-686 6237). The orchestra offers musical young people a unique opportunity to develop their talents, but it is of course immensely competitive and only a very few can expect to be accepted. Grade 8 distinction standard on an orchestral instrument is normally the jumping off point for a prospective member of the orchestra. However, if you feel you have the talent (and determination) write to the above address to apply for an audition. These are held in February in major cities all round the country. If you pass the first audition you will be asked to re-audition in the autumn, and if successful you will be invited to join the orchestra which (at the time of writing) consists of 164 young players. The orchestra meets three times a year, during each school holiday, for a ten-day to two-week intensive rehearsal session followed by concerts.

The cost to the player is about £170 per session, although this in no way represents the true cost, which is many times greater. The orchestra is very keen that talented children whose parents cannot afford the fees should not lose out, and they do have a small bursary, although it is always overstretched. In some cases your local education authority can be persuaded to give a grant although the system is haphazard and unsatisfactory. The average age for joining the orchestra is 13 to 15, and players leave when they are 20 or sooner, if they go on to a music college.

United Kingdom Federation of Jazz Bands, 4 Cemetery Road, Porth, Rhondda, Mid Glamorgan CF36 0BL. The Federation exists to promote a musical education for children by helping to teach them to play musical instruments, especially marching band instruments, by means of concerts, exhibitions and national competitions. Membership is open to boys and girls between the ages of 5 and 21.

WAC (Weekend Arts College), 15 Wilkin Street, London NW5 3NG (01-267 9421), runs classes on Sundays for 14 to 21-year-olds in jazz music, composition, mime and singing. See **Dance** for full details of WAC. The London Fusion Orchestra, which has developed from WAC, is a jazz ensemble for young people, in which they perform the blues in all shapes and forms, compositions of the great such as Duke Ellington, Miles Davis, etc and are encouraged to compose their own pieces as well as improvise their own structures. Write for more information to the WAC administrator at the address above.

• Orienteering

British Orienteering Federation, Riverdale, Dale Road North, Darley Dale, Matlock, Derbyshire DE4 2JB (0629 734042)

Orienteering is the sport of navigation on foot with the aid of a map and a compass. It is both an exciting challenge of skill and stamina and a chance to visit lovely countryside that you wouldn't otherwise see. Write to the above address and they will send you a detailed list of local clubs and lots more information. There is no minimum age limit – children and beginners can start on a 2-kilometre course – and there is both junior and family membership for those under 19 years of age. Orienteering is a competitive sport, but there is usually also a non-competitive Wayfarers' course to be explored. No special equipment is required to start with – outdoor clothes and training shoes – and the entrance fee for an event is usually about 50 pence for Juniors.

• Plane Spotting

This is really one that involves the whole family, as there is quite a lot of travelling around involved and a car is obviously the easiest form of transport. Most small airports have an aviation society or group, which publishes its own magazine, listing flight movements and the latest news of airlines and aircraft. Subscription is around £7.50 a year, which includes copies of the magazine. All airports, even the large ones such as Heathrow or Gatwick, have some sort of viewing gallery or spectators' enclosure where visitors can watch the planes arriving and departing.

• Railways

Association of Railway Preservation Societies, 3 Orchard Close, Watford, Herts WD1 3DU (0923 21280)

If you are a steam railway enthusiast, there may be an opportunity for you to help on one of the 100 preserved railways in Britain.

They need volunteers to help clear undergrowth from the tracks and to clean the trains and engines. It is hard work, but great fun, and you have the chance to ride on the railways while you are working. Write to the above address for the full lists of railways to see if there is one near you, or to apply to join the Association. Another railway club that you can join is the Watercress Williams Club, run by the Mid-Hants Railway, Alresford Station, Alresford, Hampshire (0962 733810). The club is for people under 16, who receive a regular newsletter and are entitled to a free ride a year on the Watercress Line (see page 184).

The Association of Railway Preservation Societies publishes an annual *Guide to Steam Trains in the British Isles* which will give you full details of railway museums, restored stations, passenger rides and so on. See page 184 for list of some of the major steam railways around the country.

See also **Train Spotting** in this chapter.

• Stamp Collecting

British Philatelic Federation Ltd, 107 Charterhouse Street, London EC1M 6PT (01-251 5040)
The Stamp Collecting Promotion Council, 27 John Adam Street, London WC2N 6HZ

There are two million people in this country who collect stamps, and it provides a marvellous source of enjoyment for a small outlay on the minimum amount of equipment. Obviously there is no minimum age for collecting stamps – it depends entirely on you, but once your interest is aroused it would be well worth getting in touch with the Stamp Collecting Promotion Council at the address above. They are now a committee of the British Philatelic Council, and a fount of useful information. They will let you have a list of philatelic societies – virtually every town in the country now has one, and most of them have special sections and meetings for junior collectors and beginners, and some have their own reference libraries where you can look at stamp catalogues and handbooks. The SCPC will also let you have some very useful leaflets on stamp collecting, including *First Steps in Stamp Collecting*, *The Story of Stamps*, and *Starting a School Stamp Club*. Incidentally, if your school hasn't already got a stamp club, how about setting one up with the help of this booklet? The cost of stamp collecting could of course eventually run into hundreds of pounds for a real (and very rich!) enthusiast, but you can start off with, and get hours of enjoyment out of, a collection costing only a few pounds.

• Theatre

Should you want to take private drama lessons ask at school or in your local library to see whether they can put you in touch with a drama class. You can then take exams to achieve grades in drama as you can in music. You should also contact one of the addresses below, who will put you in touch with any workshops, etc, that are run in your area, as well as nationally-run courses. Remember, you don't need great acting ability to become involved, as there are many jobs backstage that you can help out with.

It is also a worthwhile idea to approach the theatre in your own town and to see if you will be able to arrange a visit for yourself and family or group of friends to visit the theatre backstage, perhaps during a rehearsal or after a performance. Ring the manager to ask if you could have a guided tour – you should not expect them to manage more than half a dozen of you and you should, of course, be careful as theatres can be dangerous places – a lady mayoress we know of fell into the orchestra pit and broke her leg while on her way up to the stage to make a speech welcoming the touring company to her town!

The National Theatre, South Bank, London SE1 9PX (01-928 2033 Ext. 382) runs and education department which gives workshops and demonstrations on the South Bank and in schools. The department provides tours of small-scale productions, practical study courses, support for student projects and ticket schemes for the NT School Association. If your school is not already a member then encourage it to join – membership is free! The National Theatre also provides daily tours of the theatre building, which last about 1½ hours and cost £2 (reductions for groups). For further details ring 01-633 0880.

National Youth Theatre of Great Britain, 32 York Way, London N1 (01-837 0118). The National Youth Theatre is one of the great British theatrical institutions – it celebrated its 30th birthday in 1986. It needs young people for its main summer show and travelling Easter shows, so if you would like to be considered and are aged between 14 and 21 write in for an audition. These are held in London, as well as all over the United Kingdom, including Scotland and Northern Ireland, and will cost you a £3 fee. If you pass the first audition – and thousands apply for only a few hundred places – you will be invited to a second audition. If you pass this you will be able to attend a three- to four-week summer course in London, costing around £40. Then the following year you may audition again to take part in one of the NYT productions. The Theatre emphasises that it is not a drama school or a stepping stone into the profession; it prefers to encourage teamwork, and emphasises the joint efforts of everyone concerned. Acting is not of course the only possibility, there are plenty of openings on the technical side, such as lighting technology, stage management, set design and wardrobe.

WAC (The Weekend Arts College)   If you live in the Greater London Area, see also under **Dance** for full details on WAC which gives drama and mime courses on Saturdays for 7 to 13-year-olds and on Sundays for 14 to 21-year-olds.

Young Theatre Association, Darwin Infill Building, Regent's College, Regent's Park, London NW1. The Association provides training and theatre information for young people between the ages of 12 and 18. Members receive a regular newsletter and a copy of *Drama Magazine* four times a year. They are entitled to buy cheap standby theatre tickets, and to go on training courses during the Christmas and Easter holidays as well as the very popular summer schools. These take place in different parts of the country – London, Cheltenham and Torquay – they are residential and open to young people from the age of 12 as well as adults. No previous experience is necessary, and the cost is about £100 for the under-18s. There are lots of opportunities for acting experience, as well as plenty of other facilities such as tennis, swimming, riding and so on. The YTA also runs local Saturday morning workshops, Sunday production groups and weekend courses. If you are interested in the theatre the YTA is a must for you and costs only £5 membership per year.

A backstage visit to the RSC theatre in Stratford could also make an exciting outing for your school or a group of friends. Write to RSC Gallery, Royal Shakespeare Theatre, Stratford upon Avon, CV37 6BB for a provisional booking or ring 0789 296655, but in either case contact the theatre the day before, because for technical reasons, the tour sometimes has to be cancelled. The price for students is £1 and the tour lasts 45 minutes.

● Train Spotting

There is no national organisation for train spotters, although there are local groups of enthusiasts who meet informally. However there are lots and lots of books and magazines to get you started. The publishers Ian Allan Ltd, Coomblands House, Coomblands Lane, Uddlestone, Weybridge, Surrey KT15 1HY (0932 58511) are the main source for these and they will send you a full, illustrated guide on request. Among their titles, published every year at the end of January, are *ABC British Rail Motive Power Combined Volume*, *British Rail Handbook*, *Electric Trains in Britain and London's Underground*. They also publish several railway magazines, including *Motive Power Monthly* at £1.25.

Interestingly, Ian Allan himself started the hobby of train spotting in the 1940s, by compiling lists of trains, and their numbers, which ran in his area, so setting in motion what is now a nation-wide interest.

See also under **Railways** in this Chapter, and on page 184.

● Under Seventeens Car Club

Lloyds Bank Chambers, South Street, Deal, Kent CT14 7AW

The Club has been set up for under age drivers to practise driving – legally and in properly supervised conditions – and to take an active interest in cars and motor sports. Upper age limit is 17 (hence the name), and while there is no lower age limit, in practice there are

ACTIVITIES **73**

few members under the age of 10, as you have to be able to handle and control a car before driving. At the moment, club venues are all in the south of England, but the club is hoping to spread to the Midlands and North in the future. Full members pay £5 a year, and associate members £6, plus a once-only joining fee of £15 for each family. Each full member must have an associate member (usually a parent) responsible for him/her, and they will be expected to help to run the club. Members will be driving the family car so there is a strong incentive for parents to take an active interest! The aims of the club are learning and enjoyment, and producing a safe, experienced driver at the end of it.

• Young NADFAS
(The National Association of Decorative and Fine Arts Societies), 38 Ebury Street, London SW1W 0LU (01-730 3041)

Young Nadfas organises holiday activities where the emphasis is on having fun and learning at the same time. Visits to historic houses and museums are made extra special with young professional guides, and there are lots of opportunities to take an active part in crafts, such as paper making, brass rubbing, spinning, weaving, enamelling, and so on, to dress up in costumes, to re-enact historic events, to learn about medieval farming methods, early industries or modern film making. These are only a few of the events organised by Young Nadfas to encourage members to take a positive role in understanding and enjoying this country's heritage.

Write to the address above to see if there is a group in your area. Groups started originally in the south of the country but have now reached Yorkshire, and new groups are still being set up. The age range is from 8 to 18 years, and the subscription is about £2 per year, which covers the cost of letters giving details of events, newsletters and a metal badge.

3.

CLUBS AND ORGANISATIONS

There are lots of organisations specially formed for young people and their interests, and they are very much more informal and relaxed than they used to be, so you will not feel that you are being regimented or over-organised. Even if you haven't considered joining any sort of organisation before, it is worth noting that these groups often provide the cheapest and most convenient way of learning very exciting and expensive skills (eg: sailing, riding, skiing, gliding, shooting) and of participating in expeditions, adventure camps, Outward Bound courses, foreign travel etc.

We have listed in this chapter some of the main organisations in the country – they all seem to offer a wide range of inviting and varied activities in a very down-to-earth way, and most of them are open to children from the age of 8 up to adult level (ie: 18). It costs very little to join any of them, and most of them can offer year-round activities, many in your own area, to keep you busy in the winter as well as the summer.

• Air Training Corps

Air Cadets Headquarters, Royal Air Force, Newton, Nottingham NG13 8HR (0949 20771 Ext. 441)

'Venture Adventure' is the motto of the ATC, and it certainly lives up to it! The ATC is a voluntary youth organisation linked to the RAF, and open to boys and girls between the ages of 13 and 18. Its aims are to encourage a practical interest in aviation, adventure, and sport, and its training includes topics such as map reading, meteorology and first aid. Cadets also take part in competition shooting, adventure training and expeditions, a week's annual camp, and lots of sports and other activities. Older 'First Class' cadets receive training in powered and glider flying and in air navigation; and finally a scholarship scheme enables selected cadets to learn to fly in light aircraft, bringing a private pilot's flying licence within reach.

Contact your local Wing Headquarters (look under Air Training Corps in the local telephone directory) and they will give you the name of your nearest squadron. Girls, alas, are not yet accepted into every squadron, so if you are a girl, check which squadrons in your area will be open to you.

• Army Cadet Force Association

Millbank Barracks, John Islip Street, London SW1P 4RR (01-821 7196)

The Cadet Force is sponsored by the Army, but is not part of it and has no emergency or mobilisation role, nor are cadets pressured to join the Army. Membership is spread across the United Kingdom in some 1,569 detachments, and consists of boys between 13 and 18. Girls are now being allowed to enrol, but they are still a bit thin on the ground. Membership of the Cadet Force offers a club life, opportunities for sport and games, visits to foreign countries, as well as the chance to learn military skills such as competition shooting, map reading, adventure training and so on.

'The chance to learn military skills'

• The Boys' Brigade

England Headquarters, Brigade House, Parsons Green, London SW6 4TH (01-736 8481)

Scotland Headquarters, Boys' Brigade House, 168 Bath Street, Glasgow G2 4TQ (041-332 0936)

The Boys' Brigade was founded over a 100 years ago – in Glasgow in 1883 – and is in fact an older organisation than the Scouts. It has now spread worldwide to more than 60 countries. Boys can join the Boys' Brigade from the age of 6 as Anchor Boys, and carry on as Seniors until they are 18. They join in year-round activities, including helping in the local community – perhaps with old people or disabled children – as well as taking part in an award scheme which covers activities as diverse as life saving, arts and crafts, canoeing, camping and all sports from archery to table tennis. The highlight of the year is the week-long summer camp – the Boys' Brigade has outdoor centres all round the country, including camping sites and mountaineering clubs, which provide a wealth of exciting experiences. If you do not know who your local Field Officer is, write to one of the headquarters above. They are very helpful and will give you all the information you need, including starting up a new Boys' Brigade company, if you do not have one in your area.

• Bright Sparks
6th Floor, 25/27 Oxford Street, London W1R 1RF (01-437 7476)

Bright Sparks is part of Sparks which, through sporting events, raises money for research into crippling diseases.

Bright Sparks is aimed at 12 to 18-year-olds. You become a member of Bright Sparks for a small membership fee, which makes you eligible to receive a quarterly newsletter, membership badge and card. As a member you are allowed a 50 per cent reduction on entry costs for sporting fund-raising events. The organisers hope that schools, clubs, youth organisations etc will become members, and they will then arrange sporting events to raise money for the fund. If you organised a big enough event Sparks would try to send along a sporting celebrity to open it.

• Challenge to Youth
BP Oil Ltd, BP House, Victoria Street, London SW1E 5NJ

Challenge to Youth is 'designed to bridge the gap between the theory of the classroom and the practicality of the adult world'. BP has devised a number of projects to appeal to groups of young people – whether they be still at school, school leavers or unemployed – in which they have to design and construct a practical object – a robot butler, a submarine, and a hovercraft have been some of the previous challenges! Buildacar challenge was such a success that it now takes place every two years and has produced some remarkably inventive as well as functioning motor cars. First prize is £1,000, 2nd £750 and 3rd £500. In addition, Open Challenge offers a unstructured scheme for individual projects which BP will then help to finance and see through to completion. Two previous examples in the Open Challenge section have been a satellite-linked weather station launched by a school in South Wales, and a solar-powered fridge to hold vaccines in Third World countries. You can take part in Challenge to Youth through your school or as a group of individuals. So if you think you are both inventive and practical, or have friends that are one or the other, write to BP for information on current and future projects.

• The Duke of Edinburgh's Award
Head Office: 5 Prince of Wales Terrace, Kensington, London W8 5PG (01-937 5205)

The Duke of Edinburgh's Award Scheme is a programme of leisure time activities 'which challenges all young people between the ages of 14 and 25, throughout the Commonwealth, to serve others, acquire new skills, experience adventure, and make new friends'. 'The Scheme is not competitive and anyone with the necessary perseverance, enterprise and effort can gain an award, including those with some sort of disability'.

There are three awards: Bronze, for those over 14, Silver for those over 15 and Gold for those over 16. You have to compete in four different types of activity for each award, as follows: *Service*, for instance, first aid, conservation, community service, childcare. *Expeditions*: you plan, train for and undertake a journey of at least two days, on foot, bicycle, by horse, canoe, staying in tents or youth hostels. *Skills*: you choose one of over 200 activities in which – over a period varying from 6 months (Bronze) to 18 months (Gold) – you show perseverance and practice. A few examples of such activities might be: agriculture, dogs, boatwork, music (classical, jazz, etc), public speaking, driving (car or motorcycle), photography, fishing, entertaining, and so on. The last category is *Physical Recreation*, in which you take part in an organised sport, for instance, archery, cycling, trampolining, orienteering, caving, rowing, etc. Lastly, Gold Award candidates complete a five-day residential project in such schemes as work camps, Outward Bound courses or Sail Training Voyages.

Most young people take part in the Duke of Edinburgh's Award

Scheme through their schools, but you can always join as an individual. Write to the Head office (address above) for the address of your local Award Committee or nearest Award Office. Local authorities also have their own established arrangements of the Scheme. The Award Scheme is an immensely fulfilling and satisfying way of pursuing your favourite activities, it also provides the challenge of wider interests, and is a sure recommendation for possible future employers.

● Endeavour Training

17a Glumangate, Chesterfield, Derbyshire S40 1TX (0246 37201/2)

Endeavour was established to help young people develop their full potential as individuals and as members of society. It runs a variety of courses in residential centres around the country, and organises expeditions here and abroad through the John Hunt Exploration Group. It also runs Camp Endeavour which uses trained volunteers to provide holidays for underprivileged children.

● Girls' Brigade

Brigade House, Parsons Green, London SW6 4TH (01-736 8481)

The Brigade is an international and interdenominational organisation for girls, working in over 50 countries. You can join at the age of 5, as an Explorer, and continue through the Juniors and Seniors to a Brigadier, for 14-year-olds and over. The Brigade, like the Boys' Brigade, its male counterpart, is uniformed because it feels the uniform encourages a sense of belonging and responsibility. Like the Boys' Brigade too, its emphasis is on a structured training programme which combines learning new skills, making new friends, service to the community and exciting activities such as holiday camps. There is an award and badge scheme for completing different stages of the programme, and the Brigade also encourages members to join the Duke of Edinburgh's Award Scheme to work for their bronze, silver and gold medals.

● Girl Guides

Girl Guides Association, 17–19 Buckingham Palace Road, London SW1W 0PT (01-834 6242)

Some schools run Girl Guide Companies, but if yours does not, write to the Association for the name of your District Commissioner, who will put you in touch with the nearest Company. Alternatively, you can go to the reference section of your local library, who will almost certainly be able to help you. Guides cater for any activity you can think of, from flower arranging to pony trekking, swimming and camping. They run an 8-point programme for both indoor and outdoor activities and these 8 points cover the development of mind, character, physical fitness, creative ability, relationships with others, service to others, homecraft skills and enjoyment of the out-of-doors. There are three groups within the Guide framework: Brownies for 7 to 10-year-olds, Guides from 10 to 14 and Rangers from 14 to 18. Rangers are especially adventurous and may find themselves involved in pot-holing, parascending, climbing or canoeing. Costs are kept very low and the uniform is not expensive to buy.

• Girls' Venture Corps

Redhill Aerodrome, Kings Mill Lane, South Nutfield, Redhill, Surrey RH1 5JY (073 7823345)

In individual units and at national camps and courses, leadership training is encouraged. Outdoor activities include expeditions (in conjunction with the Duke of Edinburgh's Award Scheme), camping, orienteering, canoeing, sailing, rifle shooting and skiing. Flying is a popular activity and aviation subjects are taught in Units. The arts of make-up and hairstyles, flower arranging, art and crafts also play an important part in the Corps programme. Cadets also work on community and conservation projects, help the elderly and the disabled and work with young children. Girls can be members between the ages of 13 and 18 and there are currently between 5,000 and 8,000 members.

'Flying is a popular activity'.

• Inter-Action

Royal Victoria Dock, London E16 1BT (01-511 0411/6)

Inter-Action is not an organisation that young people can join or even one that youth groups or schools can affiliate with, but it deserves to be included because of the extremely interesting and unusual work it is carrying out on behalf of young people. Your school or local youth group may well find it helpful to get in touch with this group. It consists of a group of companies which seek to find ways of helping with particular problems in the community by developing new projects and techniques which can then be used by local groups elsewhere. This is the theory behind Inter-Action, but the various different companies provide the more concrete base. The ones concerned specifically with young people include:

Community Computers UK helps youth groups or schools to set up their own computer clubs, schools activities, creative play and community holiday computer camps, plus Computerama, a mobile holiday scheme, and Logo, a festival in which young people present their own practical projects.

Country Wings Country Wings is designed to teach group leaders to help children to use their local outdoor setting, whether in town or country, more positively. They use practical techniques, such as blindfold adventure trails, new games and activities, or camping out in a town, to teach young people to get the most out of their local environment.

Inter-Action in Print Handbooks on youth and community projects, computer training techniques and creative play programmes.

Occupation Preparation Systems A set of training systems for employment or constructive leisure which are designed for schools and youth clubs, including MIY – make it yourself – for practical training, and a Search System for job finding.

Youth Options Menu A scheme to help youth clubs throughout the country develop self-help skills and opportunities for employment and creative leisure.

• National Association of Boys' Clubs

24 Highbury Grove, London N5 2EA (01-359 9281)

The NABC exists to develop boys' clubs throughout the country and to offer support to existing clubs. They run a very full and exciting programme including a national drama festival, radio workshops, and annual competitions in music, photography, film and video. Sport is of course important; they organise an international soccer tournament as well as championships in athletics, boxing, canoeing, cross country, angling, etc and a national adventure trophy awarded after a tough weekend competing with the 'outdoors'. They also issue regular newsletters, magazines and so on, and can help clubs with insurance, transport, and every kind of advice and information.

• National Association of Youth Clubs

Keswick House, 30 Peacock Lane, Leicester LE1 5NY (0533 29514)

The Association is an umbrella organisation serving and representing associations of youth clubs in counties and metropolitan areas of England and Northern Ireland, Scotland and Wales. These associations provide invaluable advice, guidance and support for clubs and youth groups in their areas and offer a range of services and facilities for young people and those who work with them.

When a club affiliates to NAYC the club members immediately have the following benefits: a free copy of the magazine *Youth Club* six times a year, a varied programme of sports and recreation, information sheets and advice on any relevant topic, fund-raising support, insurance cover, various useful publications and lots of other help. Membership is open to boys and girls between 11 and 21 years of age.

• National Council for Voluntary Youth Services

Wellington House, 29 Albion Street, Leicester LE1 6GD (0533 554910)

The purpose of the Council is to 'help and educate young people so as to develop their physical, mental and spiritual capacities that they may grow to full maturity as individuals and members of society'. They act as a central umbrella advisory body to all voluntary youth organisations, and speak out for the rights of young people to the Government and society generally. This is especially important today, with so much unemployment and dissatisfaction among the young. If you are running or helping to run any voluntary youth organisation you will find them very helpful with any advice and information you may need, and if they can't help you directly, they will at least be able to point you in the right direction to find the help you need.

● National Council of YMCAs

640 Forest Road, London E17 3DZ (01-520 5599)

The YMCA, founded in England, has grown into a worldwide ecumenical youth organisation with centres in more than 90 countries. It provides a welcome for all young people which is based on a belief of the equality of the individual. In England it is one of the largest voluntary providers of health sports and youth and community facilities in the country, with over 200 centres nationwide. It provides 8,000 young people with a bed each night in safe, comfortable, home-from-home accommodation. It is the largest voluntary sponsor of places on the Youth Training Scheme and trains over 5,000 unemployed teenagers each year. It has its own international wing – 'Y' Care International – for the support of refugees all over the world and to encourage international development education. It has also a Schools Link programme to increase its work with young people.

See also **YMCA & YWCA** in this chapter.

● Nautical Training Corps

2 Old Shoreham Road, Brighton, East Sussex BN1 5DD (0273 504880)

Membership is open to boys and girls from the age of 7 upwards. The Corps provides instruction and basic training in seamanship, especially for young people who are planning to make their career in the Royal or Merchant Navies.

• Ocean Youth Club

c/o The Bus Station, South Street, Gosport, Hants PO12 1EP (0705 528421/2)

The Club exists to teach young people to sail, and to learn seamanship and navigation. It provides over 4,000 berths at sea to young people between the ages of 12 and 21 on eleven vessels based at Gosport, The Hamble, Plymouth, Holyhead, Liverpool, Belfast, Clyde, Blyth, Great Yarmouth and Ipswich. Membership entitles member to wear the Club T shirts, sweat shirts, tie and cap badge, receive the sailing programme and Club Yearbook, join the nearest Area Support Group, take part in winter refit work and join area social and training activities, and sail on any boat in any of the Area Support Groups. Membership is open to both sexes and consists of Cadets (12 to 14-year-olds) and sailing members (15 to 21-year-olds).

• The Prince's Trust

8 Bedford Row, London WC1R 4BU (01-430 0527)

The Trust was set up by the Prince of Wales in 1972 to encourage young people between the ages of 14 and 25 to help themselves. It is a charity which will provide small grants and support, and is able to respond quickly to requests for help by individuals and small groups. The maximum grant is usually around £300 and is given to disadvantaged young people for self-help schemes or for projects which may enable them to help others. The Trust is also tackling problems of unemployment in helping young people set up their own small businesses. Write for further information to the address above.

• Ramblers Association

1/5 Wandsworth Road, London SW8 2XX (01-582 6878)

The Association exists to help walkers in the English countryside by guarding rights of way and fights to protect the countryside itself. The RA is the walkers' pressure group; its benefits for members include a national service of expert advice and information; the free annual, *Bed and Breakfast Guide*, a quarterly copy of *Rucksack* the RA magazine, discounts in many outdoor equipment shops, and lots of other useful perks. Members under 18 years can join at a reduced rate of £4 per annum, and there is also a joint family membership rate of £10 per annum.

• St John Ambulance Cadets

1 Grosvenor Crescent, London SW1X 7EF (01-235 5231)

St John Ambulance gives young people the opportunity to partake in community work, attend camps, and take part in various forms of adventure training which are both exciting and enjoyable.

Apart from first aid and nursing, cadets can be awarded proficiency certificates in animal care, childcare, cookery/nutrition, hygiene, natural history, sailing, canoeing, swimming/life saving, fire fighting, road and home safety.

Membership is open to boys and girls between the ages of 8 and 18.

'Cadets can be awarded proficiency certificates in animal care'.

• Scouts

The Scouts Association, Baden Powell House, 65 Queensgate Street, London SW1 (01-584 7030)

If your school does not run a Scout Troop, write to the above address for the name of your District Commissioner, who will put you in touch with your nearest troop, or the local library will be able to help you. Cub Scouts are for 8 to 11 years, Scouts 11 to 16 and

Venture Scouts from 16 to 20 years. Although the emphasis is still on outdoor activities, to encourage self-reliance in the summer camps, Scouts can now take up a wider range of other activities including electronics, car mechanics and other technological subjects. Community Service is also stressed and the Scoutreach Programme has been planned to extend scouting into areas such as inner cities or new housing estates where there are limited leisure opportunities for young people.

• Sea Cadet Corps

Broadway House, Broadway, London SW19 1RL (01-540 8222)

The Sea Cadets is an organisation for boys and girls from 12 to 18. They have units around the country named after the town or district in which they are situated, and these units are grouped into areas. If you cannot find an address in the local telephone directory, get in touch with the London headquarters for your nearest unit. The aim of the Sea Cadets is to train young people in many activities and especially the art of seamanship by practical training. They have their own sailing brig *Royalist* and there are also opportunities to take to the water in canoes, sailing dinghies, motor fishing vessels and even in RNR Minesweepers.

• Sea Ranger Association

50 New Street, Henley on Thames, Oxon RG9 2BX

This is one just for the girls. It offers all forms of boating, rowing, canoeing, powered sailing, in dinghies, wind surfing or offshore. Members can also work for the Duke of Edinburgh Award Scheme, and they go camping in adventure holidays. Girls can join at the age of 10 as Cadets, and from 13 onwards they become full Sea Rangers.

• YMCA & YWCA

National Council of YMCAs, 640 Forest Road, London E17 3DZ (01-520 5599)

The YMCA is part of a worldwide movement of over 26 million members in 96 countries. In England it has over 200 centres with 80,000 members and one million participants. The Association is a voluntary organisation which was set up to offer opportunities to encourage all, members or not, to lead full and worthwhile lives.

There is a junior section for young people under 17 years old which runs programmes and activities specially geared to their needs.

The YMCA centres provide activities and facilities to meet local community needs, and you don't need to be a member to use them. A few examples of these facilities include outdoor/all weather football pitches, day camp programmes, 'Just Ask' – a London Central counselling service, and in addition the YMCA runs activity holiday centres in Cumbria, Northumberland, Hampshire, etc (see page 206 for full details of these).

Among many other activities, they provide housing and accommodation for thousands of young people, and organise youth training courses in leadership, sports coaching, etc, and this is only a very small sample of the work they undertake. Write to them for more information and for details on how to become a member.

See also **National Council of YMCAs.**

4.

FOR THE HANDICAPPED

Facilities for the disabled have increased greatly over the past few years, although there is still much room for improvement, and it is essential to keep pushing for more improvements. Meanwhile most societies and organisations are now aware of the particular problems of the disabled, and are making steps to meet them.

In this chapter we list organisations that are not designed specifically for the disabled but welcome them anyway, and those that were designed and so do cater for their special needs. The two most useful addresses we can give you are:

The National Children's Bureau, 8 Wakely Street, London EC1V 7QE (01-278 9441). The National Children's Bureau deals with the well-being of all children, but has also set up a committee called The Voluntary Council for Handicapped Children which is concerned specifically with improving services for handicapped children and their families. The Council provides a very important information service for parents, especially in regard to services and consumer participation, and in addition has published a book *Help Starts Here*, which details sources of help for both parents and professionals. A number of fact sheets are also available on different topics such as holidays or winter sports for disabled children.

The Royal Association For Disability and Rehabilitation (Radar), 25 Mortimer Street, London W1 (01-637 5400), is equally a mine of information for handicapped people, including children and young people. They provide very detailed fact sheets on sport and leisure activities, and we are very grateful to them for giving us so much information – we can only reproduce a fraction of it here, but write to them direct, for full details.

Sport

There are very few sports that handicapped children cannot take part in. Their special needs are catered for either under the umbrella of the national society for a particular sport, or by an organisation set up specifically to cater for them. Have a look at the chapter on sport in this book. Most of the sports associations will either be able to help handicapped people directly or put them in touch with another organisation for people with special needs. We give below the addresses of some of these organisations, but write to Radar for a full list.

British Sports Association for the Disabled, Hayward House, Barnard Crescent, Aylesbury, Bucks HP21 8PP (0296 27889). For information on all sport, contact this Association. They are the central co-ordinating body for sport for the disabled, and will be able to put people in touch with the appropriate organisations, and can provide information for disabled people who want to watch sport, as well as participate in it. In addition, they can provide help and information on sports gear or equipment which is specially designed or modified to enable a disabled person to take part in a particular sport.

REMAP (Rehabilitation Engineering Movement Advisory Panels), c/o Royal Association for Disability and Rehabilitation, 25 Mortimer Street, London W1N 1AB (01-637 5400). Remap is a group of professionals including therapists, engineers and technicians who design 'one-off' aids for disabled people to fill a special need, including aids for a particular sports activity.

In addition, local authorities should be able to help the disabled with sport in their regions, whether they want to be spectators or participants.

The Information Centre, Sports Council, 16 Upper Woburn Place, London WC1H 0QP (01-388 1277). The information centre has a reference library where people can come to look up facts for themselves. It also publishes *Sport and Recreation for the Disabled*, which is a bibliography of all the literature available on the subject.

● Basketball
Great Britain Wheelchair Basketball League, 76 Leicester Road, Failsworth, Manchester M35 0QP (061-682 9521)

● Camping
Camping for the Disabled, 20 Burton Close, Dawley, Telford, Shropshire

● Fencing
Wheelchair Fencing Association, 42 Falkland Avenue, Marton, Blackpool

● Judo
British Judo Association Working Party for the Disabled/Handicapped, 16 Upper Woburn Place, London WC1H 0QH (01-387 9340)

● Movement and Dance
National Wheelchair Dance Association, Craig-y-Parc School, Pentyrch, Cardiff CF4 8PD
Shape, 9 Fitzroy Square, London W1P 6AE (01-388 9622)

Shape is an organisation in which artists (musicians, painters, sculptors, actors etc) offer their services as performers or in workshops to people in residential care, hospitals, day centres, clubs and so on. Regional Shapes are being set up around the country and are organising training courses for artists and disabled people.

• Riding

Riding for the Disabled Association, Avenue R, National Agricultural Centre, Kenilworth, Warwickshire CV8 2LY (0203 56107)

The RDA has 18 regional branches, with 562 member groups which cater for over 18,700 riders, with many different disabilities. The headquarters will provide information on local branches.

• Sailing

Sparks, 6th Floor, 25–27 Oxford Street, London W1R 1RF (01-734 3232)

Sparks (sportsmen pledged to aid research into crippling diseases) owns a 45-foot catamaran called *Sparkle*. It can take up to 10 people in wheelchairs as well as other disabled, and is available free of charge. See page 76 for more details on Sparks and Bright Sparks.

• Skiing

British Ski Club for the Disabled, Corton House, Corton, Near Warminster, Wiltshire BA12 0SZ (0985 50321)
Uphill Ski Club, 12 Park Crescent, London W1N 4EQ (01-636 1989)

• Swimming

Association of Swimming Therapy, Tree Tops, Swan Hill, Ellesmere, Shropshire SY12 0LZ (069171 3542).

National Association of Swimming Clubs for the Handicapped, 219 Preston Drive, Brighton, East Sussex BN1 6FL (0273 559470)

• Water Sports

British Sports Association for the Disabled, Water Sports Division, Hayward House, Barnard Crescent, Aylesbury, Bucks HP21 8PP (0296 27889)

The Water Sports Division includes representatives of all water sports, including angling, canoeing, sailing, sub-aqua, etc (see Chapter 1 for the addresses of these organisations). In addition it includes the British Disabled Water Ski Association, Spastics Society, British Association for Sporting and Recreational Activities of the Blind, the Sports Council and the Department of Education and Science.

Activities

Many if not most of the activities described in Chapter 2 of this book are ones that disabled young people can take part in. The national associations given under each interest will provide information for people with special needs.

The Disabled Living Foundation, 380–384 Harrow Road, London W9 2HU (01-289 6111). The Foundation is another useful organisation to contact, and has produced an information sheet called *Leisure Activities*, at 90 pence, which provides details on hobbies, holidays and other leisure pursuits.

Radar (address on page 87), has produced some splendidly detailed fact sheets on all types of leisure activities for the disabled, including useful special equipment where necessary and addresses of relevant organisations. The fact sheets on hobbies cover needlecraft, knitting, board games, jigsaws, playing cards, photography, pottery, printing, reading and gardening and woodwork. Those on the arts include art, music, drama and dance for the handicapped. They provide useful addresses throughout the country and publications which link the arts and disabled people (for instance, *The Arts and*

Disabilities, a creative response to handicap, ed. Geoffrey Lord, Macdonald, 1981: *Arts for Everyone*, guidance on provision for disabled people, by A. Pearson, Centre on Environment for the Handicapped, 1985).

Finally, an address for adventure playgrounds: Handicapped Adventure Playground Association, Palace Playground, Fulham Palace, Bishops Avenue, London SW6 6EA (01-736 4443).

Holidays

There are many organisations which provide handicapped children with holidays of various kinds. Some of these enable less severely disabled children to take a holiday on their own, without their parents, others make provision for children and parents together. Contact the Voluntary Council for Handicapped Children (address on page 87) and ask for their fact sheet on holidays. The social services departments of local authorities should also be able to give information on local holiday schemes for disabled or disadvantaged children and their families.

The organisations below all provide holidays for the handicapped or disadvantaged children. In some cases they cater for the able bodied as well, and the children are expected to mix in together on the holiday.

British Red Cross Society, 9 Grosvenor Crescent, London SW1 (01-235 5454). The Red Cross organises holidays for children in need through their local branches, of which there are over 50.

Calvert Trust Adventure Centre, Little Crossthwaite, Underskiddaw, Keswick, Cumbria (0596 72234). This holiday centre caters specifically for disabled people, and provides specially designed accommodation. The holiday includes hill walking, sailing, riding, etc.

Children's Country Holiday Fund, 1 York Street, Baker Street, London W1 (01-935 8373). The Fund arranges holidays for unaccompanied children from 5 to 13 years of age, whose parents could not otherwise afford a holiday for them. The children go to the country or the seaside and stay either with a family or in camps.

Churchtown Farm Field Studies Centre, Lanlivery, Bodmin, Cornwall (0208 872148). This is a holiday centre owned by the Spastics Society, and its facilities include a library, audio visual aids and a heated swimming pool. It caters for groups who come with their own teaching and care staff.

Constance Holidays for the Disabled, 34–36 South Street, Lancing, West Sussex BN15 8AG (0903 750310). Multi-activity holidays at Ullenwood Manor, near Cheltenham. Activities include archery, basketball, golf, swimming and so on. Accommodation is in specially adapted rooms, with special equipment provided if required. The minimum age is 8 years. The cost is about £175 for a week.

Farm Holiday Bureau, National Agricultural Centre, Stoneleigh, Nr. Kenilworth, Warwickshire CV8 2LY (0203 555100). The Bureau publishes a book *Farm Holidays* (£1.99 from them or from a bookshop). In it are details of 90 farms which can cater for disabled people on holiday. Not all the farms can cope with wheelchairs, so make sure you check before booking exactly what they can offer.

Forest School Camps, Special Enrolments Officer, 110 Burbage Road, London SE24 9HD (01-274 7566). Ten per cent of places in Forest School Camps are reserved for children who are either handicapped or in some way disadvantaged. The children, who are unaccompanied, must be recommended by a local authority, and the cost can sometimes be shared between the authorities and the camp.

Kielder Adventure Centre, Low Cranecleugh, Kielder Water, Falstone, Hexham, Northumberland (0660 50232). The Centre is open all year round, and offers holidays to disabled people and their families. The activities include canoeing, sailing, swimming, rock climbing, cross-country orienteering, skiing, birdwatching and nature walks, fishing, camping, badminton, and so on.

Holiday information

Holiday Care Service, 2 Old Bank Chambers, Station Road, Horley, Surrey RH6 9HW (02934 74535). This service had been funded by members of the travel industry. It offers advice and help in arranging holidays for people with special needs.

For further information on holidays for the disabled, contact the holiday officer at Radar. Radar publishes Holiday Information Sheets (send s.a.e.), as well as the guide *Holidays for the Physically Handicapped* (£2 by post) which provides details of special interest holidays in this country, as well as a few abroad, suitable accommodation (including self-catering), and the amount of care available.

Useful Organisations

Here are two organisations which combine able-bodied and handicapped young people in associations which encourage them to get to know each other, and to co-operate, work and enjoy leisure and holidays together.

National Federation of Gateway Clubs, 117 Golden Lane, London EC1Y 0RT (01-253 9433). A national voluntary youth and community organisation sponsored by Mencap in which able-bodied young people help to provide leisure and fun time for the mentally handicapped. For more details see page 53.

PHAB (Physically Handicapped and Able Bodied), Tavistock House North, Tavistock Square, London WC1H 9HJ (01-388 1963). This organisation encourages the physically handicapped (PH) and able-bodied (AB) to come together and meet in clubs, holidays or other leisure activities. Page 54 provides more information.

Most of the following organisations were not specifically established to cater for the disabled, but all of them welcome handicapped members, and some of them have sections specially designed to help people who want to join the organisation but suffer some handicap and have special needs.

We do not give addresses here, as all of them are already provided in the book, just page references so that you can find them quickly.

5.

RAISING MONEY

Fund raising is now very much part of all our lives. Newspapers and television have made us much more aware of other people's problems throughout the world, and we often feel not only a deep sympathy but a great desire to do something to help these people. The efforts of Bob Geldof, Blue Peter and the like have inspired us all, by showing us very practical and positive ways to do our bit. While fund raising is a serious subject, and needs to be organised efficiently, it can be enjoyable too. If it turns into a chore then it will defeat its object, because you just won't raise the money. Equally, the fund raising must be taken seriously, and remember that any charity you support relies on a good reputation for continuous public support.

There are so many good causes these days that it is hard to single any one of them out for special help, but it is often a good idea to select a local charity that people will know about, and can feel involved in. Often such a charity will be able to give you a specific aim to support, and it can be very satisfying to know that your money is, for instance, helping to build a stable for Riding for the Disabled or providing a special therapeutic bath for a local home for handicapped children.

You could raise some money and spend some of it giving a party for old people. You would need to arrange it with the matron of an old people's home. If you want to raise money through your school, remember that many have pet charities which staff and students support, but they will probably be happy to make room for others, if you are willing to do the organising. Also, check that there isn't a local group already in operation for the particular charity you have chosen. If there is they will be delighted with your support, and may even be able to help you.

In case you need suggestions for charities we have listed some of the main ones, particularly for helping children and young people. For example, **Bright Sparks** are specifically aiming at encouraging the young and fit to raise funds for the crippled (see page 76). This of course is only a tiny proportion of those available – the Charity Commissioners tell us there are over 50,000 different registered charities – but it may give you some ideas to start with. Of course, when there is a sudden need for emergency relief, as in Ethiopia in 1984, our imaginations are stirred, and we may want to concentrate our fund-raising efforts and donations on these causes.

There is no reason why you shouldn't have the added incentive of raising some money for yourselves. Perhaps you could give 75 per cent to a charity and keep 25 per cent for yourselves? But make sure this is *very* clearly stated before the fund raising begins or you are acting illegally, and remember sometimes people are less supportive if the whole amount does not go to a charity. It is probably best to run this sort of appeal on a very small and personal level.

You may need to raise money for yourself, for example, to go abroad to work in a voluntary capacity (see page 224) or for a sport enterprise for which you need sponsorship. You will find people very supportive especially if you show you intend to *do* something to earn your share. Always explain very clearly that you are the recipient of the money so that there are no misunderstandings. We give ideas for this kind of fund raising on pages 113–120.

Organisation

If you are interested in a cause, you will want to organise most of the fund raising yourself. The younger ones among you will obviously undertake simple efforts, but the older ones could embark on more complicated events. How much help parents or other adults need to give you, depends of course on your age. It is however always a good idea to ask an adult to check over what you are doing – don't forget even they find it easy enough to get into a muddle where money is involved! You may need a certain amount of subsidising by an adult for printing expenses, raw materials, etc, prior to the fund-raising event. Even though these costs will not amount to much and can be reimbursed afterwards, they will have to be paid for, so it is up to you to convince adults that you are serious and well organised enough for them to want to help. Also in certain instances, an adult *must* be involved to supervise from safety, legal and insurance angles (see page 102).

Committees

If your event will involve a lot of people, first of all organise a group of friends into a committee to oversee the fund raising – you should have a good reliable chairperson to keep everyone up to the mark! You will need an efficient secretary to keep minutes, ie, notes on what you decide to organise, and a treasurer to be in charge of the money with the backing of an adult to show you how. Don't have everyone on the committee: about six to ten of you should be enough to get things organised, but then you will need to organise others to help on the day, etc. Do ask people who can be relied on – use other people's talents to help you but not necessarily to actually organise the events. Always keep tabs on those in charge of various jobs well ahead of the event.

Printed Forms

You may need to have printed forms, either for sponsorships, advertising, judges to keep records on, etc. These need not be elaborate but must be legible. Set out your requirements in rough, and get an adult to check the contents. Then organise them to be typed and xeroxed – again ask a friendly adult! Schools might be able to help here, a local vicar usually has some sort of copying machine or perhaps your or another parent works in a co-operative office, which will be prepared to lend its equipment for a good cause if you pay for the paper – remember that even this can be quite expensive. If all else fails, libraries and office equipment shops run a photocopying service, but they do charge.

Publicity

Posters

You want everyone to know about your fund-raising event, and there is no better way than putting up posters. You can make your own with sheets of bright coloured or fluorescent paper, which you can buy from a good stationer or craft shop. They also sell fluorescent pens (called 'Stabilo Boss' pens) for making eye-catching lettering. Make this lettering big: 6 to 8 inches high for the heading and date and venue – but then keep the rest of the information to a minimum – you don't want the poster to look fussy, or be hard to read. If you are using arrows to point people in the right direction on the big day, then make these large and fluorescent too. Cover the posters with polythene if it is likely to rain.

'If you are using arrows to point people in the right direction...'

You and your friends can put posters up at your homes, and get permission to put others up in your school, local shops or on notice boards. Don't put them on empty shop windows, or cover up other posters. Ask the local police if you can put them up in the street, on lamp posts etc, but be careful not to put them on sharp bends in the road, as they can be distracting and dangerous. Finally, be sure to take them all down once your event is over. You may well need to enlist parents or older brothers and sisters to help construct and erect simple but stable and strong boards on posts. Put up your posters at least three weeks before your event – remember to use really strong drawing pins when attaching your poster, especially if you are expecting it to withstand the elements outside.

Press and media advertising

If you are planning a large event advertise in the local press, but you will find it very costly. A possible way around this is to contact the features editor of the local papers and see if they would be prepared to do an article on your efforts and in effect give you free advertising. Local parish magazines are much cheaper than newspapers, but do not have such a large circulation. Contact the editors well ahead to ask advice. Perhaps you could insert into each magazine a typed slip of information, for example:

```
YOUTH CLUB JUMBLE SALE - VILLAGE HALL
     SATURDAY 17TH MAY AT 2.30 p.m.
     ITEMS WANTED FROM 10.30 a.m.
              OR TELEPHONE
       659 or 558 FOR COLLECTION
```

Always organise newspaper advertising well before your event – it would be very annoying to find the paper had gone to press without your publicity information. Plan very carefully what needs to go into the advert. It must be clear, concise and catchy. Go to the newspaper and discuss your plan with them – apparently it is always preferable to place the advertisement on the right-hand page of the newspaper which is more eye-catching, and page three is considered a prime position! Depending on how adventurous and large the event is, contact your local radio station. Even TV may be interested in including you in a slot. Obviously the event would have to have enough general appeal to warrant such media attention.

Door-to-door publicity
Depending on the suitability of where you live, go *in pairs* round streets dropping neat and explicit publicity into local letterboxes.

Charities
Larger charities are often very helpful in providing posters, leaflets and even in some cases printing. Once you have decided on your charity, write and ask if they do provide any such help before you start your planning. NB You will have to have some official documentation from the charity if at all possible to prove that your effort is in aid of a genuine case. This is particularly relevant if you are going around to local shops or businesses asking for sponsorship, raffle prizes, or any help with your event.

Celebrities
If you can provide a 'celebrity' of some sort, for example, a local sportsman/woman to come along and help publicise the event, then it will help with your 'drawing power' on the general public. Try writing to a suitable candidate – at worst they can only say no – but the event must be worthwhile, not just a small effort. Check that they will not want to charge for the appearance! Include their name in the publicity blurb. Bright Sparks (see page 76) will be very helpful with this if you are holding a large sporting event on their behalf.

Local firms
If you are holding a large event, many local firms, and in particular estate agents, will pay the costs of posters, printing, etc provided that their name is linked with the advertising in some way.

Money
Make sure you have someone reliable who can organise money matters – if you are very inexperienced it is best that an adult is in charge. In any case, you should have an adult overseeing your arrangements. You will not need to open bank accounts for small events, but if there is liable to be a larger sum of money involved, then choose a treasurer and open a separate account – see a bank about this. Go along with all the facts well set out and if possible accompanied by an adult to organise everything.

Depending on what sort of event you are running, you may well require a 'float'. It is probably a good idea to have at least £5 worth

'Make sure you have someone reliable who can organise money matters'

of change for each individual event. For example, if you are running a fête you will need a float for each stall. Go to your bank, and they will be able to help you change your fiver for whichever coins you consider suitable. How much you require will be governed by the size of the event – ask an adult in any case to supervise these finances and advise about the amount of change you should need.

The Law

Naturally there have to be strict laws about fund raising – otherwise people would set up bogus charities, but don't be put off by the formality! They are not a hassle if you are sensible and organised, and are not of concern for the simple fund raising which most of you would attempt. We include information here which you should know about, so that you can judge whether or not you would need to take heed!

1. You must always give the money you raise to the charity you have named as the object of the appeal. It is illegal to mislead those contributing by deciding to give your proceeds instead to any other charity. Remember this if you are splitting your proceeds.

2. If you intend to charge an entrance fee at any event then you should obtain a Public Entertainments Licence from your local government office – ask for the Chief Executive Officer. This involves filling in forms which are referred via a local authority to the police, fire adviser and certain council departments. You must give 28 days' notice, but discuss the whole position well before that to decide whether or not such a licence is required. (The licence also involves a fee.) The easiest way out is not charge an entrance fee for your event.

3. The law concerning raffles, tombolas and lotteries can be complicated, so to keep things simple:
(i)   Do not give cash prizes,
(ii) Keep your expenses (including tickets and prizes) below £50,
(iii) Sell and draw your tickets and announce the lucky winners during the fund-raising event.
(If you intend to hold a very grand raffle, involving raffling a car for example, then consult a lawyer about the 'ins and outs'.)

4. If you are under 16, you cannot legally undertake any sort of street collection. If you are accompanied by older people you will still need to have permission of the police or local authority. Remember to have proof of being attached to a *bona fide* charity while you are making collections, for example, wear a badge.

5. If either alcohol or music and dancing are involved in your fund raising, you need to check up about licences well before the event, as the police have powers to stop a function if licensing regulations have not been properly adhered to.
(i)   Liquor Licence: Since 1983 small organisations have been able to apply for a liquor licence to sell alcohol at functions connected with their activities. The procedure is very simple but all steps must be complied with and therefore we recommend anyone to apply to their Local Clerk to the Licensing Justices. The application must be made at least one month before the function, so think well ahead.
(ii) Music and Dancing Licence: It is necessary to check that the venue has a proper licence for music and dancing. This licence is necessary where the public is invited to attend. Here again the procedure is simple for an application. You should apply to your local government office for advice, and ask for the Chief Executive Officer.

Insurance

Get an adult to help you over this – it is absolutely *vital* to have insurance cover if you are holding a charity event, in case of accidents, theft, fire, etc. Even if your event is at home, check that your parents' insurance will cover you. Ask you parents' broker if there is *any* query. Consult local insurance brokers to give a public liability insurance and ask for quotations from all of them to find the cheapest cover. If you are holding an event in a hired building, always check exactly what insurance cover they have and remember some have limits on the numbers allowed inside.

We don't imagine your events will be large enough to warrant insuring against being rained off, but we are just mentioning that it can be done – at a price!

It is worth putting up disclaimer notices that no responsibility for accidents, theft, loss or damage will be incurred by the organisers. Put these in car park areas, or cloakrooms, etc.

Safety

1. Small events – check that parking is not likely to be dangerous, also that you have a fire extinguisher and fire blankets if necessary, and a first aid kit to hand.

2. If you are involved with any swimming or sports event, have knowledgeable adults trained in first aid in attendance – some sports associations have rules for instance about first aid or refreshment requirements – check if this is relevant.

3. If you are holding a large event at a hired venue, check fire and safety regulations. For any event you can always ask local fire officers and police if you have any queries.

4. Whether the event is at home or elsewhere, if there is likely to be traffic congestion always discuss this with your local police beforehand, and be guided by their suggestions.

NB Do note that your insurance might not be valid if you have not abided by safety rules.

Hints

1. If you need to approach the authorities for their help and permission over your events, always go well prepared with all the facts and figures and, depending on your age, possibly accompanied by an adult.

2. It is always a good gesture to thank personally or send thank-you notes to those who have helped you with your event, or sent donations. They will always be willing to step in again if they feel they have been appreciated! If you are on a committee either share this job between you all or give one member the responsibility as their particular contribution to the event. Often the secretary or treasurer takes this on board but if there is a lot for them to do, ask another member, even if it is the secretary or treasurer who draws up the list of those requiring thanks.

Sponsored Events

These days just about everybody knows what a sponsored activity is. The aim is for as large a group as possible of people to set themselves some sort of target, whether running a marathon or learning to spell a hundred words, and persuading as many as you can to sponsor you, ie pay you for achieving your target. Decide which activity you wish to undertake – see the list below for suggestions – and how many people there will be involved in the event. Don't panic if you don't think you can achieve Bob Geldof's Sports Aid proportions – every little bit helps!

You will need to have registration and sponsorship forms, the former are for each of the organisers, the latter for each of the participants to use when obtaining their sponsorship. How you get these printed will rather depend on the numbers of people involved. Do a rough copy (the illustration on the next page shows a typical form) with all the relevant information. You could photocopy handwritten forms, but if possible ask someone to type you a form which you can photocopy, as it does look more businesslike. You will then need to go round to friends and neighbours in good time to encourage them to sign the form and write down the amount of money they intend to sponsor you for. *Never* go asking for sponsorship on your own – it is always more fun anyway if two or three of you are together. Sometimes people prefer to simply include the maximum amount they are liable to pay you, rather than for example giving you 10p per mile or whatever. Don't rely on vague promises – you or they may well forget!

Fixing a date for the sponsored event is probably one of the most important factors. You will need to plan well ahead of time, and choose your date carefully so that you can enlist as many people as possible to partake in the event. If you wish to raise a lot of money, advertise for more participants in your local shop and any local

SPONSORSHIP FORM

Name: _JIM BEST_

Address: _10, FLEETWOOD DRIVE, BRIGHTON_

Activity to be sponsored: _SWIMMING_

AT THE SPORTS CENTRE

Name and address of Sponsors	Amount promised	Amount received	Signed by
Mrs. A Best 10 Fleetwood Drive	10p per length	£1	A. Best
Mrs. V. Hodge 9 Fleetwood Drive	5p per length	50p	V. Hodge
Mr. B. Smith 25 Green Lane	5p per length	50p	B. Smith

'Never go asking for sponsorship on your own...'

parish magazine. If it is in a good cause, you will be surprised at how many people will want to help.

If you are planning an activity on a public road or recreation area don't forget to check with the police or local authority (see page 104 for details). They will probably be co-operative if they know well in advance what you are planning, and if you go to them with all the information and the route efficiently laid out so that they know you are being serious and responsible about your plan. In general, the local authority would be the people to approach for events in local parks, recreation grounds, swimming pools, etc, also for street collections (for instance a mile of pennies in a pedestrian precinct on a Saturday morning). For events on roads or lanes outside the town contact the police. Depending on your age you may feel that it would be sensible to have an adult go with you to approach the authorities, but make sure it is you who proves that the event will be well organised – and if the interview goes well don't forget to take a sponsorship form with you and ask for their help!

• Bicycle Rides

Plan your route in advance, well away from the main roads. See page 102 for safety, the law and insurance. If the route crosses a main road, have an adult at the crossing at all times to supervise. All participants should wear fluorescent arm bands and the judges should have similar jerkins. You can buy these from good cycle shops. Stagger the starts of riders (see registration forms) if you have large numbers involved. If possible choose a circular course which is not too long, say two or three miles, and then people can do as many laps as they like. The other advantage of a circular course is that it only takes one adult to keep an eye on the correct mileage. The easiest way to check participants through would be to give them numbers to wear, and give the judge a list of these numbers which he can then check off as they cycle by. Depending on the numbers involved you may need someone to help the judge at this point. Measure the course before you start, so that the cyclists can be sponsored per mile. Make the event extra fun by asking riders to wear fancy dress, but make it optional. Remember to check that the costumes are not dangerous to wear while cycling.

You could arrange variations on a sponsored bike ride by making it a grand tour of, for example, local churches (especially if you live in the country), recreation grounds or other places of interest. You would need to have adults joining if younger children were involved on these longer treks. Also, with this type of non-circular route, you would need to organise a form to be signed at each stopping point by an adult judge to verify that the cyclists had reached there.

Exercise bicycle marathon   This would be a smaller event which could perhaps be organised at school or, if a friend has such a bike, in someone's home. The alternative ways of running this are either sponsoring people per minute or per mile. Remember it is hard work so don't let people go on too long, and gauge the gearing on the bike according to age and fitness.

• Walking, Jogging or Running

We do advise you to contact the Ramblers Association, 1/5 Wandsworth Road, London SW8 2XX, 01-582 6878, when you are first planning any kind of sponsored walk either on roads or footpaths. They have issued a leaflet setting out all the do's and don'ts and will be very helpful with any extra advice.

Choose a route in advance, well away from main roads if possible. See page 102 for safety, the law and insurance information. Decide whether the sponsorship will be for walking per mile or per house if walking between friends' homes. Make sure that everyone has a luminous arm band or chest strap for going on the roads. These can be bought very cheaply at a cycle shop. For jogging, choose a short course, for instance, around a recreation field, and charge sponsorship per lap. Running would be per 100-metre dash, say, with a breather in between. A 24-hour walk is one for all the family rather than just kids, and it doesn't mean that everyone involved has to walk for 24 hours! The walk lasts for 24 hours, and people decide when they wish to join in, during the night or during the day. If younger children are allowed to walk at night, then of course adults must go with them, and again (see above) make sure that everyone has some sort of luminous marking on them. You all start from the same point, over a set course and sponsorship would be per mile. As organisers, you will need to bring along some food and drink for the walkers, or else ask everyone to be responsible for their own sustenance. Obviously, summertime with its long daylight hours is the best time for this one.

• Swimming

First check that you will be able to use your local or school pool for a sponsored swim, and that you have an adequate number of life savers available to organise a rota for the day.

It is vital that for this event you have photocopied two sets of forms to give to the participants:

1. The first registration form is for the organiser's benefit. You will need to know what time each swimmer wishes to take part. Divide the day into sections so that not everyone comes at once, for instance: section 1 between 9 am and 11 am; section 2, 11 am to 1 pm. Ask for the telephone number of the swimmers to be included, in case you have a run on those choosing a certain time. You can then transfer some to another section. Do check that those swimming around lunchtime have *not* just eaten an enormous Sunday joint or whatever.

2. The second form is the sponsorship form for the swimmer to get filled up. It states how many lengths the sponsor is covering, and at what price. This is the form to be signed by all the swimmers' sponsors. Have a maximum swim of, say, 10 minutes – the sponsors then know that they won't have to pay out a fortune, and also it will give more children a chance to participate in the swimming.

Separate your pool into lanes (ask the pool manager if you can borrow their lane-dividers). Each lane will need a judge to verify the number of lengths the swimmer has done and to act as a timekeeper to make sure that the swimmers don't go over their allotted time. You will have to organise a shift of judges and tell them to bring pencil and paper to make a note of the number of lengths swum as each is undertaken. It is all too easy to forget the count! Each judge must be responsible for signing the sponsorship form to verify the lengths that have been achieved.

Above all else, please make sure that you have PERMANENTLY on patrol a life saver who is ready to jump into the swimming pool in case any of the swimmers get into trouble by trying to swim further than they can cope with, just to earn the money. There must be somebody there who really knows how to administer mouth-to-mouth resuscitation.

• Disco Dancing

Why not run a disco party with a difference? Everyone can have a tremendous evening but at the same time really be doing their bit to help others. See page 127 for more detailed information about running a disco party.

A disco can be a very small affair. First of all fix a suitable date when you know there isn't another party planned, and a good venue that will not cause anyone's parents a problem! For instance, someone's garage. You will need to be very organised even if you are not holding a large event, as insurance, fire regulations, music licences, etc, will all need to be checked – we feel you must involve an adult. Even if you are holding a small event do remember that parents need to be carefully considered and consulted from the beginning.

How you organise the sponsorship depends on the children's ages. For the young, why not have timed sessions lasting about 10 minutes, followed by a break? Each dancer is then sponsored per session. For older groups, just let them dance as long as they can non-stop – the dancing need not be too energetic!

• Spelling

The number of words involved will depend on the age of the participants. Make out a list of say 40 difficult (but not impossible) words and attach it to the sponsorship forms. The sponsorship will be for each word correctly learnt. We suggest you have a 'spell-in', with an adult to judge the results. This is obviously a good sponsorship to run at school – an alternative could be learning all your tables!

• General Knowledge Quiz

There are two ways of running this sort of sponsorship. Either, as with the spelling, attach a list of about 40 general knowledge questions to the sponsorship form and the participants have to simply answer as many questions as possible. Or at the beginning of the holidays hand out a similar form. The participants then not only have to answer the questions, but also learn what they think are the correct answers, to be tested at the beginning of the next term. Again this is a good sponsorship to run in schools. Ask a teacher or knowledgeable parent to devise a form or use Trivial Pursuits or any good Encyclopedia to make up your own. Keep a careful copy of the answers of course!

• Countries and Capital Cities of the World

Make out a list of about 40 countries of the world with their capital cities and jumble them up. Supply the contestants with the list plus the sponsorship form. Everyone then has to match countries and capitals correctly, and with any luck you might learn quite a lot too!

• Starve

We suggest this for the over-12s only, and not to last longer than 24 hours. Sponsorship is by the hour, and includes night time if it is really part of the starve. Obviously, this would be a particularly appropriate event to help charities concerned with famine in the Third World countries. Remember to drink lots of water.

• Silence

This is a difficult one! Organise a group of friends to sit in a room keeping silent. Sponsorship is per minute that they can keep their mouths shut. Perhaps they could have a break after about a quarter of an hour, before starting again, otherwise the strain would be too great!

• Matchbox

A very good one for younger children. The aim is to find how many objects they can fit into a matchbox (but not matches!). In the winter they can find indoor objects (buttons, paper clips, labels, etc), and in the summer they can fill the boxes with different leaves, tiny stones and so on. Sponsorship would be per object, say one penny per object because we have seen matchboxes filled with over 100 tiny things.

• Growing Seeds

Sunflowers You can do this one at school or with a group of friends. Buy a couple of packets of seeds, and give everyone half a dozen seeds (to allow for a few failures). The seeds can be started off indoors in old yogurt pots containing potting compost or earth, but this is not essential. Plant them out, or sow the seeds in May. Do protect against slugs. Get your forms signed and make sponsors promise to pay, say, one penny for every five centimetres that the sunflowers grow. Set a particular date – perhaps September 30th – on which everyone measures their sunflowers.

Pumpkins As above give everybody half a dozen pumpkin seeds, and organise that the sponsors will pay per pound in weight. If you want, you could also give a prize for the largest pumpkin. Have the 'weigh in' on November 5th and combine it with a fund-raising firework party!

• Litter Collection

Our local cubs and scouts went through the village picking up every bit of litter they could see. The village was spring-cleaned and the scouts sponsored per dustbin liner full of litter. The proceeds went towards a new clubhouse. It would be just as easy to clear litter in a town, but choose a suitable section of it, such as a park, play area or local square. Do remind everyone to come suitably dressed and wearing gloves.

• Odd Jobs

You can be sponsored to clean cars, bikes and windows, mow lawns, sweep leaves, weed, etc – the advantage of these sponsorships is that you get paid twice for doing the same job! Charge the car or window owner a fee for the work done, and then get other people to sponsor you either per job, or per hour you work. Plan it in advance, so that you are ready to start bright and early on a Saturday, and you will be delighted with the money you will make. We suggest that you *always* do these jobs in twos, which is more fun anyway.

An alternative to the above is to organise the sponsorship in conjunction with an over-60s club, so that you do jobs free to help the elderly and get other people to sponsor you again either per job or per hour you work.

Sales

Sales can run from the very simple to the very ambitious. They are great fun but also hard work, so be prepared! The more elaborate sale will definitely need some help from adults but you will be able to arrange a straightforward event by yourselves.

You will need to be extremely organised. First of all decide on the date and venue of your sale and make sure you have permission, whether it is held in your own garden, at school, in a village hall or community centre, or as part of a local fête. If you are hiring a venue, then check all the regulations, insurances, etc (see page 102). You will need to decide how many of your friends to involve in the organisation and this obviously depends on the size of event you are planning (see page 98, concerning committees). Try not to be too ambitious – it is better to run a smaller event efficiently and successfully than make a muddle of a larger one. Don't forget that you can use your experience next year, and run another larger sale if you wish. People will always return if they have enjoyed themselves.

Nearer the time, it is vital to advertise the sale widely (see page 99 on publicity), if you want a good turn-out.

Money

Organise your float the day before the sale (see page 101). Remember you will need a cash box or tin with a lid on it to keep the money in for *each* stall. NEVER leave the money unattended. We suggest you have always at least two people per stall so that if one of you is involved with wrapping something up, or taking a short break, there is someone to keep an eye on the tin. At the end of the day, count up all your takings and hand the money straight to a parent or teacher, or take it to the bank.

Remember to have all your goods clearly priced. This will take a long time to work out and organise, so don't leave it until the last minute. You may need an adult to give you some advice here, so don't be afraid to ask! We suggest you buy some inexpensive sticky labels from a good stationers with which to mark your goods.

If you are likely to have a lot of adding up to do, don't forget to suggest that stall holders bring calculators in case the maths gets too complicated!

The day before

Try to arrange with those in charge of your venue permission to set up as much as you can before the day of the sale dawns. It is amazing how long it takes to price and display the goods, and your stalls will look much more attractive if you have had time to put them out effectively. Have a checklist of all the things you will need to have thought about, for instance: the float; who is in charge of each stall; what is going to be on each stall; do you have sufficient tables to act as stalls and tablecloths to cover them? If your sale is likely to run for several hours, have a rota prepared of 'staff' so that someone isn't stuck for four hours without a break. We suggest that you have at least two helpers per stall, in any case (see *Money* above). Remember to put up disclaimer notices (see page 104). Don't forget to have helpers armed with dustbin liners for cleaning up.

Whatever sale you are having remember that you will need an Entertainments Licence if you are charging an entrance fee. The way round this is not to charge for entrance – you will probably find that people will spend more on the actual goods if they are not being asked to pay to go in!

• Garden Sale

You will need to prepare for this well in advance, and we suggest you hold your sale in late spring or early summer. Probably the best time is early to mid-June, before everybody has filled up their hanging baskets and tubs!

Depending on your age and knowledge, we think an enthusiastic gardening adult would be helpful here. This is not so that they do all the hard work and you stand by watching, but because it would be very disheartening if all your cuttings, seeds or cacti died simply because you didn't quite know how to set about things. We shall give you a few suggestions here, although we don't have room to compile a full gardening manual with information about soils, conditions and methods!

First of all well before your sale, you can start work by saving old plastic cartons: the sort that contain yogurt, cream, cream cheese, margarine, etc. You can make drainage holes by carefully pricking the bottom with a sharp skewer. (You can sometimes buy second-hand plastic flowerpots from garden centres, but you would have to pay for these.) Keep your pots neatly in a cardboard box so that they don't get broken or cracked, and are not making a mess! You may need some old seed trays for some seedlings to start off in, so collect these up too.

We suggest that, depending on how many of you want to be involved with the sale, each individual or small group takes a particular section to concentrate on. One group might grow vegetables from seed, for example tomatoes, cucumbers or courgettes; another might grow herbs; someone takes cuttings or divides plants (with permission), from everyone's gardens – it will work even if you do this in early spring, for example with geraniums, lambs' ears, saxifraga, etc; another can grow cacti or houseplants, for example crassula, trailing tradescantia and ivy will root easily; another can grow annuals from seeds, for example alyssum, lobelia, tobacco plants, hollyhocks, sunflowers, etc; maybe another group could (again with permission) dig up clumps of overcrowded bulbs, for example daffodils, tulips, crocuses, etc, and dry some off to sell (don't forget to make a note of their colour when in flower and keep them all separate so that you can tell people what they are buying).

For the sale itself you will need to have everything very clearly labelled and priced – you could go along to the local garden centre to gauge roughly the prices you should be charging, but don't 'go over the top' as psychologically people are bound to buy more if they think they are getting a bargain and so can afford to be more generous. Don't forget to do the watering – good luck!

'Simon, are you sure your Dad won't mind us flogging his roses?'

• Garage Sale

A garage sale is very easy to run and has the advantage that you can put anything in it – from old china to home-made cakes and biscuits. It can be a good opportunity to sort out the toys you no longer want, the clothes you have grown out of (but are still wearable) and anything your parents can spare. Collect what you can from your friends, but don't include any real junk, because you just won't be able to shift it. To hold a sale, make sure that the stuff already in the garage is put away, otherwise you might find you have sold your father's lawnmower! You will probably have to do a bit of sweeping out and cleaning up before the sale. Put some tables just inside for the goods, and a big 'Garage Sale' poster on the gate. As always we do think it is more fun to do these sort of things with friends, so choose whichever of you has the most suitable garage and most tolerant parents as the venue for this sale. If you had room you could have a small refreshment stall as well, selling orange squash and biscuits.

• Book and Bun Sale

Combine a homemade bun sale with secondhand books, and run it at school during the lunch hour (with previous permission, of course). Remember to organise your tables, pricing and so on beforehand as time will be limited. Collect some old paper and plastic bags for people who want to take the buns away, not eat them then and there. Also why not have a supply of soft drinks available, which you can serve in yogurt or washing powder pots (well washed, of course) for those who want to eat their biscuits or buns immediately? Look at the cookie sale suggestion list for possible biscuits and cakes to make.

• Bring and Buy

You will need lots of publicity for this sale, so that people know they must bring something as well as come and buy. Things to eat always sell well (see the cookie sale) so do pens, pencils, notebooks, plants, vegetables, freshly laid eggs, stationery, etc. Although people should bring things to sell sometimes they forget, so do have plenty there initially, otherwise your sale will be in danger of ending early! You could make a couple of simple things if you feel they are appropriate. Little girls love peg dolls made from the old-fashioned springless type of peg and a few remnants of material and felt (use a biro to draw the face). Pretty little bags made with material remnants, and filled with dried lavender, pot pourri or a tiny piece of soap are another simple idea.

• Christmas Card Sale

Some schools run a Christmas card competition and print the best ones. Persuade your school to do this and run a stall to sell them. You could, in addition, stock the stall with Christmas candles, decorations, Christmas food and even possibly the odd stocking-filler present. Remember to make the cards a suitable size to fit post office preferred sizes of envelopes.

• 50/50 Sale (only to be undertaken by the over-16s)

Try to persuade a local auctioneer to conduct the sale if valuable items are involved. This is a complicated sort of sale, and usually involves more expensive items as the point is that the donor of an item can claim half the sale proceeds back and donate the other half to your charity. Don't be deterred by this, because it is amazing how generous people will be especially if it is something they want to get rid of anyway! The major disadvantage with this sale is that you have to keep extremely detailed notes, both prior to your sale when you will have to agree what price is put on each item, and subsequently after the sale when you will have to return 50 per cent of the proceeds to the former owners.

We suggest that you give the donors a form on which they state what the item is they are giving, what the price is they wish to charge for the item, and finally, a signature to state that this is correct. Put a disclaimer note on your form so that people sign to absolve you from any responsibility if the goods were stolen or damaged once they were delivered into your hands prior to the sale. If you would prefer to insure against such mishaps you could ask for a quote for such a liability. It all rather depends on the value of the items, but discuss this aspect with an adult before printing your forms. Don't forget that after the sale you then have to return to the donor the correct amount you owe them (that is, half the sum raised by that item).

You will need to have lot numbers on sticky labels ready to put on to items as and when they are brought to you. Give the vendor a card on which you have the lot number and the item written down. Keep a very careful record yourself at the same time in a file.

At the auction have notices saying that items must be removed by a certain time – this might affect your insurance. State that any cheques must be backed by a banker's card. Finally add that no goods can be removed from the saleroom without a receipt being checked at the door.

When the bidding starts a 'secretary' must write down the name of the successful purchaser by the lot number with the amount they are liable for. Have a system of checking off items and writing out receipts as lots are collected. Double-check signatures on cheques and take down a banker's card number. Although it is unlikely that you will sell items costing more than £50, if you do, remember banker's cards are invalid in that instance. Ask for two cheques each backed separately instead. Have an adult in charge of this aspect of the sale. Have 'doormen' who will not allow goods to be removed without checking receipts. (You can buy receipt books at stationers.)

• Good as New, or Not so New Clothes Sale

Gather up from your wardrobe and your friends' wardrobes clothes that have been outgrown, but not worn out. You do not want socks, underwear or shoes. Do insist that the clothes are *clean*. Be firm about rejecting unsuitable items or you will just end up with a load of rubbish. Remember you will need ways of displaying the clothes.

If you could borrow a clothes rail from a friendly shop you could hang things which would keep them neater and cleaner. Collect lots of wire coat hangers from dry cleaners prior to the sale. Also, have prepared price tags – we suggest you pin or safety-pin 2-inch paper squares with prices clearly printed on them.

Make sure this sale is held (perhaps as part of a school fête) when there are plenty of mothers about, because they are the ones who will be buying for their younger children.

If you do have clothes left over that people do not want back, Oxfam shops or local jumble sales would probably receive them gratefully, so don't just throw them away.

• Secondhand Toy and Book Sale

One family we know simply gathered up all the toys and books they had outgrown and put them on a table by their garden gate, with a large notice saying 'Toys for Sale'. They made several pounds for Famine Relief and at the same time sorted out cupboards and bookshelves. Don't sell anything broken or too battered – it lowers the tone! Write book price on the inside leaf in pencil so that it can be rubbed out by the purchaser.

• Cookie Sale

If you like cooking, why not get permission to run a special stall at your local or school fête? Organise a group to do the cooking (and enlist a few parents to help!). Make simple things but present them well. Here is a list of suggestions:

Sweets Peppermint creams, fudge, toffee apples, peanut and chocolate balls, coconut ice, chocolate truffles, etc.

Biscuits Homemade biscuits and buns, shortbread, shortbread shapes, biscuits to hang on a Christmas tree, etc.

Jams Jams, chutneys, mincemeat for Christmas, etc. You will need help to make these items, but they are popular sales.

The vital thing about this sale is to make sure that everything looks appetising, clean and attractively presented. Here is a checklist of items you will need to buy – you will not be popular if you sell your mother's plates!

1. *Clingfilm* Vital for covering things and also for making little parcels of your sweets, biscuits, etc. (Tie the latter with wrapping ribbon made into 'twirls', by running the back of a pair of scissors down the ribbon.) You will find that the clingfilm will not stick to paper plates, so cover the whole plate and its contents then the clingfilm sticks to itself.

2. *Paper plates* It will cost you a little bit more to buy patterned coloured plates, but they look much nicer than the cream-coloured ones, and are easily available from good stationers, eg, W.H. Smith.

3. *Doilies* You could economise on the paper plates by using doilies under a cake and then completely cover it with clingfilm. However, they do not provide any support so do not use them for biscuits, etc.

4. *Remnants* of pretty materials These are for jam pot covers, and you will need more than you probably think. Use pinking shears to give a pretty zig-zag edge to your material, otherwise just cut in simple circles. Secure material either with rubber bands or wrapping ribbon.

5. *Wrapping ribbon* To tie around packets of sweets or jam jar lids.

6. *Sticky labels* (a) Naming – you will need a largish label to mark your jam jars of marmalade, etc, and it looks very attractive to decorate these, eg: rule a coloured line around the edge to match the main colour of your material cover, or do a simple logo in the corners, or even just print or write the name in a fun coloured felt tip, etc. Call things fun names eg: Clare's Chocolate Cookies – emphasising the home-made element.

(b) Pricing – You will need small self-sticking labels to write your prices on. Write the prices before you stick them on a squidgy cake! W.H. Smith, etc, sell a good selection of these.

Hygiene

Obviously it goes without saying, you must cook these items in extremely clean conditions. We suggest that you should if possible cook the day before the sale, so that everything is fresh. However, you may need to cook cakes etc ahead of time and freeze them, but if this is necessary, always attach an extra label saying that the item has already been frozen and the purchaser then knows not to re-freeze. You are advised not to cook any dishes containing meats, eg pâtés. This is a shame but it means that you can avoid all the dangers attached to selling meat products. Once items are cold wrap up carefully in clingfilm.

● Chinese Auction

This must be organised by the over-13s. For a Chinese auction you need to ask as many friends as you can to give, say, six small items each, and ask your friends to wrap everything up. For example, a tin of soup, a set of writing paper and envelopes, a reel of cotton, a bubble bath, a packet of teabags, a tape. The point is to include some good items and some tiny things, but as they are wrapped, nobody knows which is which. You then invite a group of friends' parents and friends to a supper party and tell them that you will be holding a Chinese Auction.

During supper, perhaps in between courses, begin the auction. Someone who is a good auctioneer holds up a tiny parcel and encourages the guests to bid for it! However, the bids are only 10p each, and as everyone bids they put 10p down on the table. As this is progressing – probably quite loudly! – there must be a hidden referee who cannot watch the proceedings. He decides at what point he will ring a bell. This stops the auction and whoever put the last 10p on their table has 'brought' the item. Keep the momentum going, which encourages the 10p's to be put down! It is a little like an adult 'pass the parcel'!

As for the supper, either organise this yourself or ask some adults to help with the food and arrange the drinks. It is probably simplest to ask for donations for the sustenance as this will avoid licences being required but check up (see page 102).

Other Ideas for Fund Raising

● Mile of Pennies

Run this as part of a local fête, having first asked permission, or in your local town on a Saturday morning if there is a suitable pedestrian area – your parents and you will have to clear this with the local authority first. Perhaps your school would allow you to run this one lunchtime in the playground.

Take a pound's worth of pennies with you to start off. Lay the coins touching each other on the ground to form a long line. When everyone starts adding their own money you hope that you will have something worth more than a penny – any coin will be acceptable. It may be necessary, depending on the space available, to 'snake' your line to and fro. Don't forget to advertise your event in advance with posters, and have a poster beside you during the event to explain to passers-by what you are doing, and what charity it is in aid of.

• Raffles

Persuade kind adults to donate good prizes and sell tickets at school (with permission of course) or at a party. Tickets can be bought at any stationers – cloakroom tickets are ideal. Write the name of the donor on the number on the stub and hand them their half to keep for the draw. Do not buy more than one book in one colour or you will end up with two winners holding two pink tickets, both number 28, fighting for your prize! Have a 'life and soul of the party' to draw the raffle for you to make it fun. For legal notes see page 103.

• Scrabble/Chess Championship

You can in fact play any game (but Monopoly does go on and on). Contestants make a donation in order to be allowed to play (say £1) and play in knockouts, ending with the two finalists playing each other. Organise lists of contestants in advance and ask them to bring their games sets so that you have plenty. Have soft drinks and food available during the championship for which people give donations – 5p, etc. If you are playing chess and want to do it professionally, contact a local chess club to see if you can borrow their clocks. Hire a room in a village hall or community centre for the day, or perhaps the school would co-operate at a weekend or in the holidays. Have a small prize for the winner.

• Computer Day

Organise a room for the day (hire a room in a village hall or community centre or ask your school) and ask your friends who have computers to bring them along (some will need portable television sets to operate them). Check you have sufficient sockets and adaptors. People then donate, say, about £1 to play with the computers. Offer food and drink during the day, and ask for donations towards it.

• Entertainments

Use your school premises to put on an entertainment, as it will have all the necessary equipment. The school will surely co-operate if it is for a good cause, and if you don't try to do it too often! Sixth formers could organise one by themselves, younger children will probably need some help, but you will be pleasantly surprised at all the local talent waiting to be discovered. You could organise a music hall, run an art show, hold a slave auction or a raffle and so on. Try one of these; plays, concerts, music halls, puppet shows. Charge admission and sell drinks (soft) during the interval, but see licences page 102.

• Charities Week

Combine several of the previous ideas and run them during a week at school. . . .

• Mini Fête

If you like organising then choose some of the ideas above, and run several stalls as a mini fête, either on the school sports field, or on a local recreation area. Have a refreshment stall and serve orange squash, coca-cola and packets of crisps. Try and buy the crisps at cost price, perhaps through your school or the local cash and carry.

• Dog Show

You could organise a simple fund-raising dog show. We suggest that you hold this for your pets to win the prize for the waggiest tail

Best turned-out doggie competition

rather than your West Highland to be proved the best of breed. If you embark on official judges via the Kennel Club you will be in a different ball game, and while there is nothing wrong with that, you will find yourself swamped with professional dog show entrants. Keep things simple for your friends and their pets!

Of course you could hold a general pet show for cats, budgies (not together!), fish, rabbits and hamsters – with an assortment of classes for everyone to join in.

Whatever your plans we suggest that you contact a local vet and ask if you should specify on the entry form that owners of certain pets are required to produce valid vaccination forms.

• Pyramid Teas (or Suppers)

This is a very skilful way of raising a lot of money without anyone having to do too much work! It is in fact an upside-down pyramid in that it involves fewer people at each round rather than more. This is how it works: you invite five friends round to tea (or supper, but charge more!) Each of them donates a fixed sum – say 20 or 50 pence for the privilege. Those five people then invite four to their house, and each of those four then invites three, and so on, until the last round is reached. The table shows how much money you can raise with a 50 pence contribution.

1st Round	5 guests @ 50p	£2.50
2nd Round	5 × 4 = 20	£10.00
3rd Round	20 × 3 = 60	£30.00
4th Round	60 × 2 = 120	£60.00
5th Round	120 × 1 = 120	£60.00
		£162.50

You can make £162.50 for your charity and nobody has to do more than give their friends a simple meal. The really important point of course is that everyone must do their share – obviously if the chain is broken the money won't come in. Each person is responsible for collecting the money at their function, and handing it to you, the organisers. The only problem with this idea is that 325 people will have to be involved by the end. It is easier to keep the chain going if you spread the initial guest list to cover either various age groups or try to invite people from slightly different areas – otherwise later on people may find it hard to find enough friends who haven't already been invited!

• Famine Lunch

Not quite what it sounds, luckily! Ask your school if you can hold a famine lunch during your dinner hour, or else invite friends to your own house during the holidays or at a weekend. Ask them to donate what they might have spent on lunch, say 50 pence, and provide them with French bread, butter, cheese and an apple – actually quite nourishing – and water to drink, although you could add a little orange squash if you felt very kind.

• Slave and Promises Auction

This is for the older age groups to organise. The idea is for you to collect both 'slaves' offering to take on various jobs for free, and 'promises' for different goods or services. Make up a catalogue and subsequently hold an auction at which people bid for these.

You will need to be very organised. Go round and ask people what they could offer and keep careful notes. Then draw up your catalogue – spread out the best lots in between the not so exciting to keep the interest going! For a good evening we think you would need a good 70 lots, but if you have less, hold an auction during a supper party – and ask for donations for the supper too.

We are providing a list of suggestions for you to look at. When you have a suitable catalogue you will have to make photocopies, staple the sheets, and distribute them to the people at the auction. If you have plenty of copies, hand them round to as many people as possible before the auction. You must have enough copies for everyone attending the auction.

You will have to fix a suitable venue and above all else use an enthusiastic auctioneer to get things going! This is vital to the success of the auction. Then publicise your event (see page 99), or just send out invitations if you want a smaller function.

CATALOGUE FOR AUCTION TO RAISE FUNDS FOR

. . . .

at 7.30 pm on Friday 14th March
Auctioneer: . . . .

Lot No.	Item	Donor
1.	2 trays of free range eggs	Mrs P. Harding
2.	2 theatre tickets	Hatherley School
3.	1 afternoon hedge-cutting	Mr D. Goodman
4.	2 Grobags	The DIY Shop
5.	2 hours' gardening	Mr A. King
6.	1 shampoo and set	Miss P. Watson
7.	1 load of manure	Hillside Stables
8.	1 car wash	Mr W. Hawkins
9.	A small drawing of the successful bidder's house	Miss S. Hall
10.	Family Sunday lunch for up to 5 guests	The Misses J. and K. Cumming
11.	1 evening's babysitting	Miss J. Holding
12.	1 fruit cake	Miss S. Spark
13.	A butler and maid for an evening	Mr R. Long and Miss A. Cater
14.	Lunch for 2 and a conservation trip round farm	Mr and Mrs T. Hardy
15.	A child's jersey (24″ chest)	Mrs W. W. Hawkins
16.	A day's childminding (9–6)	Miss D. Davidson
17.	6 tomato plants	Mr R. Pearse
18.	1 cuddly toy	Miss C. Winter
19.	2 hours' housework	Miss T. Rogerson
20.	1 afternoon's tennis and barbecue for 4	Tennis Club
21.	3 piano lessons for a beginner	Miss J. Turner
22.	2 carved wooden table lamps	Mr T. Good
23.	2 tickets football match	Mrs P. Hunt
24.	Picnic tea for 4	Miss J. Shepherd and Miss P. Robinson
25.	3 elementary riding lessons	Hillside Stables

• Miscellaneous Jobs

Don't forget all the obvious, simple ways of raising money: baby-sitting, sweeping snow or leaves, gardening, weeding, mowing lawns, car/window cleaning, walking dogs, valeting bicycles, collecting old newspaper or milk bottle tops.

• Parties

Small party

If you want to hold a disco party, why not organise a fund-raising one? (Parents may be more agreeable to the whole idea then!) You could include a further fund-raising activity during the evening, eg: raffle or small Chinese auction. Alternatively you could ask for donations, perhaps 2p every time anyone danced, and for food and wine. Do not charge entrance fees or you will need a licence. Do remember to ensure that your friends understand that this is a fund-raising event or they may feel miffed at being asked for money!

Large party – for older children (and parents) to organise

If you want to undertake a large fund-raising disco we will give you the main guidelines here, but refer you to our book *Parties for Older Children*, published by Piatkus Books, where we discuss in great detail their organisation and give many excellent and practical ideas for music, venues, party themes, food, games, invitations and decorations.

Organise a committee, probably 10 to 12 people, who are thoroughly reliable and with various talents to offer, someone artistic, someone who can type and someone who can add up!

You must have several adults overseeing the enterprise for various reasons:

1. As you will have to put quite a lot of money upfront for deposits and possibly insurance, etc, you may need help financially.

2. They must be in overall charge of the accounting side of the event. Costing the tickets too low could be disastrous, for example.

3. We advise you to have adults overseeing the drinks if you are serving alcohol.

4. You *must* have adult advice about legal matters, licences, etc, insurance and safety aspects (see page 102).

Don't think from this catalogue that they will end up running the show! Ultimately the project is yours – only you would know the best disc-jockey, the most popular food, and who to invite.

Venue   (a) *Hired hall*: Whether at school or elsewhere book very early. Check costs, insurances, electrics (are they suitable for discotheque equipment?), heating/ventilation, facilities (kitchen equipment, cloakrooms – always take extra loo rolls), timing (when can you have access to hall for decoration, etc, and when do you have to clear up by?).
   AVOID: halls near a pub, and advertising the party outside the building. Both will result possibly in gatecrashing. Have a father or two 'policing' outside anyway.
   (b) *Home*: Consult parents first! Best to avoid using the house if possible – garages, cellars or barns can convert well with imagination. Check if suitable for equipment. Consider noise, bar, food, ventilation or heating, electrics. Remember to warn the neighbours, but tell them it's in aid of charity – they will be more amenable!

Discotheque   *Disc-jockey*: You will know your best local disc jockey; book up very early. Check costs – plus charges for extras, eg: a strobe, bubble machine, and insurance. Is venue suitable, with enough space for equipment, correct electrics? If there are any queries he should come and inspect. What's the age group of guests – can he cope with what you require? Give directions – send a map if any uncertainty – and decide the time he will arrive. Send a letter confirming all the points raised; take a photocopy and file it.
   Hi fi equipment: DIY would be fine for a small party. If you are organising a large event, don't spoil it by false economy. It would be

cheaper to run your own show but only worth it if you are competent enough to do the job properly! Have a trial run, and check the lighting too.

Themes   Decide whether you are having a theme. This will affect the invitations, decorations, food, etc. You can have themes which involve whatever degree of dressing up or not that you want. For instance: a Black and White party, Razzle Dazzle, Dress to Impress, Dress to Dazzle, St Trinians, Glitter and Gleam, Outrageous Dress, Funky Punk, Shimmer and Shine, Down and Outs, Red, White and Blue, Multi-coloured, 1920s, 1950s, Gender Bender, Horror Party, etc. Don't forget that seasonal parties are great fun. For example: Red and Green Christmas Party, Dress to Sparkle for Guy Fawkes, Spooky Spoofs, Ghosts and Ghouls, or a simple mask party for Hallowe'en, and Valentine Parties.

When and Who   *Date*: Choose very carefully. Check that there is no other event on same date. Avoid a popular holiday period – August is the worst month for a party.

   Numbers: Invite enough guests to fill hall or room.

   Age group: Either run this for your own age group or organise a party for younger children.

Invitations: See page 129 for illustration. You will need either a tear-off section or a separate slip to be enclosed for ticket application. Design and photocopy invitations yourselves – it's the cheapest way – and you can match up with your theme (see page 129). Printed professionally looks best but will also cost you! Take a postcard with all information on it to a local printers and get a quote.

Always photostat or print extras in case of need. Check invitations fit cheap envelopes.

Advertising   Don't do public advertising, but if it is a school-based party you may prefer to put up posters instead of sending invitations. All information should be on the poster; put a final date for ticket applications – so numbers will be known ahead.

Tickets   Either design a page of tickets, photocopy them, and cut them into single tickets, or have printed ones (obviously more expensive). *Do not* hand out any tickets without being paid first.

Decorations   Organise well ahead – they take much longer than you think. Remember disco lights create atmosphere. If the venue is large, small decorations will not show up. If fixing to walls or ceilings use either blutack, double-sided cellotape or possibly drawing pins, but do not damage walls as you may be held responsible. Posters, balloons, streamers (make your own from crêpe paper), Christmas lights, foil are all very effective. Tie in ideas, colours, etc with theme of the party.

Food and Drink   *Food*: Keep it simple – finger food does not require plates. Buy crisps, etc through school cash and carry. Ask for adult advice.

Drink: Have an adult in charge. Buy on a sale or return basis from local wine merchants, whether your drink is alcoholic or not. You can hire their glasses, usually free, but check if you have to pay for breakages. It takes time to set up a bar so get drinks delivered early. Remember to make ice beforehand (four carrier bags for 50). Have an ice bucket on the bar for people to help themselves and keep the rest in insulated boxes.

Cleaning up   Have a small army to help clear up after the party.

They will need brooms, dustpans, brushes, dustbin liners, plenty of washing up liquid and drying up clothes.

Have a great party!

Raising Money for the Gap Year

Fund raising is of course mostly about making money to give to good causes, but just occasionally that good cause might be yourself. If you have decided to take a year or a few months off after school, before starting a job or going on to further education, you will want to do something positive with your free time, and this can cost money. Foreign travel and expeditions have to be paid for, and even voluntary service organisations will expect a good sized contribution from you towards your fare, sometimes as much as £1,400. This does seem a very large sum, but don't be discouraged, there are ways of raising it.

First of all have a look at *Directory of Grant Producing Trusts*. This is a good thick book which you will be able to consult in your local public reference library. It gives details of organisations that are willing to give grants to people trying to raise money for worthwhile charity projects. If you are hoping to be accepted as a volunteer in one of the foreign aid schemes we describe on page 219, such as Project Trust or Gap, or to join an expensive expedition such as Operation Raleigh or the Sail Training Association (pages 233–234 and 204) then it is a very good idea to go through the Directory very carefully, making a note of likely sounding names. You must expect to approach a lot of organisations and write a lot of letters, because it is very unlikely that anybody will give you more than a fraction of the amount you need in total.

Local Authorities and Local Firms

Local authorities have unwillingly become very much meaner than they were in the past, because they are obliged to be so cost-conscious, but it is still worth approaching your authority to see if they can help you. Even if they cannot give you any direct financial help, they might be able to suggest others who could.

Your local Chamber of Commerce or Rotary Club is well worth a try, as the members usually represent most of the town's businesses, and there are always some generous souls among them. Also, contact local firms direct, especially if you have any personal contact with them, if for instance a member of your family works there. Don't be afraid to ask – the worst they can do to you is say no!

Big nationwide firms such as Boots will sometimes be willing to contribute goods rather than the actual cash and this can be very useful if you are going abroad, either as a volunteer worker or on an adventure holiday, and need items such as pharmaceutical products, as you surely will.

Finally, don't ignore the obvious and forget to try to earn some money by getting a job yourself, however humble. Paper rounds, Saturday jobs and unskilled labour of various kinds all bring in money, and if you are living at home you may be able to save nearly all your earnings.

Children's Charities

You or your school will no doubt have your own pet charity which you support – perhaps a local one where you can see the direct results of your fund raising. For further inspiration we have drawn up a list of some of the charities which are particularly concerned with children and young people. There are many good causes and this list mentions only a very few, but many of these charities have homes or schools in your area which you could, perhaps, visit to discuss your fund raising directly with them.

Action Research for the Crippled Child Vincent House, North Parade, Horsham, West Sussex RH12 2DA (0403 64101). Provides support for research into crippling diseases and is at present funding over 200 research projects.

Bright Sparks 6th Floor, 25/27 Oxford Street, London W1R 1RF (01-437 7476). This is a very new and excellent charity. It is part of Sparks, which raises money through sporting events, for research into crippling diseases.

Bright Sparks is aimed at 12 to 18-year-olds. The idea is to become a member of Bright Sparks for a small membership fee –

you will receive a quarterly newsletter, membership badge and card. As a member you will be eligible to a 50 per cent reduction of entry costs for sporting fund-raising events. The organisers visualise that schools, clubs and youth organisations, etc will become members. You will then arrange sporting events to raise money for the fund and if you organise a noteworthy large function Sparks would try to send along a sporting celebrity!

Children's Country Holidays Fund 1 York Street, Baker Street, London SE11 4DQ (01-935 8371). Gives professional and caring help to over 6,000 children and families.

The Drake Fellowship 10 Trinity Square, London EC3P 3AX (01-488 8629). Works in inner city areas to help 15 to 25-year-old unemployed and disadvantaged people to find employment and make a positive contribution to their community.

Dr Barnardos Tanners Lane, Barkingside, Ilford, Essex IG6 1QC (01-550 8822). Britain's leading childcare charity. It has children in care and helps families in need in their own communities.

Greenpeace Environmental Trust 36 Graham Street, London N1 8LL (01-251 3020). Not strictly a children's charity but concerned with tomorrow's world to give today's children a chance. Defends the environment and its creatures with peaceful but direct action, especially in safeguarding the seas and protecting the whale and the seal.

Helen House 37 Leopold Street, Oxford OX4 1QT (0865 728251). Helen House is a hospice for children, providing respite care. Helen House sets out to give support to children with life-threatening illness for whom medicine can do no more, and who are being cared for at home. They come and stay in Helen House a few days at a time, on a regular basis.

Home Farm Trust 43–45 Queens Road, Clifton, Bristol BS8 1QQ (0272 23746). Runs eight homes (there may be one near you) to help mentally handicapped children and young people to live fulfilled and secure lives. More homes are being built all the time and parents are not charged fees.

Hospital for Sick Children Great Ormond Street, London WC1N 3JH (01-405 9200). The hospital admits children with every kind of serious illness from all parts of Britain and from overseas. Their care and treatment and research are second to none throughout the world.

Invalid Children's Aid Association (ICAA) 126 Buckingham Palace Road, London SW1W 9SB (01-730 9891). ICAA works to improve the quality of life for handicapped children and their families. It maintains four special schools, a team of practical social workers and a free information service.

National Children's Home 85 Highbury Park, London N5 1UD (01-226 2033). Runs over 100 centres for children with special needs. Also works in the community to give children with physical or emotional handicaps support in their own homes.

National Society for the Prevention of Cruelty to Children (NSPCC) 66 Saffron Hill, London EC1N 8RS (01-242 1626). During the past 100 years the NSPCC has come to the aid of over 9 million children. It provides a 24-hour service to protect children from abuse and neglect.

National Toy Libraries Association Seabrook House, Wyllyots Manor, Darkes Lane, Potters Bar, Hertfordshire EN6 2HL (90707 44571). There are now 1,000 toy libraries serving all children, especially those with special needs.

Outward Bound 12 Upper Belgravia Street, London SW1X 8BA (01-253 4286). Offers courses to provide challenging new experiences in the outdoors and in community service.

Pearson Holiday Fund 112 Regency Street, London SW1P 4AX (01-834 7444). Helps hundreds of needy children to go on holiday.

Pestalozzi International Children's Village Sedlescombe, Battle, Sussex (042 787444). Children from the poorest countries in the world come to the village to learn vital skills and then return to help other people in their own countries.

The Prince's Trust 8 Bedford Row, London WC1R 4BU (01-430 0527). See page 83 for full details. In brief, this is a charity to help young people to help themselves by providing small grants of money for self-help schemes.

Radio Lollipop   Queen Mary's Hospital for Children, Carshalton, Surrey (01-661 0666). Provides a play service at special children's hospitals for children on the wards as well as a radio service run for and by the children. Why not see if your local hospital has a Radio Lollipop?

Rainer Foundation   89a Blackheath Road, London SE10 8TJ (01-691 3124). Helps young homeless or unemployed, young offenders or those in care.

Riding for the Disabled   Avenue 'R', National Agricultural Centre, Kenilworth, Warwickshire CV8 2LY (0203 56107). This is a marvellous charity – encouraging disabled children to ride has proved very beneficial to them, giving confidence, pride and enjoyment.

Save the Children Fund   Mary Datchelor House, 17 Grove Lane, Camberwell, London SE5 8RD (01-703 5400). An international charity for children which provides basic health care, clinics and nutritional centres wherever children are in need, from Nepal to Peru.

Shaftesbury Homes and *Arethusa*   3 Rectory Grove, Clapham, London SW4 0EG (01-720 8709). Devoted to the care and welfare of under-5s at risk, deprived teenagers and needy single-parent families. They run hostels, day-care centres and a sailing barge and sailing ketch (the *Arethusa*) to give children challenge and adventure.

STA (Sail Training Association)   Schooners April Cottage, Northbourne Road, Betteshanger, Deal, Kent CT14 0EQ (0304 611336). Two schooners, the *Sir Winston Churchill* and the *Malcolm Miller* were built to give young people adventure. Every year they take 1,200 boys and girls to sea for two-week courses where they learn new skills, confidence and independence.

6.

GROUP ACTIVITIES

'What are we doing today?' is a familiar enough cry during the school holidays. Keeping up the momentum can be difficult, especially during the long summer break, and a real worry to mothers who go out to work (see page 249 for other ideas to help working mums). Think about joining forces with others in the same predicament and maybe a problem shared will prove a problem solved! This chapter is designed for the *whole family* to read as it is you who will undoubtedly be helping to choose your holiday activities, but it is your parents who will be doing the organising and forking out the necessary cash! The information is designed mainly for the 8 to 15-year-olds.

There are various ways of getting together. Some schools run holiday centres. If you have one near you make the most of it as they are not countrywide! For those without such help try an 'Activity week'. A local village here gets together for one week during the summer and all those with young organise, or help others to run, an event for each day of that particular week. These are different in the afternoon to the morning, and various alternatives could be devised depending on the size of the community or street. Then publicise the idea, put a slip in your parish magazine or get some children to deliver them round local doors, and after that meet together to get it off the ground. Similarly, a group of 10 to 12 mothers could informally devise various amusements for their children.

Alternatively start up a holiday club in your area. We tell you how to on page 137. This idea is based on holiday clubs set up in East Anglia, operating in towns and cities, as well as smaller, more rural centres. There are almost 3,000 members! It is such a worthwhile concept and ideally should be developed throughout the country to give everyone in this age group the opportunity to make the most of what's offered. Whether you belong to a club or not, you will find

the tips on helpers, insurance, age groups, information and suggestions for a programme of events, plus the organisation on planning matches, outings and tournaments all extremely helpful and practical.

How to Set Up a Small Holiday Group or Club

Some parents may feel like getting together in a small group to organise events for the children during the holidays. In our area the original group has blossomed into a club and others have grown up following their lead. They run excellent outings and events and the children really look forward to the various activities and seeing their friends. Every parent has to participate by organising, say, one event a holiday and be prepared to help supervise with others – depending on the numbers involved. Beware of the system being used as a babysitting service, but if everybody pulls their weight you will find it both great fun and a real benefit, keeping the young happily occupied during the holidays.

When you and your friends first start this, make sure you have children of similar ages so that they will be able to enjoy and partake in activities together. Don't try to have 8-year-olds combining with the teenagers, but offer junior groups one treat and the seniors another. Once children are about 14 to 15 you will find they arrange their own amusements rather than wanting to be organised! However, let them still be members as some events will still attract this older group.

To begin with, keep the numbers limited. No doubt your club will snowball gradually but think small when you are getting it off the ground. You will need to have someone who is 'in charge', a secretary and a treasurer. There will be a lot of work for these people and it is only fair that everybody has a turn in these positions if at all possible. You will also need to establish some sort of rules (see page 141 for a sample form). This may all sound rather boring, but if you want the thing to run smoothly and properly you will have to give the club an ordered framework. These 'offices' should not be held for more than two years as it is very hard work and others should take their turn. You will need to open a bank account for the club.

Insurance and Costing

If you are just a small informal group your own policies may be adequate. However, *always* check that your household insurance covers accidents at your home. Remember charging a fee for running an event is a form of business even though it is non-profit making. You *must* then contact your insurance broker and explain and confirm the situation with him. It is also wise to include a disclaimer for accidents, personal injury or theft when you send out the list of activities (see the form opposite).

If you are thinking in terms of a holiday club, then you enter a different ball game. This is partly because the cost of insurance will be the key to your membership fee. You will find that two-thirds of your fee is spent on insurance and the remaining third covers your postage, printing and stationery costs. Ask your broker if you can charge insurance costs separately each holiday. Insurance is *vital* so *never* run a club without it.

Contact some reliable brokers and explain your plans. Then choose the most reasonable quote, but check all the small print. It might be possible to insure yourselves for the holiday months only – the one drawback is that you cannot then run any events during the term. However, it is saving you money, and considering the main point of the exercise is to occupy everyone in the holidays, it is a small sacrifice. Depending on the terms of your cover, it is likely that you will only be insured for the events specified on your pro- gramme. For example, if you had not done your homework properly and you arrived at a closed museum, you would not be covered by your insurance if you decided to take the children to the local swimming pool instead – so be warned! Another probable proviso is that there is a representative of your group present at each event, even if they are not involved in it themselves, and they must be there during the times the event will last on your programme. Check with your broker what the position would be regarding visiting children who might join in as guests of members.

Please don't be put off by these grim-sounding warnings. It is really worthwhile seeing the children enjoy the marvellous fun they have, so go into details correctly. Then, if there is a problem, everyone will be safely insured and no one individually held responsible. If you want specific help about starting a club contact Mrs J. F. Swetenham, Pound Farmhouse, Rayne, Braintree, Essex CM7 5DJ (0376 26738).

This is a suggested Small Group's Indemnity Form, but see your insurance broker for confirmation that it is adequate:

Full Name ....

Address ....

....

Date of Birth ....

FORM OF INDEMNITY

I, ...
of ....
Being the Parent/Guardian of ....
(hereinafter called 'the child') agree to the child becoming a member of the Holiday Group. I shall indemnify the organisers and any employees of the Holiday Group from any liability in respect of any injury sustained by the child during any event organised on behalf of the Holiday Group.

Signed ....

Dated ....

Opposite is a suggested letter of acceptance and membership and renewal of membership for a larger club (note that you should have a sliding scale of fees for more than one child in a family as postage costs will not be increased).

Drawing up the programme

Having decided on the initial plan, you will need to make a list of events which you want to implement for the next holidays. It is best to have a get-together at the *beginning* of the preceding term – it is surprising how far ahead you need to plan outings, book up if necessary, and settle dates so that they are convenient for one and all. See what ideas everyone comes up with, that they can either organise or at least help with. You don't need to necessarily get involved in ambitious trips, especially in the beginning. Use local facilities at first – if any members have a particular talent, for instance if they paint, cook, garden particularly well, then encourage them to utilise these skills for the children's benefit by having a sketching class, icing Christmas cakes, or sowing some tomato seeds in yogurt pots etc.

It is amazing how much information local tourist and government offices provide if you go round to ask about facilities in your area. You will find your local library very helpful too. Remember to take advantage of block-booking offers to save money, as often you get discounts for over 10 people. When you have your planning meeting, do stress that once somebody has committed themselves to undertake the responsibility for the event, they must be prepared to carry it through – barring emergencies of course. Make sure that everyone comes equipped with a pencil, paper and diary to this meeting.

Booking method

The simplest way of booking the children into the various events is to send a list of each member stating what the event is, the date (plus the day of the week so that there is no confusion), the age group of the children involved for that particular project, and the amount of money it will cost per child. State the time to arrive and where to meet, whether or not they will require a picnic meal, and if possible a time for collection. Following this resumé, give the telephone number and name of the main organiser. The organiser keeps a list of those who want to be included, and will have to judge how many

Date

Dear Parent/Guardian,

We welcome your son/daughter to the membership of the   Holiday Club and hope that he/she will derive benefit and enjoyment from the Club. Our aims are:

1. To provide opportunities for children to learn and practise sports and hobbies in their locality during the school holidays.
2. To ensure an excellent standard of professional tuition in order that members may learn pursuits which they can continue in later life.
3. To promote knowledge and conservation of the countryside.
4. To encourage an interest in environment and local history.
5. To provide all facilities at the lowest possible cost while maintaining a high standard.

We require all members to abide by the rules of the Club and to behave themselves at all arranged events. For reasons of safety, we require all members to comply with any instruction given to them by an instructor or supervisor at an activity. Members must report to the supervisor of the event, both on arrival at, and on departure from, each event. Failure to observe and follow these rules may lead to the termination of the child's membership of the Club.

On joining the Club we require all Parents/Guardians to sign an undertaking that the rules have been understood and that your child has been shown and seen to understand them. We also require all parents to undertake to acquaint any guest their child should bring to an activity with the above Rules. We also must be informed if a child suffers from any specific condition (eg diabetes, asthma, epilepsy, etc).

If there are any parents who would like to organise and supervise an outing or event we should be very interested to hear from them.

Secretary

I am the Parent/Guardian of ....

I have read the Rules of the Club to him/her and will use my best endeavours to ensure that he/she will abide by them. Likewise if my son/daughter wishes to take a visitor to an activity I will make certain their guest is also conversant with the Rules.

Signed ....

Address:
Tel. No:
Full name and date of birth of child:

The membership fee is £   for the first child, £   for the second child and £   for the third and subsequent children.

(Please cut off this slip and return it to the Membership Secretary:)

she can cope with and whether or not to have a waiting list in case of cancellations. Here are some hints for making sure things run smoothly:

1. At the top of the page of events, state a final booking date. This is to encourage people to reply promptly, and to allow you to know how many helpers, etc will be required and to have time to organise them.

2. Have the rule that on booking you send off the money for the event. If the money does not arrive within a week, your child's booking is cancelled. This helps to avoid people deciding at the last moment that they won't bother to come – it is incredible how laid-back some people are. It is very annoying if you are held up leaving for a treat by someone who eventually doesn't appear anyway, or if you are planning a match and the numbers for teams are put out because a child doesn't turn up. People are less likely to be casual and forget an appointment if they have paid already!

3. Make sure that the organiser of each event checks that those involved know what time members are to arrive. It is best to ask everyone to come at least a quarter of an hour before they plan to start their event. Also they must say if they want any extras brought, clothing or picnic food etc. Whatever plan is made, do have sufficient helpers. Decide on how many you think you need for each treat and stick to it. One local club insists that for every three events your child is involved with, you have to help with one of them. This seems an excellent idea. However, some mothers may work and be unable to participate so actively in the outings. Instead, perhaps they could take on administrating the club, for instance be the secretary, most of which work could be done in their own time.

When the club evolves into something larger, you may wish to have less casual methods of booking, as follows:

1. Send to each member a list of events plus a booking form. The form must be sent back on a first-come first-served basis, with a stamped addressed envelope included and the money required for the chosen events best paid by cheque (see page 146). The secretary and helpers will then have to organise the booking, cheques, and returning of money if an event is full up. Also the secretary must have complete information from each organiser concerning ages, numbers, and if necessary, whether equal numbers of boys and girls have to be booked (for a mixed tennis tournament, etc).

2. Have a booking day. This is an alternative method that is used but it can all become rather a bun fight. The mothers have to come and book in on a first-come first-served basis. They sign up on lists pinned around a room, for whichever event their child wishes to participate in. They then go and pay the treasurer, immediately. This does avoid quite a lot of administrative work, but we think the other method of booking is less of a hassle so long as you have sufficient secretarial help to organise it.

Overleaf is a typical programme and how to set it out:

THE HOLIDAY CLUB
Easter Holiday Programme

BIRD WATCHING 8–10 years

Monday, 24th March. Trip to RSPB, Sandy, Beds. Please bring a picnic lunch. *Time* 10.30–4.30 approx. *Cost* 75p. Meet at Lower House.
Contact .... Tel. no. ....

CHOCOLATE EASTER EGGS DECORATING All ages

Wednesday, 26th March at Hazel Cottage (next but one to the village shop. Please bring plastic box. *Time* 10.30–12.30; 11+ 2.30–4.30. *Cost* £1.50.
Contact .... Tel. no. ....

SNOOKER 10–14

Thursday, 27th March and Tuesday 15th April at The Snooker Club. *Time* 1.30–3.30. *Cost* £1.75 *per session.*
Contact .... Tel. no. ....

BRIDGE IMPROVERS 12+ (Unless reasonably experienced)

Thursday, 3rd April at 1, The Hill. *Time* 6.00–10.00 p.m. *Cost* £3. Light supper provided. Instruction and help will be given.
Contact .... Tel. no. ....

WOODWORK 8+

Monday, 7th April at Hatherley School. *Time* 9.30–4.00. *Cost* £5. *Instructor* Mr Brown. Please bring a picnic lunch.
Contact .... Tel. no. ....

POTTERY 8+

7th, 8th, 10th April at the Pottery and Craft Gallery. *Time* 10.00–12.00 Daily. *Cost* £10.50 per child for three mornings to include all materials. Clay is expensive, hence the rather high cost of this event. Please bring an overall. *Instructor* Mr Potter.
Contact .... Tel. no. ....

FLOWER ARRANGING 8–10

Tuesday, 8th April at 22, The Close. To make some 'Spring Arrangements'. Please bring an old saucer and some scissors. *Time* 10.30–12.30. *Cost* £2.
Contact .... Tel. no. ....

VISIT TO HOUSE OF COMMONS Age 10+

Wednesday. 9th April. Time 9.30–5.00 approx. *Cost* £5. Please bring money for lunch at MacDonalds, or picnic lunch if preferred, plus spending money.
Contact .... Tel. no. ....
Please ring nearer the time to check where to meet up.

FIRST AID 8–11

Wednesday, 9th April at The Health Centre. *Time* 1.45–3.45. Please be prompt. *Cost* £1. Red Cross Book available on request at £2.50 per copy.
Contact .... Tel. no. ....

TENNIS 8–12

Thursday, 10th, Friday, 11th April at The Tennis Club. *Time* 10.00–11.00 Beginners, 11.00–12.00 Improvers. *Cost* £2.50. *Coach* Mrs Smith. Please bring racquets and tennis shoes.
Contact .... Tel. no. ....

ROLLERSKATING 8+

Friday, 11th April at .... *Time* Session 2.30–5.00. Allow 1 hour for travelling. *Cost* £2.00 plus pocket money – refreshments not included. Bring roller boots if you have any.
Contact .... Tel. no. ....

TENNIS 8+

14th, 15th and 17th April at The Old School. *Time* ½ hour bookings from 9.00–1.00. Individual or shared, up to 4 children. *Cost* £4.50 per ½ hour. Please be punctual, preferably early! If you are late time cannot be made up.
Contact Please book DIRECT with ....
Tel. no. .... and pay her in advance.

ICE SKATING 11+

Wednesday, 16th April at the Ice Rink. *Time* 9.00–Lunchtime. *Cost* £2.25 includes skate hire and refreshments.
Contact .... Tel. no. ....

DRUGS TALK 12+

Friday, 18th April at Greentiles. *Time* 10.30–12.00. *Cost* £1. Talk, with video film on the dangers of drugs, glue sniffing, alcohol abuse, etc by Det. Sgt. .... of the Drugs Squad.
Contact .... Tel. no. ....

CLAY PIGEON SHOOTING Girls and boys 12

Sunday, 20th April at The Gravel Pit. *Time* 9.30 but phone to confirm exact time. *Cost* £6. *Coach* Mr Shot of The Gunsmith's Shop. Please bring warm clothing. Parents are welcome to stay and watch.
Contact .... Tel. no. ....
(after 6 p.m.)

NEXT MEETING FOR MOTHERS

Monday 28th April at 11.30 at Greentiles. Please let us know if you would like a Ploughman's Lunch. (£1 per head).

PLEASE NOTE

Please let us have your booking forms and order for lunch on 28th April back by *Friday, 21st February*.

Opposite is a typical booking form. Send this with your programme of events to be completed and returned. You will see from this type of form that the cheque to cover the costs is left open. The cheques have to be filled in by the Secretary very carefully and if a child cannot be accepted for any of the events cheques must be returned. Put 'Not to exceed £ ....' on the bottom of your cheque.

BOOKING FORM

EASTER HOLIDAY 1

Name .... **Date of birth** ....

Address and Tel. No. ....

Please return this form, with your cheque open but with the words 'NOT MORE than £ . . . .' and the maximum figure written across the bottom and a stamped addressed postcard with all your options entered on it.

To: The Secretary .... + address ....
NOT LATER THAN Friday 21st February.

		Amount	Tick if you can help supervise
Bird Watching 75p	24th March		
Choc. Easter Egg Decor. £1.50	26th March		
Snooker £1.75 per session	27th March/ 15th April		
Bridge Improvers £3	3rd April		
Woodwork £5	7th April		
Pottery £10.50	7th/8th/10th April		
Flower Arranging £2	8th April		
Visit to House of Commons £5	9th April		
First Aid £1	9th April		
Tennis £2.50	10th/11th April		
Rollerskating £2	11th April		
Tennis	Book Direct		
Ice Skating £2.25	16th April		
Drugs Talk £1	18th April		
Clay Pigeon Shoot £6	20th April		
	Total enclosed		

Information for those in charge of outings and events

There are no two ways about it, you will learn about your 'friends' when you are organising an event – who's on time, who's reliable, and who's totally disorganised! If you are prepared then you will find it much easier to take in your stride! Also it is a responsibility, even having other children at your own house, let alone taking them on an outing – however it is also great fun and once you've done it you know that it will be someone else's turn next time!

Your event and you

When deciding what event you will plan don't try to pack too much into the day. Whether you choose to ice cakes at home or take a couple of car-loads ice skating, it is very important that you know your limitations and the children's. Young hands will be slower, being less practised, than yours, so the icing will take longer and the cries for help will be more frequent than you envisage. Similarly, by the time you have organised skates, drinks, mopped up the odd tear, and counted heads, don't think you can drive an extra 20 miles to go to a safari park that day too. Remember that even crossing a road with 20 eight-year-olds is really a major manoeuvre!

Numbers

You have to know how many children you and however many helpers you enlist can cope with. If it happens to be a popular event, and depending how you run your booking-up scheme, keep a waiting list in case someone drops out with the measles – there's probably going to be one. Always ask for the telephone contact numbers for those on waiting lists because if the club is a large one you will not necessarily know everyone's number. Remember you should have 1 helper to 5 or 6 children, depending on age, numbers and nature of the event. Check if your insurance is specific about this.

Drivers

Be sure if you are taking an outing that you have organised sufficient drivers to help. There is no point squashing too many into each car – better to take an extra one than have everyone, including the driver, fraught after a long journey in a sardine can.

Timing

Always allow extra time when planning your event. It's worth adding an extra quarter of an hour when working out your timing from the starting point. Pick-up times can also run later than you imagine, allowing for delays either at home or returning from a trip. On an outing, always take a telephone number of someone who could contact others, in case you are likely to be very delayed before reaching a pick-up point.

Extras
Remember to have sensible extras to hand with you, for instance extra wet-weather clothes, a packet of tissues, etc depending on what you have planned to do. They may well not be needed but it is much better if you go prepared.

Supervisors
Whoever has organised an event *must* be present all the time. This could affect insurance claims. For example: an expert may be giving a golf lesson and the parent in charge will not be actually doing anything other than waiting – but it is vital that they are there, supervising throughout. Sadly accidents can happen and someone must be responsible. If a supervisor, for some very important reason, cannot go to the event, another person must take their place. You have helpers involved so perhaps one of them could take over and enlist another helper. Everyone must do their fair share of helping and supervision (although if some cannot see page 143).

On the day you will have to:

1. Arrive ahead of the official time stated and leave after everyone else has gone.

2. Tick off on the list all those present and mark the absentees. Check that you have only the number of children allotted to the event and if you are on an outing do the odd head count to check that no one is lost.

3. Have a simple first aid kit and a telephone number of a contact in case you will be delayed on return journey.

4. If there is an accident make sure the child is treated, the remainder of the group stay together under adult supervision, and ask the other adult helpers to make notes concerning the incident.

5. Check, if necessary, that all the equipment is returned to its correct place.

6. Tidy up and lock up if necessary.

7. Remember if you have taken children on an outing that they must be returned to the place named on the programme and not allowed to leave your care until they are picked up. If no one arrives to collect a child, the supervisors must take him or her home.

Background information for you

It is most important if you are going out somewhere to have a recce first and really know what you are embarking on. For example, if you want to organise a sailing course, go down and check the whole set-up. It's not just a safety measure, it also means that you have made personal contact and you have real knowledge before you get there with your 'brood'. Double-check dates and opening times, as they may have been changed since the year before, and one telephone call could avoid a huge disappointment – well worth it!

Before your event list goes out, have bookings written for and provisionally organised. If there are handicapped children in your group check that your venues will be suitable for their needs, for instance that there is access for wheelchairs. If you need information there are excellent tourist information centres all over the country. Ask for your local one from the British Tourist Centre, 12 Regent Street, Piccadilly Circus, London SW1 (tel. 01-730 3400). Any local centre will give you a Directory of Tourist Information Centres. Having compiled all the facts you need, keep the information in a file. This is not just for your use! When your children grow up and dispense with the club, you can hand on all your experience and information to the next committee.

Costs

Cover yourself for the costs of the event. Obviously no one is out to make a profit here. The cost of an instructor, materials, and transport must be fairly shared. If you are providing some refreshment, don't go over the top as simple fare is all that is required. (A chicken drumstick, chipolata, peas and chips followed by ice cream and chocolate sauce would be a perfectly adequate lunch without being too pricey.) The expense of events will vary but some, such as sailing or shooting, can seem very costly while others, such as a nature walk, could be free. Put a good variety on your programme.

Visitors

Check with your insurance that visitors can come on outings and will be covered by the club's policy. Club members must take priority over visitors when bookings are being worked out.

NB If events are going to last all day, or even several hours, organise, say, two-hour shifts for supervisors and helpers. If you are on an outing where this would be impractical, just be sure you have enough members helping. No one must leave, even if their time has expired, until the replacements have arrived.

Group Outings and Events

All the activities we suggest in this section are to help you in setting up a holiday club. However, they will also give you ideas for keeping your own family amused during the holidays, for planning a day's group outing or for organising a birthday treat for one of your children.

There are so many possibilities here including canoeing, computing, glass engraving, judo, photography, sailing, or water sports as well as visits to a local farm, factory, fire station, newspaper or back stage in a theatre that you are sure to find one to suit your individual needs.

You will find more detailed information and addresses concerning many of these activities in the previous chapters, Sports and Activities.

• Badminton

An hour's class is enough. You could run an event for beginners and intermediates if this is a popular sport in your area. Most public courts require players to wear white plimsolls. Racquets can normally be provided. Check these points when booking the court and write them on your form.

• Barbecues

These include preparing the meal, cooking and eating it! Run the event from 11 am to 2 pm and have a few games before lunch while the barbecue sizzles. Remember to state that when writing the programme. Tell the children to bring an apron. For an older group you could do an evening barbecue and then camp out (see **Camping Out**).

• Birdwatching

You may need to make this a long outing depending on where you live. If you are within striking distance of somewhere like the RSPB at Sandy, Bedfordshire (see page 172) then you will have a marvellous time. Remind children to come with binoculars if at all possible, sensible walking shoes, or boots, plus wet-weather clothes in case of need. Do make sure your helpers are interested in ornithology too or else the children's questions might not get answered; try and arrange guides in any case.

• Board Games

There are various ways of using either a single board game or several of them, to provide a fun get-together. You would need a couple of hours at least to really make the most of a tournament. Here the children play a variety of games and if you time everyone so that they can play as many games as possible you will keep all the children occupied. Have the rule that whoever is winning when time's up scores two points, and the loser scores one, then you will find a *victor ludorum* but everyone will have at least scored something! Remember to have enough helpers if rules need explaining, and enough umpires for the event to run smoothly. Many children often do not really understand rules without an adult there to remind them, so be prepared to help. Perhaps you could serve a drink and biscuit at half-time!

An alternative is to hold a chess party – you will need some people to bring chess sets so put that on the programme. Again allow two to two and a half hours and have specified on the programme what level of experience the players should have reached. Have a few lessons for beginners one holiday and follow it next holiday with a party.

Bridge lessons are a good idea for the older children – they have to be able to hold a hand of cards easily. It is fun to make this a bridge evening followed by supper. Again have sufficient helpers as before and specify on the form what standard player you are aiming at – see chess for suggestions.

• Brass Rubbing

Find out if there is an authoritative brass rubbing parent who will organise this event. Do remember that you must ask permission before you arrive with children in tow. Some brasses cannot be used as they are wearing out. The length of time for this activity rather depends on how far you will have to travel to find the brasses. If you are all novices about this activity, there are plenty of brass rubbing centres now throughout the country and you can contact one of these to help arrange a session. See page 173 for further details.

• Calligraphy

You need to find an art teacher to help with this. It would probably take three mornings, two hours each day, to learn basic skills. Do not include children who are too young, 10 upwards would be best. The teacher will need to provide equipment.

• Camping Out and Barbecue

The organiser will obviously need a lawn for this activity. Be firm and keep this one between 9 to 13-year-olds. If the children are too young they may become frightened, and if too old the high jinks start! Tell them to come equipped with sleeping bags and pillows, warm clothing, anorak, torch, and depending on your requirements a tent and ground sheet (check how many the tent will sleep and if it needs a ground sheet, when booking is organised).

Give them a barbecue supper and play some games before they turn in. Be prepared to have fairy footsteps coming in and out of the house during the night. We definitely advise that some adults camp out too in any case.

• Canoeing

Contact a local canoeing club (see page 15) and ask their require-ments. Children who participate in this must be strong swimmers and you must stress that on the form. We think unless children are very keen it is best to avoid wet suits, etc, so only suggest this for summer. Then they can wear swimming trunks or shorts and old trainers or plimsolls. They will need a towel and some clothes to change into, plus a plastic bag for wet things. This will probably be a two-hour session but you could arrange several days of instruction so that there is an opportunity to really learn something. As it will be in the summer it could take place in the evening, say 6 to 8 pm, and perhaps some parents could help run it.

• Car Maintenance

A keen mechanical parent could run this session. Tell the children to wear old clothes or overalls and allow at least three hours, depending of course on what the person in charge is prepared to do! Tell them also to bring a packed lunch, and run the course from 11 am to 3 pm. Start the age limit at 11 at the minimum, or keep it as an event purely for the older group as it can be hard to find events for them.

• Carpentry

Contact a woodwork master at the local school and run two grades of classes, one for the younger age group – boys and girls – and one more advanced. Tell the children to wear old clothes or take an overall – they may need a pencil, rubber, and ruler each too. To make this worthwhile the older group may need two sessions of three hours each but ask the master what he suggests. Check costs involved as the wood will be quite expensive.

• Clay Pigeon

This is very popular with the older group, both boys and girls. Don't allow anyone under 12 to participate. It is vital to find a good teacher who will above all instruct them on safety. Have hour-long sessions with beginners separate from the more experienced. It will be necessary to be sure that your venue for this is 100 per cent safe – so either hold it at a shooting school or clear it with the police before you start, if it is to be in someone's field – check there isn't a footpath running through it!

• Coach Outings

You will need to be sure that your event will be popular if you are embarking on a coach outing as the costs are high. However, if you are taking large numbers very many places of interest give discounts – for example in London there is a Group Sales Box Office (4 Norris Street, London SW15 4RJ, tel. 01-930 6123) who offer substantial reductions for group of 15 or more for many West End theatres, and some concerts. Similarly, some safari parks offer reduced entry fees for large numbers, for example Windsor Safari Park (The Sales Manager, Windsor Safari Park, Windsor, Berks), give reductions for 20 or more. Contact your choice of venue well ahead of time to apply for these. Look in the yellow pages or contact the British Travel Centre (12 Regent Street, Piccadilly Circus, London SW1, tel. 01-730 3400) for local tourist office addresses and telephone numbers and they will give you relevant information for your area. For a list of suggested places to visit see the next section, Outings of Special Interest.

Always have sufficient helpers on board and let each have a checklist of the children. Do plenty of head counts during the outing and always arrange a meeting place preferably under cover, where everyone should assemble if anyone does get split up. Above all else tell the children not to go off with any stranger no matter what the person says.

• Computing

You will need to have a computer expert in charge! Organise somewhere where you have sufficient computers for several children to play games, plan programs or whatever all at the same time. Obviously a school computer room would be ideal. The session would last between an hour and a half and two hours.

• Cookery

Seasonal cooking   At Christmas organise a group to cook mince pies (let anyone bring home-made mincemeat if they prefer). You can make shortbread biscuits to hang on the Christmas tree or ice a precooked and marzipanned (or egg-whited) Christmas cake and even prepare some brandy butter. In the Easter holidays organise a class for decorating chocolate Easter eggs or baking an Easter cake.

Ethnic cookery   See if there is a knowledgeable mother to teach the children to cook a real tandoori chicken, or try African cookery, etc.

For cookery sessions you will probably need three hours, and remind everyone to bring aprons, any necessary equipment, eg rolling pins for the mince pies, and boxes to take things home in. You may need to ask them to bring cooking containers too. Remind organisers to have ingredients prepared beforehand as it saves so much time.

● Crafts

If there are any talented craftsmen amongst your group, encourage them to run a class, whether this is making patchwork, masks, batik, collage, corndollies, jewellery, shell or pasta pictures, Christmas crackers or pomanders, etc. Organisers will need to plan carefully beforehand what materials they require and what equipment they want the children to provide, such as scissors, etc. Allow two hours per session and possibly have two or three sessions per course to get the children going.

If there is no one available from amongst you, the best way to find possible craftsmen to help is to visit a local craft fair and ask anyone who has likely-looking pieces, if they would be willing to come and teach the children. Most people are very enthusiastic and will give you one of their cards – keep all the information in your file. Although you may not need the event then, you can look it up when you have a gap in your programme.

• Cricket

Coaching County clubs run their own coaching (see page 17), but local schools may well be very happy to let you use their grounds to hold a less formal coaching. This is best done in the Easter holidays before the summer term, but can be run during the summer too.

A match The problem with organising a cricket match is ensuring that you have enough players, as during the summer so many people are away. So we suggest you run this event early on in the holidays or right at the end. However it is a popular activity and well worth attempting. First of all organise your pitch. As it can be a week-day match you should not have any difficulty. Persuade an elder brother to organise umpires and scorers.

You will need to balance your team and keep the age range narrow – if necessary running a match for the younger group one day and one for the older teams another day. Do arrange the teams so that the good players are evenly distributed, and be firm about it! You may find wicket keepers hard to come by, especially in the younger set, in which case switch people around during the match. Make sure that everyone has a chance to bat and bowl if possible. It is best to have an arrangement whereby a child is retired after either, say, six overs, or 20 minutes. You may think this unnecessary for an older group when the standard of play is higher.

You will need to have two bats, six stumps, and four bails, two balls, three pairs of pads, one pair of wicket-keeping gloves and two pairs of batsman's gloves, plus score sheets, a pencil, and a coin to toss with for who bats first. Ask a school if you may borrow any equipment. Older children may have some of their own gear but bring sufficient with you in case anyone forgets. Children should wear suitable footwear.

The match may well last an afternoon so have some tea prepared – a variety of sandwiches (allow two halves each), crisps and biscuits or cake would be fine, but above all, and especially if it is hot, plenty of squash. If you are allowed to use a pavilion at the pitch check the equipment you can have there; otherwise provide paper or plastic cups, etc. If your match finishes early play a game of 'tip and run', ie: you have to run if you hit the ball at all.

• Cycling

Cycle proficiency The course would be run by a Road Safety Officer so contact the police for information. It lasts five days, an hour each session. The bicycle must be roadworthy and will be inspected on the first day. There will be a special indemnity form which parents have to complete, sign and hand in at the first session. On the last day there will be a written test, so remind children on the form that they must bring a pencil. (See also page 19.)

Cyclo-cross A new idea of cross-country fun. You will need to have a suitable course near you (see page 29). The event will last about two and a half hours, say 2.30 pm to 5 pm. Tell children to bring a picnic tea or lunch if you prefer a morning session. Probably not suitable for under-10s.

• Decorations

Younger age groups love making Christmas decorations and cards or Easter presents and cards. Whoever organises this must be sure of what equipment the children should bring, for instance: a candle, scissors, etc, and make a note of this on the form. They will need to be very well prepared themselves – collecting plastic lids, fir cones, oasis and ribbons well ahead. This will need to last about three hours.

• Diving Course

This will be a popular activity. You will need to approach your local sports centre or pool and through them book an ASA diving coach. Everyone will be required to be able to swim at least a length of the pool. To make it worthwhile have a three-day course of hour-long sessions. Remind children to bring money for locker keys if necessary. Ask at the pool if there are other relevant notes that should be mentioned on your programme.

• Drawing, Painting or Sketching

Be guided by your teacher as to what age groups they are prepared to take on but it is probably best to have one class for the younger age group and another for the older ones. Tell children what equipment they need and include an overall. A three-hour session is probably necessary but the younger ones may have less.

• Drugs Talk

This could be undertaken either by a doctor or a member of the police Drugs Squad. The talk may well be accompanied by a video film on the dangers of drugs, glue sniffing, alcohol abuse, etc. This would be for the 12+ age group, and last about an hour and a half.

• Farm Walk

If you live in a city, a farm walk is a fascinating activity. Contact your local NFU branch to ask if they could suggest a farmer with an interesting farm to approach to undertake this. Don't forget visiting city farms can be great fun (see Outings section).

• First Aid

Persuade a local nurse or doctor to help on this. There is a good Red Cross book which could be purchased for the children to keep. A full blown Red Cross course lasts several weeks with an exam at the end of it – we do not imagine you will undertake to organise this. However, even a two-hour session of instructions on basic first aid might prove invaluable in the future.

• Fishing

You would need to enlist the help of a keen angler with access to fishing. You may want to organise an instructional talk prior to the expedition. Do state exactly what equipment is needed and if a picnic will be required.

• Flower Arranging

If one of your membership is an accomplished flower arranger encourage them to hold a class, if not, contact a professional instructor (see page 63). Young children could undertake a simple creation and the older ones something more ambitious after a little talk on basic hints. Allow two hours and give instructions to bring any equipment, such as scissors, and a suitable container so that the children can take the arrangement home.

• Football Match

First of all find a suitable pitch. If you play on a full-sized pitch remember that the juniors will find it hard work, so maybe have extra players. Also you will be amazed at how lost an 8-year-old goalkeeper looks standing in the gaping hole! Instead have two goalies per side and change them with others at half time. Keep the juniors and seniors in separate matches – two years' growth at this stage makes such an immense difference in size and strength. Try to make your teams as evenly matched as possible. If you play mid-week organise an elder brother to be the referee. The game should last 40 minutes each way but we suggest you allow only 30 minutes a half for the juniors. You will need to provide a referee, a whistle, a coin to toss with, orange segments (4 oranges cut) for half-time, plenty of squash and mugs for thirsty players at the end!

On the programme tell the boys to wear football boots or trainers and later contact them to tell them to come in, say, blue or red for the team colours. You cannot expect to arrange this until you have fixed your team.

• Glass Engraving
If you can find an engraver to organise kits and tuition for the children this is a very popular event. The kits are expensive but then the children can use them again – in fact you had better lock up your own glasses or you will find everything has a picture on!

• Golf
See page 22. Contact a local golf club and ask if they will assist you by arranging instruction by their professional. This would be a good event for the older children but younger children can start learning too, so see what the pro suggests.

• Hockey Match
See page 24. If you have a group of keen hockey players run a match (11-a-side) for them. You will need to book a school or club pitch, organise a referee and come armed with a ball, half-time oranges, orange squash, mugs and a coin to toss with. Have a first aid kit in case of accidents. Tell players to bring their own pads and sticks.

• Ice Skating
See page 36. This is a very popular outing. Contact the local rink

and check costs and opening times. The cost can include hire of skates so quote that when working out your charges for the programme, as most children will need to hire. If you want them to have tuition this can be arranged but will cost extra. If you have beginners in the group we suggest that you go at a quiet period so ask at the rink what is the best time to come. On the programme tell the children to bring change for locker money (check the amount when you telephone), and for refreshments afterwards. Also state that they should wear gloves, in case they fall over (these protect fingers from other skaters), and trousers to protect knees. Thick socks are suggested not thin tights to cushion the feet as the hired skates can be rather worn. Take sufficient helpers as you may well have to help lace up skates and also in case of accidents and anyone having to go to hospital – having experienced this we know it can happen! (If helpers are sitting out rather than participating, do advise them to wrap up warmly.)

• Judo, Karate, or Self-Defence for Girls

If you contact a local judo or karate club, you could ask if they would be willing to do an introductory course for children. Similarly ask them or the police if they would be prepared to teach 11+ girls some self-defence in a short two-hour session (see also page 26).

• Local Visits

Museums (See Outings section.)   Inquire at your local museum if and when they run special holiday activities for children. For example, some have quiz sheets which the young visitor completes while going round the museum, others organise lectures, videos, etc.

Radio stations and TV   Contact your local commercial or BBC stations and ask if they would take a party on a tour. You may well have to book in advance if it is a popular one.

Factories   Dairies, breweries, potteries, sweet, glass and car factories, etc often allow visitors to go around their works. Some have age limits so check this, some do not have access for wheelchairs if there are disabled in your group, and some have maximum and minimum party numbers. Always ring well in advance to organise bookings as there are sometimes waiting lists for visitors.

Newspapers Some newspapers allow parties to watch the paper being printed on certain days of the week. For example, the *Daily Mail* (01-353 6000) has tours at 21.00 and 23.00 hours on a Tuesday or Wednesday; the groups are maximum of 12 and no children under 14 are permitted – there is a 4 to 6-month waiting list!

Backstage at theatres Some theatres have tours behind the scenes. These are very popular, and if you are travelling some distance to get there it might be worth trying to combine taking a packed lunch and seeing a matinée performance with this trip (see also page 70).

Other local visits These might include the vet; racing stables; football clubs; police dog training establishments; fire station; magistrates court; army barracks and air force bases. Contact the secretary or officer in charge and see what could be organised. People are very helpful when they know children are involved!

• Model Making

Children are often given models to make up for birthdays and Christmas which either sit around half-finished, or not even opened. It is much more fun to make them up with friends doing the same thing. So either provide simple models and show beginners how to get going, or invite older children to bring their own ones to assemble. It will depend on the degree of difficulty and whether or not you want to paint them as to how long and how many sessions you choose for this event. This will be for 8 to 12-year-olds. Make sure you have some spare equipment such as glue, paint brushes, enamel paints, in case anyone comes without, and specify on the programme what is required.

• Nature Walk

On the programme tell the children to bring boots and anoraks whatever the weather, and, depending on the timing, include either a picnic lunch or tea. This would only interest younger children and would probably last two and a half hours. Many country parks organise special guided walks (see page 59).

• Orienteering

This is a country activity which could be turned into a competition, ie the winner is the first person to find the route. But it need not be run in this way; simply finding a route can be just as much fun. Combine a picnic with this event. This is for older children – tell them to bring boots and an anorak, whatever the weather, together with their picnic.

• Photography

Run a photography course including lighting, composition and general technique information. If any school with a dark room will allow you access to this, you will find the members will discover developing their own film extremely exciting. The instructor must decide what equipment the children need, how many sessions to run and the time involved.

• Pottery

Any pottery course will obviously be run in a proper studio with a wheel and a kiln so find a teacher and a suitable venue, which will determine the numbers on the course. Tell the children to take an overall. The course will probably last two hours.

Either you will have to arrange to collect the children's work on another occasion following firing, or else have another session when they could glaze their work. This would probably last about 45 minutes to an hour.

• Riding and Stable Management

Contact your local riding school and ask them to run a one-day course of riding tuition, fun, games and including a talk on stable management. This could be for all ages but have different days for each level of ability. On the programme state that the children must note their level (honestly) and that they should wear shoes with small heels, not trainers, provide pony club approved hard hats (although some riding schools can lend pupils them) and bring a packed lunch – with a couple of carrots! The course would probably run between 10 am and 4 pm. (See page 177 for other horse events.)

• River Outings

It depends whereabouts in the country you live as to the suitability of this suggestion. However, there are a couple of points to make. Do check if you plan a canal trip that you can see over the canal bank as you travel along – there was a bit of a disappointment once when the banks were so high that the children became bored.

If you are in an area accessible to punting, remember that after 11.30 am on a fine day you will have a long queue to contend with, so get there early as punts often cannot be booked ahead. Don't expect young boys and girls to be able to punt far either – the pole is very heavy and the manoeuvring is actually difficult for a 14-year-old to undertake – so try and persuade parents to be in charge, even though everyone will want to have a go! You can take six per punt.

For all river trips you will need a picnic meal (state to bring this on the programme), but check up that there is somewhere under cover to eat it if necessary. Tell members to bring waterproofs. It is probably worth a supervisor taking some spare kit in case there is a man overboard! The outing would probably last half a day.

• Roller Skating

This can be fast and furious, so if you are taking any beginners telephone the rink to find the quietest time. Tell children to bring locker and refreshment money. Include the hire of the roller boots in the charges and give an allowance for those who bring their own. The times involved will depend on how near your local rink is.

• Rounders

The wonderful thing about rounders is that you can play with a few or lots of players, and everyone can enjoy a game even if they are not very sporty! Officially you need 9 a side but extra fielders can stand behind and between the posts. There should be four posts, marked by, for example, bean poles. Use a proper rounders bat if possible, a light cricket bat, or even (with a tennis ball) a tennis racquet, although then you need extra deep fielders as a tennis ball could be hit a long distance. A proper rounders ball is best but not essential. The match will last about an hour (allow 15 minutes per innings and each team has two innings). On the programme tell the players to bring a sweater or sweatshirt and a picnic tea or lunch.

• Sailing

You will need to do a recce and find a suitable club for your needs. There should be several sessions and the length of time specified on the programme will depend on how far you are from the coast, reservoir or wherever. Participants must be able to swim at least 50 metres in light clothes. They should wear canvas, rubber soled shoes, old clothes and bring a towel and a change of clothes. Life jackets are provided, but always check this. The children may need a packed lunch but tell them to bring extra money if they want to buy additional refreshments there.

'Knotting and splicing' could be run as a separate winter event to teach children the mysteries of such skills.

• Scottish Reels

Contact a local dancing teacher and see if she is interested in teaching reels to a class. Locally there are three sessions of about an hour each followed by a fourth which is in the form of a party and much enjoyed. This is really for the 8 to 11-year-olds. Alternatively if a group of children know how to do Scottish dancing, give a party which includes a little disco dancing and the reels.

• Shooting (Air Rifles)

You need to approach a school with a shooting range to ask permission to run an event under the supervision of their instructor. Children are usually requested to wear gym shoes. The age would not include anyone under 11 and the lesson would last an hour.

• Skin Care and Make-up

This is a very popular event for teenage girls. There may be a professional amongst you, but if not contact a local beauty salon and ask if they would help. The talk would probably last about an hour and be prepared for one or two of the girls to act as models if required. Some Health and Beauty centres will combine a keep fit or aerobics class with a make-up demonstration. Alternatively, a talk on hair care and/or nail care would be equally successful for this age group. If anyone knows anything about stage make-up, this is a popular demonstration too.

• Snooker

You will only be able to hold this event if you have a snooker club nearby as you really need enough tables for several children to play on and if necessary to have instruction. This is a very popular one for the boys, although some girls do play too. The session would probably be about two hours, you will have to organise with the club which time would be best.

• Sports Halls

Sports halls are springing up all over the country and offer an amazing range of sports. They usually require children to wear tennis shoes or sometimes trainers, but check and state on the programme. You can organise with them to stay for a day and have many activities going on from, say, 10 am to 4 pm (let supervisors do two hours each). For example, archery, trampolining, basket ball, short tennis for the younger children, badminton, roller hockey, and roller skating may well all be on offer – and you can finish off with a swim! Tell the children to come in suitable clothing, such as a tracksuit, and to bring a swimsuit and a towel. Stress the need for correct footwear. Some halls run a restaurant, but check what yours has to offer and word the programme accordingly. If locker money is required please specify.

• Squash

Approach a squash club and organise a booking of say three or four sessions each lasting an hour. Do split the beginners from those who can play and run them at different times. Clubs insist on white tennis shoes being worn and racquets can normally be supplied if required. Tell the children to bring money for refreshments.

• Swimming

If you have a group of beginners or unconfident swimmers see if you can organise some special tuition for them at your local pool. For those who can swim, stroke improvement lessons are often a great help. These would probably last about half an hour. Allow the members just to have a fun swim for the rest of the session. Remind them on the programme to take locker and refreshment money and not bring any jewellery with them. Alternatively run courses for award schemes – discuss this with the pool supervisor. Children passing the test would get badges to sew on their costumes.

• Tennis

Coaching   Organise with a local school or club to use their courts for tennis coaching. Keep the players' standards comparable and run courses for each level. These should last an hour each.

Run a tennis tournament   American tournaments are where each couple play every other couple but they never change partners. In some ways this is the easy way to organise a competition but it means that if one child is with a bad partner they are stuck with them all day. The other way of playing is to change partners every match which is in many ways far fairer but harder work to arrange! The best way of understanding the system is to study the sample tournament chart. There the losing couple stay on the same level next round, but play each other with new partners. With the winning pair the boy moves up a game and the girl moves down one.

Always provide plenty of squash for refreshment.

• Water Sports

Remember to stress on your programme whichever sport you are referring to, that children *must* be able to swim. The age of those involved will depend on the sport and the time of the event by the distance involved in travelling. Popular water sports include windsurfing (run two levels of courses for beginners and intermediates), water skiing (again run two levels), snorkelling, and for the older ones sub-aqua. Always ensure there is a life saver on duty.

TOURNAMENT CHART

TO BE COMPLETED BY ADULT

Round 1	Round 2	Round 3	Round 4	Round 5
3 Edward/Ann v Nicholas/Clare 2	4 Nicholas/Alison v Gary/Clare 1	Gary/Lucy v Sam/Clare		
1 Sam/Kate v Gary/Jane 4	3 Sam/Ann v Charles/Kate 2	Charles/Alison v Jonathan/Kate		
2 John/Susan v Charles/Julia 3	5 Jonathan/Susan v John/Jane 0	John/Ann v Edward/Jane		
5 Jonathan/Alison v Tom/Lucy 0	1 Tom/Julia v Edward/Lucy 4	Tom/Susan v Nicholas/Julia		

WINNING BOY MOVES UP   WINNING GIRL MOVES DOWN   Losers stay same level but play each other

• Workshops

Drama Ask a local drama teacher to run a day's drama course and even produce a little play or mime at the end of the session. Give the children a simple lunch or ask them to bring a packed lunch. Make sure you keep the course either for seniors or juniors.

Music For the younger group. Find a music teacher who would teach the children a few fun songs (something along the lines of 'Joseph and his Amazing Technicolor Dreamcoat') during a two-hour course.

Outings of Special Interest

We have divided this section into headings covering a variety of interests. Under each we give a brief resumé of what you will find and where. This is not a definitive guide; rather we are aiming to point you in the right direction, and give you addresses and telephone numbers so you can find out exactly what you want to know before selecting your choice for an outing.

We are not including opening dates, times nor admission charges as arrangements do change and we have decided it is far more satisfactory for you to telephone and check the queries you have yourselves. Do this well ahead of your planned visit. Also if you want a group booking most places require prior warning, so be organised.

Museums throughout Britain have shed their dusty, fusty image and are delighted to welcome young people with many varied interests. As one said during our inquiries, 'This is not a museum where children primarily look at things, it's where they *do* things.' So don't ignore your local museum – get in touch and see what it can offer you. In addition it will be able to supply you with lists or brochures on other places of interest in your region, not just museums but also galleries, country houses, castles, mills, forts, nature reserves, the list is endless! See also **National Trust**, page 57, and contact local tourist centres. We are mentioning a very few of the more unusual museums which may appeal to those with an associated interest. We also include some major national museums and if you look under the London Outings section you will find others.

The sections on animal and bird life are intended to give you main centres from which you will find information about reserves, etc in your locality. They are wonderful to visit as great care is now taken to exhibit wildlife in its natural habitat.

We suggest that if you want further information about possible places to visit, that you buy the *AA Stately Homes, Museum, Castles and Gardens in Britain Guide*. Members of the AA can buy it through the AA outlets, or it is distributed by Hutchinson's Publishing Group Limited, 3 Fitzroy Square, London W1T 6JD.

• Air Shows and Museums

If your children are particularly interested in flying and would like to go to either an air show or a flying museum, we suggest that to get the best information you should buy the 'Air Show' number of the *FlyPast* Magazine. This is a special annual issue which comes out normally in March and April, once all the air show dates have been fixed. The *FlyPast* magazine is available at good newsagents, but if you have a problem, contact Key Publishing, 1 Wolthorpe Road, Stamford, Lincs PE9 2JR (0780 55131). This is an excellent magazine which lists all the major air show events throughout the whole country. There are detailed travel guides as to how to get to the various venues, and telephone numbers so that one can check in case the event has been cancelled. This magazine also produces a comprehensive guide of *British Aviation Museums*, which is available from specialist aviation bookshops, or direct by post from the publishers. We will include here just some of the most important air museums.

Aerospace Museum, RAF Cosford, Wolverhampton WV7 3EX (090722 4872). The biggest collection in Europe (there are three hangars with 38 aircraft inside if it rains). Altogether a marvellous place for an enthusiast to visit. Not open all the year.

Imperial War Museum, Duxford, Duxford Airfield, Cambridge CB2 4QR (0223 835000/833963). There is an amazing collection of military and civil aircraft on display here. It is well worth a visit, and right by the M11 motorway, very easy to get to. Special events such as airshows take place here so check dates. There is an adventure playground and a little shuttle service to ferry you around on.

Royal Air Force Museum, Hendon, London NW9 5LL (01-205

2266). This is an absolutely fascinating RAF Museum which records the history of flying. There are two hangars with 40 aircraft in if it rains plus many other exhibits, dioramas, cinema, etc. You can try a flight simulator too! Well worth a visit.

The Shuttleworth Collection, Old Warden Aerodrome, Biggleswade, Bedfordshire SG18 9EP (076 727 288). This is a world famous and unique collection of flyable aeroplanes (1909–1942). There are usually flying displays here from April to October, but check exactly when.

Torbay Aircraft Museum, Higher Blagdon, Nr Paignton, Devon (0803 553540). There are about 19 exhibits, some are replicas, and galleries showing the development of flight – for example the story of the Bouncing Bomb. There are spotter sheets for those going round the aircraft section. In addition, in case some of the group are not aircraft enthusiasts, there is one of the largest indoor model railways in the country, and a period costume collection. Not open all the year.

• Army Museums

Aldershot Military Museum, Queen's Avenue, Aldershot GU11 2LG (0252 314598). The history of the home of the British Army, Aldershot, is portrayed here. Outside exhibits include guns and tanks, and inside there are dioramas of military aviation (including ballooning), a barrack room re-created from the 1890s, and from summer 1987 there will be more displays from the World War II era. It is suggested that this museum is for the over-9s.

Grange Cavern Military Museum, Grange Lane, Holiway, Hollywell, Chryd (20352 713455). This museum is inside a limestone cavern! The army stored bombs here during the last war. There is a large amount to see including an Anderson shelter, a First World War reconstructed trench, medals, vehicles, tanks you can get on to, and videos to watch.

The Imperial War Museum, Lambeth Road, London SE1 (01-735 8922). This is a museum of warfare in the twentieth century in the broadest terms. At the moment there is redevelopment going on, but there is still plenty to see. There are two general historical displays on World War I and II, including not just uniforms, weapons, etc, but also art and literature connected with the wars as well. The museum provides quizzes, film shows and talks during the holidays.

The National Army Museum, Royal Hospital Road, London SW3 (01-780 0717). The history of the army from 1485 to 1914 is told here. For those who are army-mad there is a Summer Holiday Club run by the museum – its activities include lectures, gallery trails, model making and films for its members.

Don't forget that local barracks often hold open days to which the general public are invited. These are great fun, especially for aspiring young soldiers!

• Bird Centres

The following reserves are well worth a visit – it goes without saying that quietness is the order of the day!

Bird and Underwaterworld, Holt Pound, Farnham, Surrey (0420 22140). There are thousands of birds here! Within the 14 acres of grounds some roam free and some are in aviaries. In a separate building you can watch highly coloured tropical fish including the dreaded sharks and piranhas! An absorbing place to visit.

Falconry Centre, Newent, Gloucester (0531 820286).

The Hawk Conservancy, Weyhill, Nr Andover, Hampshire (0264 772252). You can watch the various birds of prey and see their amazing flying demonstrations if the weather is suitable.

Royal Society for the Protection of Birds Reserves, The Lodge, Sandy, Bedfordshire SG19 2DL (0767 80551). The RSPB state that their prime aim is to provide 'rich and undisturbed habitats for wild birds' but also to allow all of us 'to enjoy' the reserves for birdwatching, using the nature trails, hides and information centres the Society has established.

There are at present 43 reserves in England, 29 in Scotland, 9 in Wales, and 5 in Northern Ireland. If you are a member you will be able to visit free, but the general public have to pay. Groups of more than 10 must arrange visits well in advance. Remember the rule is 'No dogs'.

The Wildfowl Trust Centres, Slimbridge, Gloucester GL2 7BT (045389 333). If you apply to Slimbridge they will provide a brochure on the other centres at Arundel, Sussex; Welney, Norfolk; Washington, Tyne and Wear; Martinmere, Lancashire; Peakirk, Peterborough and Caenlaverlock in Scotland.

If you book in advance, parties of 20 or more can apply to have a guided tour. To give you some idea of what is on offer Slimbridge has the world's largest collection of wildfowl. On the 100 acres there are hides from which you can view the birds and the whole centre is really fascinating.

• Brass Rubbing

There are several brass rubbing centres throughout the country which will help you get started for a small fee, and provide materials, etc (which you also have to pay for, of course). Not surprisingly they use replicas to avoid wearing out the originals. The main ones are:

Brass Rubbing Centre, Little Cloisters, Dean's Yard, Westminster, London SW1.

Brass Rubbing Centre, St James Church Hall, 97 Piccadilly, London W1.

Canterbury Brass Rubbing Centre, Old Weaver's House, Kings Bridge, Canterbury (0227 62329).

Exmoor Brass Rubbing Centre, Lynton, Devon (05985 2529)

Gloucester Brass Rubbing Centre, The Cathedral, Gloucester (0452 28095).

Lincoln Cathedral, Lincoln.

Manchester Cathedral Brass Rubbing Centre, Manchester (061-834 9031).

Ouse Bridge Brass Rubbing Centre, 35 Micklegate, York (0904 641404).

Oxford Brass Rubbing Centre, St Mary the Virgin, High Street, Oxford.

Stratford Brass Rubbing Centre, Summer House, Avonbank Gardens, Stratford upon Avon, Warwickshire (0789 297671).

• Butterfly Farms

The London Butterfly House, Syon Park, Brentford, Middlesex (01-560 7272).

This is a marvellous butterfly farm where a child's delight as one of these beautiful creatures lands on his or her head, registers the success of this project. There are special exotic plants which feed this wonderful collection.

Other butterfly farms include:

Butterfly Centre, Royal Parade, Eastbourne (0323 645522).

Edinburgh Butterfly Farm, Melville Nurseries, Lasswade, Edinburgh (031-663 4932).

New Forest Butterfly Farm, Nr Ashurst, Southampton (0421 292166).

Stratford upon Avon Butterfly Farm, Tramway Walk, Stratford, Warwickshire (0789 299288).

Weymouth Butterfly Farm, Lodmoor Country Park, Greenhill, Weymouth, Dorset (0350 783311).

Worldwide Butterflies, Compton House, Nr Sherbourne, Dorset (0935 74608). This is also the silk farm where the material for the royal wedding dress was spun.

• Canal Boats

Inland Waterways Association, 114 Regent's Park Road, London NW1 8UQ (01-586 2556).

Write to the Association and apply for junior membership. They will send you their magazine and any information you would like on particular canals, points of departure, boats and so on. Just remember some canals have deep banks and you won't see the view. Check up before organising an outing.

The Association will give you lots more ideas for places to visit and boat trips, but here are just a couple:

Clock Warehouse, London Road, Shardlow, Leicestershire (0332 792844). You can take a boat trip or visit the restored canal boats and warehouse with its exhibition on canal transport in the last two centuries.

Old Wharf Canal Cruises, Trevor, Llangollen, Clwyd (0978 823215). Canal boat cruise, including a viaduct, tunnel and lift bridge.

• Farms and Farming Museums

There are many farms open to the public where, although children cannot actually help in the farm, they can go in among the animals, sometimes stroke them or pick them up, and where they can learn about early farming methods, how to look after animals, and so on. We list some of the main ones, but consult your local tourist board to see if there are others in your area. Some sheep farms now hold open days at lambing or sheep-shearing time, so ask around or look out for adverts in the local papers. We suggest that you ring up first to check on opening times for all these farms.

Church Farm, Coombes, Lancing, Sussex (07917 2028). You go on a tractor-drawn trailer for a tour round the farm (1,000 acres) to see animals, wildlife, etc. The trip lasts for 1½ hours so might not be suitable for very young children. Ring in advance to book.

Cotswold Farm Park, Guiting Power, Cheltenham (04515 307). Indoor study centre, plus a 1,000-acre farm on which you can see old breeds of farm animals, go on a farm trail, take a car ride, etc.

Dairyland Farm Park and **Country Life Museum**, Treffilian, Barton,

Summercourt, Newquay, Cornwall (08725 246). Farm park with lots of small birds and animals (ducks, donkeys, pigs) which you are allowed to feed. Country Life Museum and 550-acre farm where you can watch cows being milked.

Farm Park and National Exmoor Pony Exhibition, Bossington, Porlock, Somerset (0643 862816). Plenty of Exmoor ponies to admire, many of them working, also lots of old breeds of farm animals – pigs, geese, goats, etc, and a farm museum.

Hunday National Tractor and Farm Museum, Newton, Stocksfield, Northumbria (0661 842553). There are at least 80 to 90 tractors on display here and stationary engines of various agricultural machines. The water wheel can still work the mill, although they do not use it to do so in case they wear out the millstones. You can see what farming used to be like, with section-ploughing and old methods of harvesting on display. There is a row of shops full of old equipment and a narrow gauge railway to take visitors to the lake and back – the engine came from a mine. There are animals too. (In the picnic area the tables are old millstones and the seats are old tractor seats!)

Newham Grange, Leisure Farm, Coulby, Newham, Northumbria (0642 245432). Lots of different breeds of animals on a working farm. Also farming implements from the old days.

Shirley Holms Activity Farm, Lymington, Hampshire (0590 682667). Rare breeds of pigs, goats, horses, etc, as well as demonstrations of milking, buttermaking and so on. Also a place for children to spend holidays.

Standalone Farm Centre, Wilbury Road, Letchworth, Hertfordshire (04626 5211). Different kinds of animals and farm birds. You can watch the milking and go on a farm walk.

Wimpole Home Farm, Old Wimpole, Royston, Hertfordshire (0223 208987). There are 360 acres of beautiful farming land, rare breeds of farm animals and fascinating old farm machinery.

The Yorkshire Museum of Farming, Murton Park, Murton, Yorkshire (0904 489966). This is a museum of farm and rural life. It stretches over an eight-acre site with plenty of buildings, housing various pieces of equipment connected with life on a farmstead. There are farm animals and sometimes craft demonstrations. If you go at Easter, there may be competitions with the winner's rewards of Easter eggs.

• Horse Events and Museums

We are sure there will be keen riders amongst some of your children – who would consider a trip to a major three-day event, a point-to-point or any horse show, the greatest outing.

The best way to find out information regarding dates is through the *Horse and Hound* weekly publication. The point-to-point fixtures will be listed in the edition on the second Friday in January. The show numbers which list all the events for the summer, are published in the first and second Friday in March. If you need a copy you must book it well in advance from a newsagent. Sometimes isolated newspaper orders never materialise, so if you want to be 100 per cent sure of getting a copy, send a letter well before to: Horse and Hound, The Editorial Office, 21st Floor, King's Reach Tower, London SE1 9LS. They will forward your request to the post sales department who will organise payment. The main three-day events are listed here, together with the month they are held, but you would need to check the exact dates by contacting the secretary of each event at the numbers given below.

Badminton, Avon.	mid-April	0454 21272
Branham, Yorks.	end-May	0937 84465
Windsor, Berks.	end-May	0420 38131
Burghley, Lincs.	beg-Sept	0780 52131
Osberton, Notts.	end-Sept	0909 472206
Wylye, Wilts.	end-Sept	0985 6281

The main indoor London events are as follows:
Horse of the Year Show at Empire Pool, Wembley (01-902 1234).
Royal International Horse Show at Empire Pool, Wembley (01-902 1234).

If you take a picnic to any of the outdoor events you will have a good day out – weather permitting. There is always plenty to see even if you are not particularly 'horsey'. Even the very young are catered for at our local point-to-point, with a bouncy castle the main attraction. Be prepared though to queue if you don't arrive early, and take waterproofs in case of need. Also remember it will take a while to get out from these events so allow sufficient time in your schedule to cover this; for example, telling parents when you will be home.

National Racehorse Museum, Newmarket, Suffolk (0638 667333). Combine a visit to the museum with a tour of the important sights of the mecca of horseracing. This is arranged through the museum. The tour includes seeing the gallops where the horses are exercised, the famous 'Boy's Grave', the racecourse itself, Tattersall's world-famous sale ring and the return to the not too large, fascinating and beautifully set out museum. The museum organises a quiz, provides a clipboard and quiz sheet and offers a prize for the best answers! There is a charge for this 'package' outing but it is very reasonable and there is a 10 per cent reduction for booked parties of 20 and over. Allow a week's notice when booking up. This was one of those museums where the curator's attitude was very enthusiastic; for example, when asked if parties could come, the reply was 'The more the merrier!' You would have a really super outing here!

• Maritime Museums
Maritime Museums are fascinating for both boys and girls to visit. Obviously they are partly out of doors, but there is still enough to see under cover even if it does rain. See London Outings section for The National Maritime Museum, Greenwich, the *Cutty Sark* and *HMS Belfast*.

The Boat Museum, Dockyard Road, South Wirral (051-355 5017). There are more than 40 canal or estuary boats at this museum and much more besides showing the life of those involved with inland waterways. You can take canal trips too.

Exeter Maritime Museum, The Quay, Exeter (0392 58075). Indoor and outdoor exhibits from an Arabian dhow to an early Brunel steam boat. This is the largest museum of international boats, so well worth a visit. Open for most of the year.

The Mary Rose Trust, Portsmouth (0705 750521), will give you information concerning the amazing *Mary Rose*. This wonderful Tudor ship, raised in 1982, is well worth a visit. The hull is now in a dry dock workshop. You will see many of the objects found plus re-creations of scenes of life on board the warship and interpretation of Tudor social and maritime history.

Merseyside Maritime Museum, Pier Head, Merseyside (051-709 1551). There are floating exhibits, for example a pilot boat which you can go aboard, and a Boat Hall where you can see how dockers handled cargo or watch boat restoration. The story of emigration to Australia and America is retold here and, on Saturdays, actors depict scenes connected with this. This is still a 'museum in the making' with exciting restoration of the waterfront buildings. There are boat trips off Canning Docks too. Part is closed in winter so telephone for information about what is going on.

Royal Naval Museum, Portsmouth Harbour, Portsmouth (0705 822351). This harbour is where Nelson's ship, *HMS Victory*, is on display and is next door to the Royal Naval Museum. This is the only museum telling the entire history of the Royal Navy. There is a set of dioramas (models) showing the Navy at work from the mid-nineteenth century to the twentieth century. These do not show great sea battles but rather the other side of the Navy, for example, the capture of a slave trader's ship. There are no quiz sheets for children but after 1987 there will be a children's activity book.

The Welsh Industrial and Maritime Museum, Bute Street, Cardiff (0222 481919). The history of industrial and maritime growth in Wales is traced over the last two centuries. Many engines and a collection of vehicles of all sorts are on view, plus the steam boat, *Sea Alarm*, and the sailing pilot cutter *Kindly Light*. There are relevant video films, and the Cardiff Shipstores Building will be open in 1987, telling the history of the port and its ship owners. Some Saturdays are 'Steam Days' when certain engines are driven – check up when these are.

• Model Railways

If you are a model railway enthusiast you will enjoy visiting some of the wonderfully intricate displays around the country. Here are just a few to whet your appetite:

Dawlish Warren Railway Centre, Dawlish Warren, Devon (0626 862131). Thirty model trains, some old, some new.

Great Exmouth Model Railway, Exmouth, Devon. Twelve thousand feet of track with 40 trains running around it.

Mevagissey Model Railway, Meadow Street, Mevagissey, Cornwall (0726 842457). Old and modern trains on half a mile of track. There are nearly 2,000 models to see.

Model Railway Exhibition, Box Bush, High Street, Bourton on the Water (0451 20467). Four hundred square feet of railways in a beautifully landscaped setting. You can work the trains by push button.

If you live near London, or when you visit it, don't forget there are some marvellous permanent exhibitions of model railways and other models at some of the museums, for instance the Imperial War Museum, the Science Museum and the London Transport Museum.

• Motor Shows and Museums

Doune Castle Motor Museum, Central Scotland (078 684 203). This is the Earl of Moray's collection of old cars. Open in the summer only.

Midland Motor Museum and Bird Garden, Stanmore Hill, Stonebridge Road, Bridgnorth (0746 261761). Over 100 exhibits of sports and racing cars and motorcycles dating from 1913 to 1981 (plus the bird garden of 8 acres of aviaries, etc).

Motor Cycles Stortford Hall, Lutterworth LE17 6DH (0788 860250). There is a collection of 65 motor cycles as well as the stately home here. The Hall is open for the summer only.

The Motor Fair, Earl's Court, Exhibition Buildings, London SW5 (01-385 1200). The Motor Fair at Earl's Court is a public show where one can buy anything from an accessory to a car. This now takes place in odd years, while the Motor Show, held at the Birmingham National Exhibition Centre (021-780 4141), is a trade show, where the public are admitted but they cannot buy. This latter show takes place in even years. Both are always held in October. We suggest that you telephone to find out which are the least crowded days, but apparently you should always avoid weekends, and the middle Wednesdays of these shows.

National Motor Museum, Beaulieu Abbey, Beaulieu, Hampshire, (0590 612345). This is a very exciting museum with something for everyone to appreciate. The vehicles are immaculate and very impressive. There are about 300 exhibits and sometimes you can ride in veteran buses. The 'Wheels' exhibition takes you on a 'pod' ride, through 100 years of motoring and even into the future. (The palace, house and gardens offer an extra interest here.)

RAC London to Brighton Veteran Car Run   This is held annually on the first Sunday in November and the cars start from Hyde Park Corner in London at 8.00 am. For any veteran car enthusiasts this would be *the* great experience as you see so many cars in action.

Stratford upon Avon Motor Museum, Shakespeare Street, Stratford (0789 69413). This museum specialises in exotic sports and touring cars.

Transport Museum, William Street, Belfast (51519). Excellent collection of transport in Ireland from cars to fire engines.

• Museums

Most big art galleries and museums have education departments which run services for schools in term time and activities for children during the holidays. We don't have the space to list them all, but contact your local gallery or museum to see what activities they have lined up for children and you will be pleasantly surprised. If they don't have anything interesting on offer, then why not try applying a little pressure or encouragement to see if you can help get things moving? Local schools might be able to make a positive contribution here as well. Here are just two examples:

The National Gallery, Education Department, Trafalgar Square, London WC2N 5DN (01-839 3321). The Department offers a particularly lively and interesting variety of free services for schools, with an age range from top-infants through to A level. Activities include talks, quizzes, worksheets, and the gallery even offers a sandwich room where groups can eat their packed lunches. Teachers will need to book up in advance, and they can then discuss their group's special needs. Holiday activities at the National Gallery are also catered for. There are special quizzes, lectures, demonstration of artists' methods, tape slide shows, and lots of other things (including, dare we say it, courses for teachers themselves!). Ring the number above for up-to-date information at the beginning of the schools holidays.

The Royal Museum of Scotland, Chambers Street, Edinburgh (031-225 734). This is a museum which really encourages children to 'do' and not just look. There is an amazing workshop programme run for the 8 to 14-year-olds. Recent posters for Christmas and sporting events included for example a Christmas Cracker workshop, Eggstra Special Paint your own Easter Eggs, learn to write Arabic, puppet making, be an archaeologist, a Chinese New Year Dragon mask workshop plus many more activities. The numbers involved are limited so you must book in advance. Contact the information desk for the Young Museum programme. It really does appear to be excellent and an example to others of how to involve the young in the museums of today.

We are including below a few examples of some rather unconventional museums. This is to illustrate that if you want to take children on a rather original historically educational outing, there is plenty on offer.

The first two suggestions are for industrial museums:

Abbeydale Industrial Hamlet, Abbeydale Road South, Sheffield (0742 367731). This is a restored waterpowered site mainly concentrating on making agricultural tools. The process of steelmaking as manufactured here from 1785 to the 1840s, is seen through to the final product. The original manager's house and the artisan's cottage show how the workers lived in the 1840s. At least three of the four waterwheels are shown in working order.

The Big Pit Mining Museum, Blaenavon, Gwent, Wales NP4 9XP (0495 790311). This is a proper coalmine! Witness the history of mining and ironworks in the raw. At the Big Pit you experience how the miners lived and worked above and below the ground from the nineteenth century onwards. Go down the 300-foot deep shaft, kitted out in safety helmet, cap lamp, belt and battery, and escorted by ex-miners. See the underground stables, workshops, haulage engines and coal faces. Imagine 6 or 7-year-old children working there with their parents. There is also plenty to see on the surface associated with the life of a mine. Numbers are limited for each underground tour, so ask for their excellent group visit brochure and book according to your requirements.

There are also many fascinating museums showing history in action:

Beckonscot Model Village, Warwick Road, Beaconsfield (04946 2919). This is not exactly a museum but it is both an amazing work of art and a perfect reflection of rural life in southern England in the 1930s, providing a visual dimension to a period of social history. It is almost unbelievable that the houses, churches, cricket game, windmill, railway, etc could all be so perfectly scaled, built and maintained. The proceeds from Beckonscot have always gone to charity and this amounts to about £20,000 per year.

Jorvik Viking Centre, Coppergate, York (0904 643211). This is seeing and smelling life under the Vikings in the twentieth century! You travel back in special 'Time Cars' to find a reconstructed Viking street. This 'trip' takes about 12½ minutes. You see reconstructions from original finds and then finally, in the artefacts hall, you can look at the Viking objects which were found in York.

Mountfitchet Castle, Stansted, Essex CM24 8SP (0279 813237/815035). This is a newly undertaken, amazingly complete, reconstruction of a Norman motte and bailey castle, with its contemporary village! There are live animals, animated figures and siege weapons, etc. Worksheets are provided if required, one set for the under-11s and another for 11 and over; all the answers are found by looking around the castle. In 1987 a study centre is to be added.

• Railways

We only have room here to list some of the major steam railways around the country which offer you the chance to ride in the trains, have a look at the engines, and in some cases act as volunteer helpers/restorers. Ring up before you go to find out about opening times. Most of them do not run trips in the winter. A marvellous idea for real steam railway enthusiasts would be to plan a week's holiday taking in as many of the railways as possible *en route*. As we mention, several of them are full day expeditions.

Bluebell Railway, Sheffield Park Station, Uckfield, Sussex (0825 72 2370). The Bluebell Line, one of the earliest preserved railways, with restored stations and five miles of track. Some very old trains dating from 1865. Join their Preservation Society and help as a guard or even driver (when you are 18).

Darlington Railway Museum, North Road, Station, Darlington (0325 460532). Museum includes Stephenson's 'Locomotion', the first steam train on a public railway. There is masses more including a model railway. Take a train ride as well.

Dart Valley Railway, Buckfastleigh, Devon (0346 42761). Museum with vintage locos which children can climb into, and also watch restoration work in progress. Seven miles of track through the beautiful Dart Valley.

Didcot Railway Centre, Didcot, Oxfordshire (0235 817200). There is a restored railway station, and a locomotive depot with 20 steam trains – they always have room for volunteers to restore these. They don't have rides on the trains every day, so check first.

Mid-Hants Railway, Alresford Station, Alresford, Hampshire (096 273 3810). The Watercress Line, so-called because it used to carry watercress to market. Allow a full day for this one, and there is lots to do. Over ten miles of track by steam train from Alresford to Alton (which connects with British Rail). You can stop *en route* to see trains being restored, or have a picnic at Ropley. They are keen for volunteers to help with restoring and running the trains.

National Railway Museum, Leeman Road, York (0904 21261). This is *the* railway museum. With two acres of exhibits, it is a must for all enthusiasts.

Nene Valley Railway, Wansford Station, Stibbington (0780 7822584). Five miles of track through very attractive countryside.

North Yorkshire Moors Railway, Pickering Station (0751 72508). Allow a full day for this, as there is so much to do. The train takes you into the National Park, and stops at places where you can get out to go for forest walks, to see engines being restored, and so on. Then you can take another train to the next stop. They need volunteers to help to run the railway, but you would have to be 16 plus.

Railway Preservation Society of Ireland, Excursion Station, White-head, Co. Antrim, Northern Ireland (09603 78567). Another full day trip (in late July and August) starting at eight in the morning, which takes you on a round trip to the seaside. There are also many other trips you can take, all by steam, eg to Dublin from Belfast and back. Lovely old restored coaches and engines.

Severn Valley Railway, The Railway Station, Bridgnorth (07462 4361). A museum of steam and diesel trains (which is open all year round) and steam train rides (summer only) along 12 miles of the Severn Valley.

Snowdon Mountain Railway, Llanberis, near Caernarfon, Wales (0286 870223). A rack and pinion railway (the only one in Britain) opened in 1896, which climbs nearly 1,000 metres in 5 miles. Wonderful scenery and views during the two and a half hour journey.

Strathspey Railway, The Station, Boat of Garten, Inverness-shire (047 983692). Wonderful old engines and coaches in the museum, and a beautiful ride, with lovely scenery and restored stations. Part of the former Highland Railway.

• Zoos, Safari and Wildlife Parks
We are not including a great list of zoos and parks as there are just so many in the United Kingdom, but if you are stuck here are some useful names and addresses:

Lampton Pleasure Park, Lampton, County Durham (0385 3311).

Longleat House and Safari Park, Warminster, Wiltshire. (Safari Park: 0985 3328; House: 0985 3551).

The National Federation of Zoological Gardens of Great Britain and Ireland, Regent's Park, London NW1 4RX (01-586 0230). Write and ask for their comprehensive list of members – some zoos and safari parks are not members and therefore omitted.

Woburn Abbey and Wild Animal Kingdom, Woburn, Bedfordshire (0525 25666).

Do remember that often safari parks are closed for the winter, so ring and check the date if you plan an autumn or spring visit.

Country and wildlife parks These are marvellous places to see wildlife and go for good rambles. The Nature Conservancy Council, Northminster House, Peterborough PE1 1UA (0733 40345), is a government body which advises on nature conservation, and runs a series of National Nature Reserves in England, Scotland and Wales. Many of these reserves have visitor centres and nature trails to enable people to observe the wildlife. Write to the Council for a list of these nature reserves.

London Outings

We thought we should include a special section with some ideas for you if you wanted to bring the children to the capital. First of all a few general hints that may sound rather obvious, but they are the sort of thing one wishes one had thought about before! Then follows a list of different types of activities.

1. Well ahead of the planned expedition, check opening times, etc. Remember that some places may be closed at certain times of the year, so always double-check. Contact the London Visitors and Convention Bureau, the Official Tourist Board for London, 26 Grosvenor Gardens, London SW1W 0DU (01-730 3488). They produce very good information booklets, such as *Group Visits to London*.

2. Don't bring too many children, as in a busy city atmosphere you will be exhausted trying to keep an eye on everyone, but have plenty of helpers in any case.

3. Don't try and pack in too much in one day – it is amazing how tiring it is tramping around, and especially if you have had a long journey to London.

4. Make sure you know exactly where you are going, and what form of transport gets you nearest to your chosen venue. London Transport, 55 Broadway, London SW1 (01-222 1234), have excellent information concerning maps, guides, costs, etc.

5. Plan to eat early so as to avoid great queues, or pre-book a meal (see London Tourist Board and Convention Board booklet **Where to eat.**).

6. Have wet-weather alternative plans if you have chosen a fine-weather outing. If you are part of a holiday club state these on your programme for the insurance cover (see page 138).

7. Probably the most important of all, always organise a contingency plan with children in case anyone gets lost.

• Major Events
You could plan a trip to include attending a major London spectacle, the Trooping of the Colour, the Lord Mayor's Show or the Royal Tournament.

The Lord Mayor's Show   This event is to introduce formally the new Lord Mayor of London to the Lord Chief Justice. The procession, which includes all sorts of floats, takes place on the second Saturday in November, starting off from the Guildhall. You can stand anywhere *en route*, but if you wanted to get tickets for seating points which are for example at St Paul's, Temple Place and the Victoria Embankment, you should apply to the Pageant Master (01-882 1083). There is a charge.

The Royal Tournament   At Earl's Court. Tickets from Royal Tournament Office, Horse Guards Parade, Whitehall, SW1 (01-930 7148), but from March 1987, Royal Tournament Box Office, Earl's Court, SW5 (01-371 8141). This is an annual event in aid of charities for the services. It takes place in July and is a spectacular show especially for children, with drill displays, dramatic reconstructions and the very exciting musical drive, etc – it just goes on and on! Beware of taking very young brothers and sisters though, as it is extremely loud and they may be frightened. Not only is the show itself exceptional, but there are masses of stands behind the ring, and you can visit the stables too. It is a very large place so do have a meeting point in case any of your party gets separated.

Trooping of the Colour   The Trooping of the Colour takes place at Horse Guards Parade, normally on the second Saturday in June to honour the Queen's official birthday. To get tickets for seats for this occasion, you should apply in writing to the Brigadier Major, Head Quarter's Household Division, Horse Guards Parade, Whitehall, SW1A 2AX. Send your application in between the 1st January and the 28th February. If you want to take a group of children, explain that this is the point of your application. The tickets are issued through a ballot allocation which is made in the middle of March. If you are not lucky enough to get seats for the actual day, you might be given some for the two rehearsals which take place prior to the event. For the first rehearsal the seats are usually free, for the second there is a small charge, and on the actual day the tickets are more expensive. If you are lucky enough to get tickets, you will find all the information you require about, for example, the time to arrive and where to go, on the back of your ticket.

● Museums

Bethnal Green Museum of Childhood, Cambridge Heath Road, E2 (01-980 2415) – Bethnal Green tube station. This is a really lovely museum of all sorts of toys, and very well set out.

British Museum, Great Russell Street, W1 (01-636 1555) – Tottenham Court Road, Goodge Street, Russell Square or Holborn tube stations. A huge, fascinating general museum, which houses amazing collections of treasures from all over the world including the controversial Elgin Marbles. There are just too many things to list here but an awe-inspiring place. Very good holiday museum trails and film shows, etc.

Geffrye Museum, Kingsland Road, E2 (01-739 8368) – Liverpool Street, Old Street tube stations. This is a small museum of furniture – we have included it as it is so well set out for the children to see the different periods of furniture. The young are very well catered for with a special area for project work.

Imperial War Museum, Lambeth Road, SE1 (01-582 2525) – Lambeth North or Elephant and Castle tube stations. Excellent museum for the general history of recent war connected with this country. It is broader in its approach than a service museum would be, offering more of the social history. There are plenty of weapons, etc, but mixed with, for example, war paintings. There are two general historical displays of the First and Second World Wars. There are plenty of holiday quizzes and film shows.

The London Museum, London Wall, EC2 (01-600 3699) – St Paul's, Barbican, Moorgate tube stations. This is an excellent museum explaining the history of London from prehistoric times onwards. It has very vivid displays – for example, watching the Fire of London!

National Army Museum, Royal Hospital Road, SW3 (01-730 0717) – Sloane Square tube station. The history of the Army from the Tudors to 1914 is illustrated here. The summer holiday club is very popular with outings, army lectures, and films, etc.

National Postal Museum, London Chief Office, King Edward Street, EC1 (01-432 3851) – St Paul's tube station. We have included this for those keen on stamp collecting – it is an amazing collection.

Natural History Museum, Cromwell Road, SW7 (01-589 6323) – South Kensington tube station. This is a fascinating museum especially for dinosaur enthusiasts! Everything here to do with animals, birds, butterflies, insects and fish. Very geared up for children's holidays from activity sheets to field trips for older children.

Pollocks Toy Museum, 1 Scala Street, W1 (01-636 3452) – Goodge Street tube station. This is a very small museum but full of goodies!

Science Museum, Exhibition Road, SW7 (01-589 6371) – South Kensington tube station. A large museum with many working models with something for all age groups. There is a fascinating new permanent exhibition called 'Launch Pad', which allows children to experiment with the latest technology. You must book parties (one adult to eight children) well before visiting. Particular age groups are given specific dates.

Victoria and Albert Museum, Cromwell Road, SW7 (01-589 6371) – South Kensington tube station. This is full of the most beautiful collections of, for example, porcelain, armour and furniture, etc. The costume display is really fascinating and beautifully presented.

• Places of Special Interest

Covent Garden *The* place to end up – it is expensive to shop here but lovely and has a pedestrian area, which is a great relief! Teenagers will just adore the atmosphere.

London Planetarium, Marylebone Road, NW1 (01-486 1121) – Baker Street tube station. The 35-minute performance is excellent for both budding astronomers and anyone interested in the stars.

London Zoo, Regent's Park, NW1 (01-722 3333) – Camden Town tube station, or there is a water bus from Little Venice (Warwick Avenue tube) with a special fare which includes admission to the Zoo. There is so much to see here you could stay all day.

Madame Tussauds Wax Works, Marylebone Road, NW1 (01-935 6861) – Baker Street tube station. This is next door to the London Planetarium so it is sensible to 'do' both. Do telephone to find out the best times to avoid the crowds and queues.

The Tower of London, Tower Hill, EC3 (01-709 0765) – Tower Hill tube station. This is the most amazing place, but again beware of the queues. You can see the Crown Jewels, wonderful armour, etc – the list is endless.

● The River

River trips are fantastic fun on a fine day! Contact LT and CB information service (01-730 3488). For example, an ideal trip for 'a granny's outing' is to take the grandchildren from Westminster or Charing Cross piers, down the Thames to visit the Tower or Greenwich to see the sailing clipper *Cutty Sark* and *Gypsy Moth*, or to go round the National Maritime Museum (01-858 4422). There are lots of destinations to choose from but do research times, costs and boarding points well ahead of your visit. Remember you can see the Thames Flood Barrier now.

HMS Belfast, Symons Wharf, Vine Lane, Tooley Street, SE1 (01-407 6436) – London Bridge or Tower Hill tube stations or go by boat from Tower Pier. This is a marvellous floating naval museum and an excellent treat for boys. NB, if wet, don't bring elderly grandparents, as there are steep metal steps everywhere which do become slippery in the rain. If windy weather, mothers should wear trousers!

HMS Discovery, Victoria Embankment, WC2 (01-836 5138) – Temple tube station. Captain Scott's ship full of memorabilia of the 1901/4 expedition.

● Sight-seeing Trips

The sight-seeing buses are marvellous if you want to go and see all the various sights in London, but they are useless if your child is not old enough to really appreciate the tour. (It is best to take younger children to a specific place in which you know they will be interested.) Contact London Transport regarding these trips at 55, Broadway, London SW1 (01-222 1234).

7.

HOLIDAYS AWAY

Adventure Holidays

Adventure or activity holidays, which have been popular for a long time in America, are now catching on in Britain. They are a wonderful way for young people to have a taste of adventure, try out new activities and begin to learn a little independence. But they cost quite a lot and there is no point in booking your children in if they are going to be miserable or if your money is not going to be well spent. We have therefore gone into the subject rather thoroughly to help prevent you making any mistakes and to make sure that your children have a good time. Although we have addressed this chapter to parents, because they will be paying, do encourage your children to read it with you, and discuss the whole subject with them first so that they know what is involved.

The first object of the exercise is that the children should enjoy themselves! If your child has not been away from home before, and if you think that he/she might be homesick staying for a week, then the best thing would be to send him/her to a day camp, providing that there is one not too far from you. Day camps run just the same activities, but the children come home in the evening. The camps are very efficient at arranging transport and will organise pick-up points where the children can be taken and collected every day. If they enjoy this then you may well find that they are ready for a full residential week the following year. But don't worry if your children don't take to it – maybe they just love their home best!

Any good residential holiday centre will give you plenty of advance information on the children's activities, what they will be eating and what clothes to pack for them. All good camps should have a high staff/children ratio so that they can keep an eye on all the children, and they will ring you if there is a real problem. They do suggest, however, that you don't ring them for the first couple of days to give the children, especially the ones away from home for the first time, plenty of time to settle.

They will probably ask you to pack simple and sturdy clothes such as jeans, trainers, boots, T shirts, anoraks, etc. Where extras are required, for instance, sleeping bag, eating utensils and so on, these will be specified. It goes without saying that children should not take valuable possessions with them, and money is usually handed in to the camp director on arrival. As far as clothes are concerned, most mothers find that the clean clothes in the suitcase tend to stay there, while the clothes the children are wearing, plus the children themselves, come home absolutely filthy!

Having decided that your children would enjoy a week's activity holiday, the first question is how to go about finding a good one. It is a sad fact that any unqualified person can set up their own holiday centre at present without any legal restrictions. And there are plenty of horror stories about the bad ones – lack of activities, no proper supervision, terrible food and so on – so do make sure that your children only go to a really reputable centre. You may know of such a one through personal recommendation, and this is often the best way, because you will learn about the bad points, as well as the good ones! If not, write to the British Activity Holiday Association. This group has been set up by the activity holiday industry, and already has 80 members. Their address is PO Box 99, Tunbridge Wells, Kent TN1 2EL (0982 49868). They are planning to publish a handbook of reputable holiday firms and centres, and will certainly be able to advise you about the ones they can recommend. They stress the two words 'competent and caring' and emphasise that parents must be prepared to ask a lot of questions before committing their children to the care of a holiday centre. Visit the place if you can, and ask about staff, equipment, safety, insurance, extras, food and so on. Also, don't be afraid to complain if you feel your children have had a raw deal – a good centre should be prepared to accept criticism in a positive way in order to improve their standards for the next time.

Try and book up in good time. Advertisements for activity holidays start appearing immediately after Christmas, which might be the last time you feel like thinking about them, but the good ones do get booked up early, and some will offer special rates (eg two for the price of one) if you book before the end of January.

Some adventure holidays like to offer children a taste of everything, and others tend to specialise in one particular activity, for instance, tennis, riding, drama, and so on. We list the general holidays first, followed by the special activity ones, although in many cases these will overlap to some extent. Some camps run both day and residential holidays and we specify where this is the case. Obviously we do not have room to go into much detail here, but if you write to the addresses we provide you will receive lots of information, usually in the shape of a glossy and very tempting-looking brochure. The prices we give are only approximate, as they are likely to go up at the start of each season, and they do not include VAT, which at the moment is 15 per cent.

The English Tourist Board produces a book called *Activity and Hobby Holidays* for £1.99, available from large book shops. This has a very useful selection of children's holidays.

The YHA (Youth Hostels Association) produces a brochure called *Adventure Holidays*, and you can get a free copy by writing to them at Trevelyan House, St Stephen's Hill, St Albans, Herts AL1 2DY. It covers holidays for young people from the age of 11 upwards at YHA hostels, and includes details of canoeing, caving, water sports, pony trekking, explorations and many others.

Adventure Holidays is also the name of a book published by Vacation Work, 9 Park End Street, Oxford, and obtainable from book shops or direct from the publishers; price £3.95 (and 75 pence postage). It covers holidays in this country and abroad, listing every kind of activity you can imagine, including cycling, hiking, riding, sailing, scuba-diving, wildlife, windsurfing and so on.

Multi-Activity Holidays

Ardmore Adventure Ltd, 23 Ramillies Place, London W1 (01-439 4461). Day and residential multi-activity camps, especially sport, based at centres in Buckinghamshire, Dorset and Sussex. Age range from 3 (day camps only) to 16-year-olds. Day camps are about £70 per week, residential camps about £150.

Camp Beaumont, Corpus Christi House, 9 West Street, Godmanchester, Cambs PE18 8HG (0480 56123). Camp Beaumont prides itself on being the first in this country to start running day camps. They also do residential holidays (both are multi-activity) in centres around London, including Essex, Kent, Surrey and Sussex, as well as Cheshire, Warwickshire and near Edinburgh. Endless list of activities (my son voted go-karting and mini-motor bikes top favourites), catering for 3 (day only) to 16-year-olds. They are especially strong in water sports – canoeing, sailing, scuba-diving, windsurfing, etc as well as land-based sports and activities such as abseiling, orienteering, drama, pottery, etc. Costs are about £70 for a week's day camp, £150 for residential.

Countryside Holidays Association, Birch Heys, Cromwell Range, Manchester M14 6HU (061 225 1000). An organisation which provides specialist holidays for adults, but also runs young peoples' holidays in several of its centres, such as the Lake District, Cornwall and Yorkshire. Parents and children can share a holiday, but parents are free to do their own thing, while the children have an adventurous week canoeing, sailing, pony trekking and so on. This might be a good compromise for parents who are not quite happy at sending their children away unaccompanied, and yet want them to have a taste of adventure on their own. Costs are about £150 per person for a week.

Dolphin Activities Ltd, 34–36 South Street, Lancing, West Sussex BN15 8AG (0903 750310). Twenty-five holiday centres based in prep and public schools around the country, also one in France (residential only obviously!). The other centres provide both day and residential holidays, some multi-activity, some specialist (see below for details of these) for 8 to 16-year-olds. Costs are about £70 to £90 for a five-day course, and about £150 for a residential week.

H.F. Holidays Ltd, 142/144 Great North Way, London NW4 1EG (01-203 1113). This is an organisation which provides holidays for school groups and, because it is non-profit making, is able to charge very reasonable prices. They aim to take all the hassle out of school trips by organising all the travel for you, providing all specialist equipment at no extra cost, and supervising each course with expert instructors. They run a Lake District multi-activity course with canoeing, sailing, windsurfing, climbing, pony trekking, an assault course and BMX course, mountain walking, archery and so on. A week, according to the season, costs between £90 and £120. Group leaders of more than 10 children go free. They also run centres for field studies in beautiful locations all over Scotland, Wales and England, and in addition will organise a group holiday in London for you. These centres offer a mix of study and fun, with opportunities for lots of holiday activities. Why not persuade the school to organise a week away? Costs vary but at the moment are under £100 per week.

John Ridgway Adventure School, Ardmore, Rhiconich by Lairg, Sutherland, Scotland IV27 4RB (097182 229). John Ridgway runs an international summer school for boys and girls aged 12 to 15 and 15 to 18 years old. The purpose of the school is to teach self-reliance, positive thinking, and leaving people and things better than you find them. With these aims in view, the course includes survival on an uninhabited island, a two-day expedition to climb the Ridge of Foinaven, an orienteering course plus sailing, abseiling (down a cliff into a boat), canoeing and rock climbing. All activities are very carefully supervised. Accommodation is in simple but comfortable dormitories, and there are two hot meals a day plus packed lunch. The courses take place between June and September each year and cost £250 plus VAT for two weeks. Incidentally, the centre also provides adult adventure courses, so if parents like sailing, hill walking and so on why not get everyone into it as well?

Lake District Outdoor Pursuits Centre, Falbarrow Hall, Windermere, Cumbria LA23 3DX (09662 5454). A week of quite strenuous outdoor activities, such as abseiling, canoeing, orienteering and so on. Children from 7 to 17 are catered for and the costs are about £130 for a week.

National Association of Youth Clubs, Keswick House, 70 St Nicholas Circle, Leicester LE1 5NY (0533 29514). Members of a youth club, or those helping to run one will be able to take advantage of nearly 30 holiday centres run by the Association, in beautiful countryside locations throughout the UK, including the Outer Hebrides, Northern Ireland, Wales, Yorkshire, Hampshire and so on. In addition, the Association runs a houseboat (in Berkshire), a canal narrow boat (in Warwickshire) and log cabins and canvas camps in Wales. Write to the above address for a copy of their brochure *Going Places*, which gives details of the individual centres that can be booked by youth groups or, in some cases, individual families with children.

Outward Bound Trust, Chestnut Field, Regent Place, Rugby CV21 2PJ (0788 60423/5). Outward Bound exists to encourage young people to develop their skills and confidence through challenging courses which include navigation, search and rescue, rock climbing, canoeing and so on. They run different courses for different age groups; an adventure course for 10 to 13-year-olds, school courses, junior outward bound (14 to 15 years), wilderness and discovery courses (14 to 16 years) and even a city challenge course which concentrates on community service. The courses take place in one of the five fully equipped residential centres in Wales, Cumbria and Scotland. In some cases financial help to go on a course may be available. Write to Outward Bound for details.

PGL Young Adventure Limited, 2–5 Market Place, Ross-on-Wye, Herefordshire HR9 5LD (0989 65556). Twenty centres in the British Isles based in schools, university buildings, farmhouses, and so on. Most centres cater for day and residential holidays. It has a long list of skiing sports and activities including sailing, canoeing, windsurfing, pony trekking, as well as more specialised ones such as caving, pot-holing, cycling and so on. Age range between 8 and 16, costs about £70 per week for a day camp, and £170 for a residential. PGL also run adventure holidays in Europe (in the Massif Central and on the Mediterranean) and America, and skiing holidays in the winter.

Specialist Holidays

You may find that your children develop a particular interest as they grow older, whether it be for computers, tennis, drama, music, riding, sailing, and so on. There are now holidays to cover almost every kind of specialist interest and they can be a most valuable experience. Obviously we cannot list them all, but we give you addresses to contact which will provide you with further information on your chosen subject. In addition we provide details of school group holidays, either here or abroad, which do provide cheap and well organised trips. You hear such horror stories of some of these trips, for instance, one holiday when the children had bread and butter for breakfast while the other guests, in full view, tucked into bacon and eggs! The ones we recommend promise to care for the children and to feed them well!

There are a number of organisations which offer a week's camp to their members, as one of their special attractions. If anyone is specially interested in a particular activity, for instance to do with boats or flying, it is well worth joining one of these organisations for their year-round activities as well as the annual summer camp or course. We provide full details, addresses, membership qualifications, and so on in Chapter 3, but here are some of the names (in alphabetical order) which might interest you: Air Training Corps, Army Cadet Force, Boys' Brigade, Endeavour Training, Girls' Brigade, Girl Guides, Girls' Venture Corps, Nautical Training Corps, Ocean Youth Club, St John Ambulance Cadets, Sea Cadet Corps, Sea Ranger Association.

• Birdwatching

The Young Ornithologists' Club, The Lodge, Sandy, Bedfordshire SG19 2DL (0767 80551).

This club runs holiday courses based at youth hostels or field centres – write to the above address for details, and see page 51 in this book for more information on the Club.

• Camping

The Camping and Caravanning Club, 11 Lower Grosvenor Place, London SW1W 0EY (01-828 1012/7)

Camping has always had a special appeal for young people, with its independence and outdoor life. Even if your parents are not members of the Club, you can be a youth member if you are between the ages of 12 and 17. At first you camp at particular sites under the guidance of a youth leader – write to the Club for details – and eventually you take the Youth Camping Test, which is largely a test of common sense and basic safety rules. This entitles you to all the benefits of full membership and to use the Club camping sites with full adult status.

Forest School Camps, 23 Station Avenue, Walton on Thames, Surrey KT12 1NF. Camping for children from 6½ to 17. An informal back-to-nature approach is provided by camps located in various parts of the country as well as one or two abroad. Costs are about £98 for two weeks.

• Computer Holidays

Many multi-activity holiday organisations now offer computers as a special activity.

Camp Beaumont (address on page 195) offers computer sessions as a special option.

Dolphin Activities Ltd (page 196) offer a non-residential five-day computer course, plus drama, archery, shooting, swimming, etc.

PGL (page 198) have a week's holiday which can include 6 half-day computer sessions.

Young Leisure, PO Box 99, Tunbridge Wells, Kent TN1 2EL (0892 31504), runs a week's computing course at Felsted School in Essex. The mornings are spent on the computers, and the afternoons offer swimming, shooting, canoeing, dancing, cricket and so on.

There is an organisation called Inter-Action (see page 80) which has a division called Community Computers UK. One of its many functions is to help set up holiday computer camps in non-residential centres throughout the country. They advise on hardware, tutors, funding and all the information needed to organise such a scheme. They work through youth groups or schools rather than with individual young people – so if you would like to help run or take part in a computer camp, get your own school or youth club on the move and contact Inter-Action. They also run Computerama, a mobile holiday scheme – details from the Inter-Action organisation.

• Cycling
The Cyclists Touring Club, 69 Meadrow, Godalming, Surrey GU7 3HS (048 68 7217)
   The Club arranges cycling tours for groups of about 16 around the more attractive parts of the country such as the New Forest or the West Country. Accommodation is in youth hostels or guest houses. The minimum age is 11, but you do need cycling experience.

The YHA offers cycling holidays (the address is on page 205) for young people aged 11 to 15 years in Norfolk (flat), Wales (hilly), and cross-country cycling using mountain bikes in the Peak District.

See the book *Adventure Holidays* published by Vacation Work (details on page 194) for more ideas on cycling holidays in this country.

• Farm Holidays
Farm Holiday Bureau, National Agricultural Centre, Stoneleigh, near Kenilworth, Warwickshire (0203 555100)

The Bureau provides an information service on reasonably priced holidays where the whole family can stay on a farm, share in the farm life, and help with some of the work, such as feeding the animals. Write to them for their book *Farm Holidays* (price £1.99, also available from bookshops). It gives details of farms where you can stay for a holiday, from one night to a fortnight.

• Moto-cross

Many activity holidays offer some form of moto-cross on mini-motor bikes, but if you are very keen why not spend a day at the Team Green Training School, at the *Isle of Ely* moto-cross track at Chippenham? The course is run and subsidised by Kawasaki and costs a fairly nominal £10 to £15, but you will need to bring your own motor bike. Ring 0753 38255 for full details.

• Music

If you are really interested in music you may well want to go further than merely playing at school. The ideas we have here for you are mostly for holidays, when you might have time to tackle the subject more thoroughly. There are several music courses where you can join in making music, playing or singing.

Junior Orchestral Summer Course, 39 Cassiobury Park Avenue, Watford, Herts (0923 25547). The one-week course is for 12 to

17-year-olds and is held in Bradfield College, Reading, Berks. You could join one of three orchestras, playing your favourite instrument. Rehearsals in the mornings, and sport (optional) in the afternoons.

National Association of Youth Orchestras, Ainslie House, 11 St Colne Street, Edinburgh EH3 6AG (031-225 4606). A four-day residential Easter course for 14-year-olds and up, and an Anglo-German Youth Music Week for 15 to 25-year-olds. The NAYO publishes a register of youth orchestras, of which there are over 300 around the country. If your school is not a member of the Association write to them to see if there is one in your area.

National Children's Music Camps, 56 Station Road, Long Marston, Tring, Herts HP23 4QS (0296 668485). Four one-week summer camps are held in Buckinghamshire (in Johnny Dankworth's house), two for 8 to 12-year-olds and two for 13 to 17-year-olds. You will have a chance to play all kinds of instruments – string, woodwind, brass and percussion as well as jazz, pop and electronic music. In addition there is drama, arts and crafts and outdoor sports.

National Children's Orchestra, c/o Fitznells School of Music, Ewell, Epsom, Surrey KT17 1TF (01-393 1577). The Orchestra organises an eight-day residential Easter course called Mainstream, held in a different centre each year (eg, York, Manchester, Sussex, etc). There are also five-day summer courses in Edinburgh, where the accent is on music-making but also on sports, theatre-going, treasure hunts and so on. Children have to audition for places and the selection is competitive.

• Nature Studies

Field Studies Council, Preston Montford, Montford Bridge, Shrewsbury SY4 1HW (0743 850 674)

The Field Studies Council runs nine residential field centres, which are dotted around the countryside, in places as far apart as Suffolk, Wales, Devon and Yorkshire. They run weekly or weekend courses, on a wide variety of subjects, such as natural history, birdwatching, conservation, archaeology and so on. Family groups are very welcome on many of these: for instance 'Exploring the Pembrokeshire Coast', 'Exploring Exmoor', 'Basic Horse and Pony Management', 'Mostly Mammals', 'Introducing Minibeasts', and lots more. Some of the courses, for example, 'The Young Naturalist in Shropshire' or 'Wildlife Adventure in Pembrokeshire', are particularly designed for children (aged from about 9 upwards) – as long as they are happy to stay away on their own. The cost of the week varies from course to course, but is usually under £100 for children. Accommodation is fairly simple but comfortable. Membership (you should be a member before going on a course) is £3 or £6 for family or group, ie school membership. Why not get your school to organise a group to go on a course during the holidays?

● Riding

If you would like to go on a riding holiday there are lots of opportunities. Contact the British Horse Society, British Equestrian Centre, Stoneleigh, Kenilworth, Warwickshire. Their leaflets *Where to Ride* and *Pony Trekking* cost £1.95 and 50 pence respectively. Ponies of Britain, Brookside Farm, Ascot, Berks SL5 1LU also do a leaflet, for 85 pence, with a full descriptive list of approved pony trekking and riding holidays.

The riding centres vary enormously – some provide family holidays, others specialise in unaccompanied children, but there is such a large number of riding or trekking centres spread through the UK, that you are sure to find one to suit your own requirements.

● Sailing

A keen sailor (or starting sailor) would love the idea of a sailing holiday. The RYA (full address on page 34) has full lists of all the different courses, including dinghy sailing, cruising, tall ships, wind-surfing and so on. Decide which course appeals to you and write for a list. Certain courses are more suitable for different age groups, so let them know how old you are when you write.

Sail Training Association (STA), 2A The Hard, Portsmouth PO1 3PT (0705 832055). The aim of the STA is to provide young people (boys and girls) with an exciting and demanding two-week cruise in a sailing ship. You do not need previous sailing experience, but must be willing to learn, because the cruise is not just a holiday, but an opportunity for challenge and adventure. The association has two sailing ships, the *Sir Winston Churchill* and the *Malcolm Miller* which each take 39 volunteers, plus their permanent crew. Each cruise includes a visit to one or more overseas ports, where you will have time off to go ashore. While aboard you will spend time either on the bridge, learning about navigation, or on deck, helping with the sails and even going aloft. The minimum age for the trainees is 16. It may be possible to get a grant to cover all or part of the cost of the trip. Write to the STA for advice.

See also page 83 for the Ocean Youth Club, which arranges over 4,000 sailing holidays every year for young people from the age of 12 upwards. PGL (address on page 198) arranges sailing and cruising holidays for 12 to 18-year-olds during July and August. No previous experience is required, and all equipment is provided.

Sea Cadets (page 85) have sailing holidays among their activities, and Operation Raleigh (page 233) is a more ambitious adventure cum expedition on a sailing ship.

• Tennis

Keen young tennis players now have the opportunity to go on special tennis camps, with plenty of tennis coaching at different levels, plus lots of other activities. Write to the Lawn Tennis Association, Palliser Road, London W14 9EG (01-385 2366) for a list of tennis camps for different age groups. The organisation Tennis-breaks UK, PO Box 197, Windsor, Berks (0753 863301), runs courses for 8 to 15-year-olds which are both residential or by the day. The courses are held in Dorset and Berkshire and the level ranges from instruction for beginners to low tournament standard.

The cost is about £89 for a week's day course and £149 for a residential course (plus VAT).

• Theatre

The Young Theatre Association, Darwin Infill Building, Regent's College, Regent's Park, London NW1

The Young Theatre Association runs residential drama training courses during the Christmas and Easter holidays as well as summer schools. They take place in different parts of the country, and involve opportunities for plenty of acting experience as well as other holiday activities such as riding, swimming, etc. See page 71 in this book for more details.

• Youth Hostels

Youth Hostels Association, Trevelyan House, 8 St Stephen's Hill, St Albans, Herts AL1 2DY (0727 55215)

The YHA was formed to give people, especially the young, the opportunity of finding out more about the countryside by providing inexpensive places to stay. The minimum age limit is 5 (accompanied!) and the minimum unaccompanied age limit is 12. Membership for the under-16s costs £1, and accommodation is between £1 and £3. Most hostels provide breakfast and evening meals, again at very reasonable prices. The YHA is able to welcome disabled holidaymakers to a number of its hostels (write for details). There are 260 hostels in England and Wales, most of them in very beautiful parts of the countryside, but also in London and other cities. If you go abroad you will find hostels all over the world in any country you could think of (don't forget to take your membership card). The YHA also organises weekend breaks (Friendly Faces Weekends), field study groups (how about going with your class at school?) cycle hire and adventure holidays (including water sports, ski sports, pony trekking, climbing, etc). Write for their special brochure on each activity. They are also actively engaged in conservation, and some local groups do practical conservation work. Write for the YHA Guide (£1.25), which will give you full details of all the hostels, plus help on transport, clothes to wear, how to book and what to see and do.

The YMCA also runs National Centres for educational, training, activity, camp and adventure holiday purposes. At all the centres you can go as a member of a group or as an individual. Write to the different addresses below for full details:

1. Fairthorne Manor, Curdridge, Southampton, SO3 2GH (04892 5228).

2. Lakeside, Ulverston, Cumbria LA12 8BD (0448 31758).

3. Otterburn Hall, Otterburn, Northumberland NE19 1HE (0830 20663).

4. The Y Holiday Centre, 25 Grand Parade, Eastbourne, East Sussex BN21 3YP (0323 26214).

Skiing

We are including this section to give information for those children or students whose families do not ski but who would love to go by themselves. It is quite easy to find excellent trips for children and they will have a wonderful time.

Firstly, many schools take parties skiing. These are ideal because everyone knows one another and often a couple of parents go along too to help, so it's not just pupils and teachers. Do encourage your school to organise a party if they have not done so already. The secret seems to be to find a young skiing fanatic on the staff and work on them! One small hint though, our children went on a positively cheap trip with a school. However, at the very pleasant and clean hotel, they were segregated from other guests in the dining room, and were given very inadequate food whilst watching (and smelling!) others tucking into delicious fare! We would have much preferred to pay that little bit extra to avoid that. 'You gets what you pays for', but check that by paying a small amount more you would not get a much better deal. Obviously this sort of thing is up to the organisers to double-check when they do a recce prior to the trip.

Secondly, the Ski Club of Great Britain, 118 Eaton Square, London SW1 9AF (01-245 1033), runs excellent parties for unaccompanied member children. If they find a friend to come too, this is an excellent way of the young going skiing minus their family. The parties are run for children between 11 and 15 years, and for those between 16 and 18 years. The leaders are specially trained by the club. There is a leader for every 8 to 12 members. There are a few rules ('Guidelines') which will be sent with the booking confirmation. The children can take tests, enter races or competitions according to their standards. There is informal après-ski entertainment, for example, skating, swimming, games, etc for the younger group, and the older ones are allowed out in groups so long as the leader knows where, and also so long as they are back by midnight. Advice is given on amounts of pocket money that should be given.

Thanks to an experienced teacher who has taken several school parties, we have been able to include here a suggested clothes list for a week's trip. (See page 221 for checklist on what to take abroad: choose relevant parts for you. You must not forget a passport, of course, if going abroad but also you will need two passport photographs for your ski pass.) The list was vital to us when our children skied for the first time as we had never been ourselves, and we hope it will be of use to you!

Many stores now stock reasonably priced ski wear and at the moment C & A have a very good reputation. If you are skiing at Easter you can usually take advantage of the January sales. Sometimes you can buy secondhand ski outfits at local 'swap shops'. For children's outfits they are usually excellent value as they have probably been outgrown rather than worn out! If you do not wish to buy ski outfits you can hire them, for example: Moss Bros, 21–26 Bedford Street, Covent Garden, London WC2E 9EQ; Ski World

Hire, Ski World House, 39a–41 North End Road, West Kensington, London W14 8SZ (01-602 4820).

If you go with a party the hire of equipment would not be your concern. It is much more sensible to let those who are taking you sort out the correct size of skis and boots for you. Also they are often given a discount for a group booking.

Before you go off skiing do remember to get fit and possibly to practise on dry ski slopes. The advantage to beginners is that at least you can have the feel of the boots, skis and sticks before you start!

Suggested list for a skiing holiday for 1 week

- *Anorak and ski trousers or salupettes or ski suit*

These must be snow- and wind-proof, and have zip pockets for preference. Sailing gear – with a slippery surface – is unsuitable. Absolutely taboo are jeans and tracksuits – these have hardly any insulation.

For choice children seem to prefer salupettes – dungaree-shape insulated trousers – to trousers. Sweaters, etc do not pop out at the waist then.

- *Sweaters*

Two thick and two thinner sweaters can be used in whatever combination you require whether for warmth or, if the weather is good, to keep you warm but not be overheated. A sweat shirt would be ideal for one of the thinner sweaters – but only if cotton.

- *2 cotton polo-necked sweaters, optional*

NB: Do not buy nylon as this will just make children hot. These are to wear underneath other sweaters. You could wear ordinary cotton shirts but the polo-neck is a bit cosier.

- *3 pairs ski socks*

Special ski socks with the thick looped stitch pile are ideal, being both warm and a cushion for the feet in ski boots.

- *3 pairs normal thickness socks*

For boys: for indoor wear or as another layer for skiing if necessary. Girls: socks or tights or pop socks for indoor wear.

- *Tights, long-johns or extra cotton pyjama trousers*

In case of need for extra warmth.

- *Mittens or gloves*

Best to get proper ski ones because of wet snow, etc but often gloves are preferred in that you can hold the ski-sticks more easily.

- *Sun cream*

Vital: specialist protection against the combination strong sun and snow. Factors 4, 5, 6, etc depending on your skin – do not buy any old cream as these can fry you. Also buy specialist lipsalve. If you have ever seen a child's blistered skin after skiing you will know how important this is.

- *Headscarf*

Boys and girls – this should be small and white – or pale – to be worn as a 'bandit' if necessary to protect against the sun.

- *Goggles and/or sunglasses*

Vital: to avoid eye problems. Buy special goggles with inter-changeable lenses or the self-varying type – not necessarily expensive. Older children prefer glasses. (Sometimes these are cheaper at resorts than in England but if you are going without parents on a school trip it is probably wise to have something organised before you go.)

- *Ski-clips*

These are very inexpensive rubber straps for holding the skis together, and useful for carrying equipment. Buy two and mark them clearly.

- *Waist packs known as 'Bum-bags'*

Which are light, nylon zip pouches. These are very reasonable and while not vital they are very useful for children to carry creams, etc in. On return home they are great if going on a cycle ride so not just confined for use in skiing.

• *Moon Boots*

These are very light warm boots to wear for après ski. They are not necessary if you are skiing at Easter when the weather is warmer but they are very comfortable (and can be worn at home in bad weather). However, if you are skiing in very bad weather, if the streets are deep in snow they are useful, especially as they have very good gripping soles.

• *Ski hat*

Make sure it fits snugly and yet does not give a headache.

• *Other required items*

Passport
Two passport photographs for ski pass
Casual wear for evenings
Underwear and pyjamas
Trainers – plus plimsolls if there is a sports centre at the resort
Swimwear – plus hats for boys and girls if required, as they are in several continental countries. Check up
Dressing gown and slippers
Sponge bag and towel
Pack of cards, pocket chess, etc
Something to write the p.c. home with
Handkerchiefs or tissues
Travel sickness pills if necessary
Camera and films, flash, battery, etc
Scarf
Alarm clock

Exchanges and Foreign Visits

These are perhaps not entirely holidays, because they are usually undertaken with the idea of improving one's knowledge of a foreign language, and so there is an element of work involved. But they are a wonderful way of learning about another country, making new friends and, if all goes well, having a good time as well.

There are several different methods of going abroad to stay with another family, and we describe them in this section. Exchanges involve a child or young person staying as a guest with a family who has a child of similar age so that either the next holiday or during the same summer the visit can be returned and the foreign child stay with the other family. School exchanges are arranged in term time for a group, often a whole class, to stay in a town abroad with individual families, and attend the same school during the day. Again, the visit is returned the following term or the same summer term.

The advantages of the exchange system are many. First, if you stay with a family abroad, it is almost impossible *not* to pick up some of the language. The GCSE French exam now awards 25 per cent of the marks on the oral test, and so a working knowledge of the spoken language is even more important than it was. Obviously when exams start looming up, this becomes one of the most vital reasons for wanting to make an exchange. In addition, staying with a family is perhaps the only real way of getting to know another country, its customs, food and way of life. And if you make a new friend by sharing their life for a few weeks, such a friendship can become lifelong. A small test of independence – perhaps staying away from home alone for the first time – can be a big plus. Finally, it is not at all an expensive holiday because the only costs are travel, pocket money and entertaining your visitor on the return trip.

There can be drawbacks of course, and one of these is the possibility of loneliness and homesickness. If there is a chance of this, and some people find it harder to cope than others, it is better to take part in the kind of group or school exchange that we have described, or to postpone making an exchange until you are a bit older. Some children can start as young as 10 years old, others are happier waiting until 12 or 14. One expert has very sensibly suggested that parents should start building up a family contact while the children are still quite young, so that the two families can visit each other, get to know each other and establish a friendship well before an exchange takes place. This particular expert has expressed a wish that many more families would do this, instead of waiting until the GCSE is rearing its ugly head!

If for any reason you don't want to take part in an exchange you can still go to France and stay with a family as a paying guest *en famille*. This costs a bit more as you have to pay board and lodging, but you are treated as a member of the family and share their life in exactly the same way as if you were on an exchange.

Finally don't forget that a young person will need his/her individual passport when travelling alone.

Exchange and en famille agencies

Exchange visits

The business of arranging an individual exchange is a fairly arduous and lengthy process because of the care needed in matching up the children concerned – their ages, interests, time and length of stay, type of family, country or town dwellers and so on. For this reason, and also because of the very many foreign contacts that need to be built up, there is not a very large number of agencies who can arrange exchanges. You or your school may know of one in your area through personal recommendation – which is really the best form of advertisement – but we can vouch for the excellence of the ones we list below:

Continental Connections, Cranford, Church End, Albury, Ware, Hertfordshire (027974 541). This agency can arrange exchanges, paying guests, visits to residential colleges abroad, or a language course with accommodation with a local family in either France or Germany for young people between the ages of 11 and 18. The agency will send a detailed form with a number of questions about the family and the child concerned – interests, preferences, and the type of foreign visit you wish to arrange. A great deal of care is paid to matching children of similar age, interests, hobbies and backgrounds, and visits can be arranged to take place during the Christmas, Easter, or Summer holidays.

Amitié International des Jeunes, 10A Woodborough Road, London SW15 6QA (01-788 6857). Amitié International arranges exchange visits for French and English children from 10 to 18 years old, and as they have been operating for nearly 40 years are extremely experienced in coping with all the problems that can arise. They take great care in matching individuals of similar interests and background and to do this they ask you to fill in a detailed questionnaire. The exchanges take place in the Easter and summer holidays on fixed dates. All the travel – by rail and boat – is arranged for you, and both French and English children are accompanied to and from Paris. In addition AIJ operates an escorted coach service to the Midlands and the north of England, so that parents can be assured that travel will be both safe and easy. The agency also issues a detailed list of what to do and not do when staying with the foreign family, and this can be a great help for someone who has perhaps never stayed abroad before.

The Robertson Organisation, 44 Willoughby Road, London NW3 1RU (01-435 4907). The Robertson Organisation has been arranging family-based visits since 1948, so they have had plenty of experience! They organise exchanges or paying-guest visits to France, Germany or Spain, and will accept children from the age of 11 upwards. They ask you to fill in a detailed booking form so that you can be matched as carefully as possible with your opposite number.

Travel is by train and boat and is accompanied either to Paris or Cologne. They are a very friendly and helpful organisation and offer a personal service so that all the arrangements can be well prepared. If it can be arranged they like to meet you in advance to iron out any possible worries or problems.

Mrs Fay Forrest Evans, 50 Cypress Avenue, Whitton, London TW2 7JZ (01-894 1151). This agency is the English representative of Séjours Internationaux Linguistiques et Culturels, which is based in Angoulême. Séjours Internationaux is a non-profit making concern which arranges 'language baths' (ie intensive courses) in a wide variety of countries including France, Germany, Austria, Italy, Spain and even Japan, Brazil or Mexico. In addition they arrange three-week *entente cordiale* (paying-guest) visits in France, as well as exchanges and 'sport language' stays which include a week's sporting activity. They organise group travel, or you can make your own travel arrangements, and visits take place in the Christmas, Easter and summer holidays. They run a very full programme so write to the address above for more details.

En famille or paying-guest visits

Some people might prefer to go as a paying guest living *en famille* with a family abroad. This means that there is no obligation to receive a guest in return, which may not be easy for some families. (Paying guests, of course, unlike exchange visitors have to pay for their accommodation abroad. It is impossible to give an exact figure, but slightly under £100 a week full board would be about right.) All the agencies listed above can arrange for English people to go abroad *en famille*, but in addition there are others who deal especially with this category:

En Famille Agency (Overseas), Westbury House, Queens Lane, Arundel, Sussex BN18 9JN (0903 838266). En Famille specialises in arranging individual visits for young people (and indeed people of all ages) to stay with a host family to improve their knowledge of the language. Most of their host families are in France, but they can also arrange visits to several other European countries.

In addition they offer a range of language holidays in France for A level students as well as a seaside group holiday at La Rochelle in France, which combines a language course with swimming, tennis, windsurfing, etc.

The Agency will ask you to fill in a form, giving as much detail as possible, as well as the names of two references and a registration fee.

The French Embassy will send you a list of exchange or paying-guest agencies if you write to them at:

The French Embassy, Cultural Department, 22 Wilton Crescent, London SW1 (01-235 8080).

Most of these agencies are based in France, although of course they are quite used to dealing with inquiries from England (in English!). Here are just a few of the agencies in France which specialise both in exchanges and paying guests:

Club des 4 Vents, 1 rue Gozlin, 75006 Paris (01033 1 354 7025),

Comité d'Accueil, 21 rue St Fargeau, BP 313, 75989 Paris (01033 1 358 95 23).

Dragons International, 4 rue de Port Marly, 79750 Mareil, Marley (01033 3 916 5413).

Other foreign embassies are not quite so organised to help with finding agencies, perhaps because there is less demand for their services. The Spanish Institute, however, will send you a very useful list of Spanish and English addresses if you write to them at:

Instituto de España, 102 Eaton Square, London SW1W 9AN (01-235 1484/5).

We cannot give all of them here, but these are just a few:

Anglo/Spanish Student Exchanges, 14 Birchfield Close, Worcester WR3 8LQ (0905 612799 evenings). This agency deals with individuals and with school groups from 10 to 18 years of age.

Euro-Academy, 77a George Street, Croydon, Surrey CR0 1LD (01-681 2905). They organise home-stays as paying guests in France, Germany, Italy and Spain for children from the age of 12 upwards. In addition, they arrange language and arts courses in the four countries.

John Galleymore, 24 High Street, Portsmouth PO1 2LS (0705 824095). Runs courses in Austria, France and Spain for 16-year-olds and over. Can also arrange for exchange visits and paying guests.

School exchanges

Many schools have a twinning arrangement with a foreign school, usually in France, by which an entire class of, say, 14-year-olds will cross the Channel to stay with the parents of pupils at the French school, go to school with them in the day, and share their lives for a week. One or two teachers come with them to organise the travel and act as troubleshooters. Then later the same term or the next year the process is reversed and the French pupils come over to England. There are several advantages to this system, the main one being that the children, in a foreign country perhaps for the first time without their parents, do not feel isolated and lonely, because their friends are in the same town and they meet them every day at school. Other advantages are cheap group travel, the security of travelling in numbers, and the presence of an adult of the same nationality as themselves. The disadvantage of a group exchange, however, is the possibility that all the foreign children, whether English or French, will gang up together during the day and in the evenings and not really try to speak the language, so that they will come home without having learnt very much. It is really up to the children themselves to decide to make the most of their trip and learn all they can – after all they can be with their friends for the rest of the year! If you find that you get on well with your French family on a school exchange you may well like to arrange further individual visits with their children. In any case, a school exchange means that your school will have lists of foreign families and will be able to help in organising an individual exchange (indeed many schools do this on a regular basis). Some schools have a working arrangement with a particular agency who arranges the school trips but will also arrange individual exchanges through the school.

The Central Bureau
If your school does not have a twinning arrangement, but would like to organise one, write to:

The Central Bureau, Youth Exchange Centre, Seymour Mews House, Seymour Mews, London W1H 9PE (01-486 5101).

In Scotland: 3 Bruntsfield Crescent, Edinburgh EH10 4HD (031 447 8024).

In Northern Ireland: 16 Malone Road, Belfast BT9 5BN (0232 664418/9).

The Central Bureau will put UK schools in touch with similar schools abroad, and advise schools on how to go about setting up an exchange. It not only deals with schools in France, it can also arrange links with schools in Austria, Belgium, Denmark, Germany, Italy, Switzerland, Spain as well as Russia and the United States.

The Bureau publishes a book called *Help*, which is a guide to International Youth Exchanges for anyone who is organising an exchange project for young people. It includes chapters on Making Contact at home and Abroad, Travel Planning, Accommodation, Travel Insurance, Involving Young Disabled People, Cultural Differences and Planning Timetable. It is invaluable for any school, youth club or other youth group which would like to set about organising an exchange, but its up-to-date and revised information will also be a great help to organisations who have already had experience of exchanges. It costs £5 and is obtainable from the Youth Exchange Centre at the addresses above. In addition, the Bureau publishes a booklet called *Home from Home* (£3.50 direct from the Youth Exchange Centre) which covers the subjects of exchanges, paying guests, agencies and so on – another very useful problem-solver. It also provides a newsletter for schools once a term called Pupil Exchange News (PEN) which is free (but send an s.a.e.).

8.

TIME OFF

The Gap Year

You will soon be finishing with school and feel you deserve a break after working so hard! Perhaps you are planning to go on to further education or are hoping to land a job, but want a breather first, either a few months or a full year off? And why not? It will perhaps be the only time in your career when you have no commitments, no exams to worry about, no one depending on you, when you can give yourself time to look around and see what this life is really all about. The most important thing, though, is not to waste your time doing nothing, but to make plans, well in advance if possible, and decide exactly what you want to do in your time off, and what you expect to gain from it. There are several possibilities for you to consider, involving travel, work and holiday, or a mixture of all three.

Travel
If you are taking a full year off and would like to spend it abroad, you could try for one of the various projects for voluntary work abroad, for instance working with destitute people in India, or refugees in Hong Kong. We give details of organisations such as Gap and Project Trust, which, if they accept you, can provide you with an experience that you will never forget and that will teach you a great deal about the way other people live. As one volunteer wrote when he got back home, 'I truly feel I have been given a new lease of life through working in Calcutta.' When the work is done then you can travel to places you might otherwise never get the chance to visit again.

Even if you cannot set aside a full year but feel you want to spend

some time on voluntary work, there are many schemes lasting either for a few months, or a few weeks, which you could consider. Have a look at Concordia, International Voluntary Service, Kibbutz Representatives and the others we describe. Some of these are in the UK and some abroad. Again, if abroad you can take the opportunity to travel and take full advantage of all the student concessions on offer – cheap fares, accommodation and so on. On page 237 we provide details of cheap rail and air fares respectively.

If you have decided that taking a job is not for you and you intend simply to travel, then of course the possibilities are endless, and so too the amount of help and information you can get. Have a look at our book list on page 244 and you will find a lot to interest you. *Adventure Holidays*, *Volunteer Work Abroad*, *Traveller's Survival Kits*, all give you advice on where to go, how to go and how to get there safely (and cheaply!).

Work

You may be feeling either that it is about time you earned some money of your own in your year off, or that you would like to get your teeth into a job where you will gain invaluable experience, even if not a great deal of cash. Many employers look favourably on applicants who can show that they have already worked at some kind of a job, even if it is an unskilled one such as grape picking, waiting at table or putting up tents. It shows that you are prepared to make an effort on your own, that you have initiative and have learnt some sort of independence.

If you are going on to further education, parents and teachers (and you) might think it a good idea to get some kind of work which will help you directly in the subjects you will be studying. Languages of course are obvious – it is essential to stay in a country if you are ever to speak its language fluently. You could also get in some direct job experience (and earn some money), if you are going on to study electronics or one of the science subjects, by applying for a job with one of our major industries (a few of them are listed on page 243) and getting a chance to help with a bit of research.

Funding

Now for the practical considerations, the first of which is money! If you are not looking for a job that will be able to keep you in the style to which you hope to become accustomed, you are going to need some money because most of these schemes do cost something. We have been assured by an expert that 'parents are potty' if they give their children a penny towards the costs of a trip – this news may cheer parents up, but it puts the onus right back on you. You could do some job in this country for a few weeks, however lowly, in order to save money; grants are sometimes possible, and local firms or major industries can sometimes be persuaded to cough up a contribution to your costs. Have a look at page 131 in the chapter on raising money, where we go into more detail.

It is essential that you get yourself organised with the practical details. Don't leave the arranging to someone else – after all they can't have your injections for you! If you are going abroad you will obviously need a passport, visas (for some countries), and sometimes injections for cholera, typhoid, yellow fever or tetanus. Depending on where you are going, you will need to take the right clothes, warm or cool as the weather requires. Find out how much money you should take with you. Even if you are going to a paying job, you will need some, and find out the best way to carry it. Last but not least, see about insurance – it wouldn't be much fun to be left stranded up the Alps with a broken leg and no money to fix it or get yourself home. Be prepared and it may never happen. Have a look at our detailed checklist to see what else you will need to remember.

Finally, congratulations if you have managed to plough through all this information, and made sense of it. Have a good trip!

Checklist for Travelling Abroad

Passport
Make sure it is still valid and not about to expire.

Visa
If required – see separate list on page 224 for full details of countries requiring visas.

Money
Take a small amount of money (say £40) for immediate expenses in the currency of the country where you are going. You may need some as soon as you arrive, and if banks are shut, you may not be able to get a good rate of exchange for sterling.

Travellers' cheques are the safest way of carrying larger amounts of money – but keep them somewhere secure. Eurocheques are very useful if you are travelling in Europe, and if you have a bank account in the UK. Ask your bank for details.

Never be tempted to change money in the black market – in most countries this is illegal and could land you in trouble.

Return ticket
Always have the means of getting home before you set off – ideally a return ticket or, failing this, the money to buy one.

First aid kit
You would be wise to take one of these if you are planning to visit places such as Africa, the East or South and Central America. Dispensing chemists, such as Boots, will provide you with a complete kit which would contain some or all of the following:

First Aid in Few Words (a small leaflet)	Paracetamol
	Throat lozenges
Sticking plaster	Laxative tablets
Absorbent lint	Travel sickness tablets
Dry dressing	Anti-diarrhoea tablets
Safety pins	Insect repellent
Scissors	Antihistamine tablets
Antiseptic lotion	

Boots Trip Kit and Boots Holiday Kit each contain some of the above and cost £6.25 and £5.95 respectively. If you want a kit containing everything on the list write to Jacksons Chemists for their Travelaid Kit which costs £7.95. Their address is: 36 Newmarket Street, Skipton, North Yorkshire.

Injections
Check with the embassy of the country where you are going, with your travel agent, with your own doctor, or the *ABC Guide to International Travel* (see page 247) as to what you will need. Some countries require proof that you have received cholera, yellow fever and typhoid injections. Allow plenty of time to have the injections before you travel as some (for instance tetanus) require two or more separate injections and some (eg cholera and typhoid) can also make some people feel rather ill for a day or two. An anti-malarial course of tablets is also recommended before visiting some countries.

Insurance
It is worth being properly insured for loss of luggage, money and medical expenses – and even repatriation costs. If you are travelling with a group then insurance may be arranged for you and the extra cost should be indicated when you pay – but do make sure that this is the case.

Clothes
First of all, if you are going to be doing a lot of travelling or taking part in an expedition, take soft kit bags, rucksacks, etc rather than suitcases – they are much easier to heave around and stand up better to rough handling. Find out what the weather is going to be like where you are going and take cool or warm clothes accordingly. If you are heading for a hot country do take pure cotton clothes rather than synthetic – they are so much cooler. Ditto with shoes – any kind of plastic footwear is hopeless. Long sleeves and headgear will protect you against the sun until you are acclimatised.

Don't try and pack too much – you are the one who will be carrying it!

When you get there
Don't forget that you are a visitor in someone else's country and are expected to obey the laws of their land and conform to their customs, even though they may seem strange to you. For instance, in some countries girls are expected to wear skirts or keep their arms covered, alcohol is strictly forbidden in some Muslim countries, such as Saudi Arabia, and so on.

Check on the dates of public holidays and opening days for shops, museums, etc, as places such as banks have a disconcerting habit of being shut when you least expect it. Make sure that you have your home address and telephone number in this country in a safe place, like your wallet, and if you are staying in an hotel arrange to keep your passport and valuables in their safe.

Each capital city contains a British Embassy, and each major city a British Consul. They are *not* there for tourists or student travellers, but they will not turn you away in a real emergency.

Miscellaneous items to take
- A phrase book of the relevant language.
- A camera – check that you have enough batteries for the flash
- A torch plus spare batteries.
- A universal bath plug (to fit any size).
- A universal electric adaptor to fit different electrical systems.
- Small presents, especially cigarettes or sweets to give to people on your journey. They may generate good will when you have need of it.
- Sun tan preparations are not just for vanity – they can prevent serious burns, rashes and even illness if you are going to a hot country. Get a high protection number – an eight or a nine – to start with if you have not been used to the sun. Take a sun hat.

Visas

A number of countries now require all visitors to have visas, and you must check this before you go. If you are going with a tour operator, they will let you know what is required, and sometimes even get your visa for you, but if you are travelling independently, get hold of a copy of *ABC Guide to International Travel* – any good travel agent will have one. This is a magazine, constantly updated, which covers travel to every country in the world, and provides information on passport and visa requirements, journey times, addresses of British Consuls abroad, currencies, customs requirements and much more. Here is a brief summary, for British passport holders, of countries that do or do not require a visa. If you have difficulty getting a visa, contact Blair Consular Services Ltd, 10 Fairfield Avenue, Staines, Middlesex (0784 54952) who will be able to help you. The cost of a visa varies from country to country.

VISA REQUIRED

Afghanistan	Ethiopia	Philippines
Albania	Germany (East)	Poland
Argentina	Ghana	Romania
Australia	Hungary	Ruanda
Bangladesh	India	Saudi Arabia
Bulgaria	Iran	Sri Lanka
Burma	Iraq	Sudan
Burundi	Jordan	Tanzania
Chad	Liberia	Thailand
China	Mongolia	Uganda
Cuba	Mozambique	USA
Czechoslovakia	Nepal	USSR
Egypt	Nigeria	

NO VISA REQUIRED

Algeria	Greece	Pakistan
Austria	Hong Kong	Peru
Bahamas	Iceland	Seychelles
Barbados	Israel	Singapore
Belgium	Italy	Spain
Bolivia	Japan	Sweden
Botswana	Kenya	Tunisia
Brazil	Malaysia	Turkey
Chile	Mexico	Yugoslavia
Finland	Morocco	Zambia
France	New Zealand	Zimbabwe
Germany (West)		

Voluntary Service

The following description of one person working in India for Mother Teresa shows what an incredible experience volunteer work can be. We hope it will inspire you – not put you off! Immediately after, we list in alphabetical order organisations involved in volunteer work.

No words are sufficient to convey my feelings of complete solitude on that first night in a dingy hotel with no working electricity, candles, rats omnipresent and peculiar hotel employees, mostly young, one of whom, a boy of about eight, repeatedly came laughing into my dormitory and offering everyone tea. . . .

Calcutta is a city of staggering dimensions: there I glimpsed utter squalor, soul-stirring beauty, unbearable noise, sweet peace of mind. I came up against a previously unrealised streak of rabid intolerance which surged up inside me during the interminable waits for train tickets and the constant parryings of beggars with my conscience. I saw streets full of energetic human beings radiating the sweetest smiles full of pure happiness shining through threadbare costumes and slender frames. It is impossible to try to communicate the emotions felt in the teeming capital city of Indian art, culture and politics. . . .

Among the several homes in Calcutta of the Missionaries of Charity, founded by Mother Teresa, the first and dearest to nuns, patients, volunteers and all commentators on her work is Kalighat, the official name of which is Nirmal Hriday – Place of the Immaculate Heart. The sister in charge is Sister Luke – a woman who possesses so many different qualities at once that she would be larger than life were it not for the quality which pervades the human operations of the entire Order of Missionaries of Charity: modesty and simplicity. She is truly a mother to everyone at Kalighat – sisters, volunteers and patients alike; it is impossible to associate the latter with the pictures we've all seen in newspapers, books and magazines – of people in the Third World dying from malnutrition. They are just like the images we see in pictures, but an image come alive is a different phenomenon. Before my eyes I became aware of these people as living human beings and then witnessed them dying. . . .

Every evening at six o'clock I would emerge from the building into the milling crowds feeling slightly sick and very exhausted and wind down drinking a revolting, sweet tea from a filthy little glass sitting on a wooden bench with one or two of the other volunteers and in this state of mental exhaustion we absorbed the energy of the crowds of cheerful and life-giving people before our eyes, constantly joking and bantering amongst themselves and laughing behind our backs in a shy unmalicious way. So I imagined myself to be slowly 'discovering India'.

• Camp America

37 Queen's Gate, London SW7 5HR (01-589 3223)

Camp America sponsor young people (but you must be a student aged 18 or over) to find places for them in children's summer camps in the United States. (The word 'camps' does not have anything to do with canvas, by the way: these are permanent holiday centres for children spread across the length and breadth of the country.) Volunteers (if selected) will be working with the children, supervising them and helping in the running of the camp, as well as providing instruction in the various sports such as riding, canoeing, swimming, tennis and all the other activities. The camps run for nine weeks, but the volunteers stay in America for three months, which gives them three weeks to do some independent travelling around the country. Your return fare, accommodation, food and some pocket money will be provided, but you will need to bring some extra money of your own. The scheme is hard work but is a wonderful way to visit a great country.

• Community Service Volunteers

237 Pentonville Road, London N1 9NJ (01-278 6601)

CSV was set up by Alec Dickson, who also founded VSO (Voluntary Services Overseas). It welcomes everyone who really wants to help the community and who can offer from four months to a year's work. Projects include working in youth custody centres, probation hostels, night shelters for the homeless, organising young people as volunteers, helping with adventure playgrounds, and many more. Volunteers receive full board and lodging (if they are working away from home) and pocket money of about £15 a week.

• Concordia

(Youth Service Volunteers Ltd), 8 Brunswick Place, Hove
BN3 1ET (0273 772086)
Write to them for an information sheet giving details of voluntary
work in Europe from June to September. The kind of work they can
offer includes digging roads, forestry, archaeological work or helping in children's camps. There is also a section on paid work abroad.

• Gap Activity Projects (GAP) Ltd

7 Kings Road, Reading RG1 3AA (0734 594 91415)
Gap is a non-profit making charity which places school leavers
abroad, in countries such as Australia, Israel, India, the United
States, Egypt and so on for periods of time ranging from six months
to a year. Over 180 schools subscribe to the scheme, but if yours
does not, you may still apply as an individual and take out your own
subscription.
If you would like to be considered as a volunteer you should apply
as early in the year as possible, and you will then be interviewed at
Reading and your school asked to provide a report in order to assess
your possible reactions to stress and loneliness. It is important for
everyone, especially you, to make sure that you will be able to cope
in a strange country on your own, living and working in very
unfamiliar conditions. If you feel you can handle all this, then the
time spent will be very rewarding, in giving you a wider outlook, and
a chance to experience an entirely different culture and make lots of
new friends.
If you are selected you will be expected to pay your fare both
ways, so you will need to find time before you go to raise the money
for this, as well as paying your own insurance and administrative
costs. (Have a look at pages 131–132 for some ideas on how to raise
the money you will need.) Once you have arrived in the country,
your food and accommodation will be paid for, and usually you will
be provided with some pocket money, but you will need to take
some more money with you, particularly if you are combining your
Gap project with some extra travel, as most people try to do.

• The Institute of Cultural Affairs

277 St Ann's Road, London N15 5RG (01-802 2848)
The Institute sends volunteers to rural self-help projects
throughout the Third World. It runs two programmes, one is a

Voluntary Service Programme (VSP) in which volunteers are sent overseas to India, Zambia, Kenya, Peru, Brazil or the Philippines. The other programme is called Village Volunteer Programme for Africa. In both schemes you will work in rural village settings as members of a permanent team to initiate new schemes such as irrigation, community industries, women's health education and so on.

Prospective volunteers (who must be aged 17 or over) are invited to attend a Volunteer Orientation Weekend. Volunteers are shown, in a very practical way, how they will participate and what will be expected of them. Information about possible placements will be available, as will returned volunteers to talk about their experiences. The minimum posting is for nine months, following a four-week preparation course in London. Volunteers are expected to pay their own fares, but the Institute will give them help and advice on how to raise the necessary funds.

• International Voluntary Service
Ceresole House, 53 Regent Road, Leicester LE1 6YL (0533 541862)

To take part in a IVS scheme volunteers must have reached the age of 18 and they are expected to have had some previous experience of voluntary community work in this country. IVS run international work camps in Eastern and Western Europe, and different parts of Africa. Volunteers may be allocated to manual projects such as building and farming work, or social work with children or disabled people. The work camps usually last from two to four weeks and run from late June to early September. Volunteers are usually expected to pay their own fares, but the cost of board and lodging is provided.

IVS also run work camps in the UK in which volunteers might be asked to help with conservation, inner-city play schemes, children's holidays, disabled people and other forms of community help. The terms for volunteers are the same as for the international work camps. Write to the above address, stating which form of work particularly interests you.

• Kibbutz Representative
1A Accommodation Road, London NW11 (01-485 9235)

A kibbutz (plural kibbutzim) is a working commune in Israel which is largely self-sufficient, with its own social and cultural life, and where work is shared on an equal basis. Visitors must be prepared to stay at least five weeks, to work an eight-hour day, six days a week on whatever project they are given, whether to do with farming, domestic work or childcare. In return they live as one of the community and share its close knit social life. Tough but rewarding. Volunteers pay their own fares, and the kibbutz provides food and accommodation, with a little pocket money. Write to the above address for an application form and more information. You will then be interviewed before being offered a place on a kibbutz. (You don't need to be Jewish.)

● The Project Trust
Breacachadh Castle, Isle of Coll, Argyll, Scotland PA78 6TB (087 93 357/444)

The Trust aims to give young people the opportunity to live and work abroad for a year, especially in the Third World countries such as Zimbabwe, Kenya, Sri Lanka, and so on. Volunteers should be school leavers aged between 17 and 19 and prepared to commit a full year to the project; in addition they will be expected to raise £1,400 towards their own costs. Hard but rewarding work, and a chance to gain some understanding of life in a totally different culture.

● Toc H Headquarters
1 Forest Close, Wendover, Aylesbury, Bucks HP22 6BT (0296 623911)

One of Toc H's functions is running summer camps in the UK for children and the disabled. It needs volunteers to help with these and also with conservation work. They publish a free leaflet giving details of all their schemes – write for a copy to the above address.

● World Community Development Service
27 Montague Road, Botley, Oxford OX2 9AH (90865 725607)

The WCDS runs a Junior Volunteers Scheme which provides young people (up to 40 at any one time) with voluntary work in India, Sri Lanka and Kenya.

Conservation Work

These are mainly working holidays in which volunteers spend a week or more helping on restoration projects. For instance they may be asked to help on archaeological digs, restore meadowland, clear streams and ponds, repair cathedrals, look after nature reserves and other schemes involving a lot of hard but satisfying work. On page 55 we also list conservation organisations, such as the Friends of the Earth or the Young People's Trust for Endangered Species. If you are interested in the long-term ideals of conservation you may like to join one of these, and they will be able to provide you with more ideas on practical conservation.

• Archaeology
Archaeology Abroad, 31–34 Gordon Square, London WC1 (inquiries by letter only). If you have already had some practical archaeological experience you could find further opportunities abroad by contacting the above address. They are in touch with the British archaeological schools and institutes, as well as societies in Egypt, Libya and so on. Obviously they mainly want qualified helpers, but there are some vacancies for school leavers, especially in France. You can get a copy of the annual *Archaeology Abroad* from the above address, for more details. You would pay your own fare and any extra costs, but board and lodging are usually provided.

The Council for British Archaeology, 112 Kensington Road, London SE11 6RE (01-582 0494), provide details of courses, study tours and digs in this country. Again, some experience is helpful. They publish *British Archaeological News* (nine issues a year on subscription), which contains details of digs around the country.

• Bird Reserves
The Royal Society for the Protection of Birds, The Lodge, Sandy, Bedfordshire SG19 2DL (0767 80551). The Society has over 100 reserves in the UK where birds are protected and where the land and plant life has managed to provide a suitable habitat for wild birds. Most of the reserves have a permanent warden, and also some

permanent or temporary assistants. When you are 17 you can apply to be a voluntary warden for a minimum period of a week, but longer if possible. You will be helping with visitors, keeping records of bird sightings, and keeping the land clear, cutting reeds, thinning scrub and so on. Your accommodation will be provided but you supply your own food and pocket money. See also page 51 for details of the Young Ornithologists' Club.

● Other Projects

British Trust for Conservation Volunteers, 36 St Mary's Street, Wallingford, Oxon (0491 39766). The British Trust for Conservation Volunteers has about 400 sites around the country which it is working on, and one of its recent projects has been making a wildlife reserve out of a derelict area in the gardens of Lambeth Palace, London. They need volunteers from 16 years upwards for a week's stay. Volunteers do not need special skills, just lots of enthusiasm. There are over 300 local groups, so contact the headquarters (address above) for the address of your regional area office.

Cathedral Camps, Manor House, High Birstwitt, Harrogate, North Yorkshire HG3 2LG. Cathedral camps are looking for volunteers over 16 to help restore cathedrals. The work involved can be cleaning the stonework, indoors and out, painting or helping professional craftsmen. Volunteers are asked to stay for a week and pay £20 towards accommodation, which is fairly simple.

National Trust Acorn Camps, The National Trust, 42 Queen Anne's Gate, London SW1 (01-222 9251). The National Trust runs Acorn Camps and Young National Trust Groups, PO Box 12, Westbury, Wiltshire. The objects of Acorn Camps are to achieve vital jobs of conservation and to give volunteers a chance to join in a rewarding activity in some of the Trust's most exciting countryside. Volunteers, who must be 16 or over, pay part of their costs (about £14 a week) and travelling expenses. Write for the annual Acorn Camp programme which lists projects through the country.

Thistle Camps, Youth in Trust, The National Trust for Scotland, 5 Charlotte Square, Edinburgh EH2 4DU. Thistle Camps undertake voluntary restoration projects in Scotland. The camps last for one week, except for the Fair Isle Camp which is for two weeks. Volunteers, who must be at least 16 years old, make a contribution of about £12 towards the week's expenses.

Expeditions

The activities in this section do not come under the heading of work, but they could hardly be called holidays either. They are strenuous and demanding and if you enjoy a challenge you will find them immensely rewarding.

One possible snag is that they will cost you money, and unlike voluntary service, you will not receive free board and lodging. In a few cases (Sail Training Association and Operation Raleigh, for instance) it might be appropriate to apply for a grant – consult your local authority or have a look in your public library at a large volume called *Directory of Grant Producing Trusts*, which gives details of bodies who might be prepared to give money to worthwhile projects. Otherwise, have a look at some of our fund-raising ideas on pages 131–132.

• British Schools Exploring Society

The Royal Geographical Society, 1 Kensington Gore, London SW7 2AR (01-584 0710)

If you are aged between 16½ and 20 and like the idea of adventure and exploration why not apply to the Society for an opportunity to take part in one of their expeditions? Young people still at school, school leavers, those between school and further education as well as those in apprenticeships on day-release schemes or on full-time training, such as nursing, police cadets, etc are all eligible to apply. There are also some places for the disabled young person.

If you are selected, and there is great competition for each place, you will undergo an experience that previous expeditioners have described as a turning point in their lives. The expedition will test your powers of leadership, endurance and initiative, and is certainly not a holiday. Until recently the Society concentrated on polar and cold weather exploration but it has now introduced expeditions to hot climates, and in 1987 will visit Papua New Guinea as well as the Arctic and 1988 will see an expedition to North West India. To make things more difficult you will be expected to raise most of your share of the cost of the expedition yourself – about £1,500 at the present time – although the Society can help out when essential.

• Operation Raleigh

CHQ, Alpha Place, Flood Street, London SW3 5SZ (01-351 7541)

Operation Raleigh is a marathon four-year expedition organised by the Scientific Exploration Society and supported by the Explorers' Club. It offers places to 4,000 young people between the ages of 17 and 23 from all over the world to join over 40 different expeditions. Successful applicants, called Venturers, will serve in the field for about three months. Their project will involve them in scientific or community work in a foreign country, sometimes in very arduous conditions. They might, for instance, collect data on tropical rain forests, coral reefs or threatened species, to name but a few of the planned projects. There are two ships, the Flagship *Sir Walter Raleigh*, the operation headquarters, and the sailing ship *Zebu* on which volunteers will receive navigation instruction and radio training as she sails around the world.

If you wish to be considered as a volunteer, go to the nearest branch of the Trustee Savings Bank, as they hold the application forms. Volunteers are selected at one of 48 weekends each year which are great fun and very stimulating, even if exhausting. Even if you are not selected as a volunteer you will receive a certificate and will be given comprehensive information about the many youth and adventure organisations throughout the country.

• Outward Bound Trust

Chestnut Field, Regent Place, Rugby CV21 2PJ (0788 60423/5)

Outward Bound emphasises team work and leadership, planning and organisation, and aims to increase self-confidence and self-awareness in the individual. They do a 21-day course for the 16 to 20-year-olds (but see page 197 for course for younger groups), which includes rugged activities such as rock climbing, orienteering, canoeing and so on, as well as discussions and reviews, which are all part of the course. There are five Outward Bound centres (two in Wales, two in the Lake District and one in Scotland). There is also a City Challenge course, again lasting 21 days, in which volunteers look after handicapped children, the old, or the deprived, in city centres. Write to the address above for full details on all these courses.

• Sail Training Association (STA)

2A The Hard, Portsmouth PO1 3PT (0705 832055)

Young people from 16 upwards take part in a two-week cruise on a sailing ship, which combines a very exciting holiday with the opportunity to learn about ships and sailing, and to cope with difficulties and adventure. More details on page 204.

Overland and Trekking

At this stage in your life it may well be the moment to make time for an adventure holiday or overland expedition that you might never have the chance or the freedom to undertake again. The three great continents of Asia, Africa and North America are now not too far away for young people with determination and a sense of adventure. Across Asia to Katmandu or China, across Africa to Kenya or Cape Town, or to Peru and the Andes – the very names are enough to stir the imagination. Have a look at our book list – page 244 – the guides published the Lonely Planet and Vacation Work are specially written for travellers planning distant trips.

You do not have to spend months on an expedition if time is short – many of the trips are for two to three weeks, although others may be longer, and if you set up your own, then obviously it is up to you.

We can give only a small selection of adventure holidays here; but any good travel agent will put you in touch with other organisations that run overland trips or trekking expeditions. The book *Adventure Holidays* (published by Vacation Work, 9 Park End Street, Oxford) also provides plenty of information on various holidays with a difference. The YHA (Youth Hostels Association) has a free booklet called *Take Off* on holidays abroad. Write to them for a copy at 14 Southampton Street, London WC2E 7HY (01-240 5236). They organise adventure trips, activity holidays, safaris, and so on.

The costs of most overland trips are relatively low because transport, often in four-wheel drive trucks, is fairly basic, and accommodation is equally so, usually in tents or simple hotels. It must be admitted that the words 'comfort' or 'luxury' do not make much of an appearance in any of the brochures describing overland expeditions, but that is not really the purpose of the trip: roughing it, at least to an extent, is part of the adventure, as is learning to cope with difficult conditions – extreme heat or cold, disagreeable insects, unfamiliar food, strange surroundings.

Do go well prepared as to clothes, medicines and any equipment that you may need. If you are going with a travel organisation, they will give you all the necessary information about visas, injections, money and so on. If you are travelling independently have a look at the checklist (page 221) of what you will need. Get hold, too, of a copy of *The Traveller's Handbook*, published by Wexas (full details

on page 237), which is full of useful information for people planning to organise expeditions abroad.

The Dales Centre, Grassington, Near Skipton, North Yorkshire (0756 752757). The Centre organises three-week hiking holidays in California, beginning in San Francisco and including the Yosemite National Park, Death Valley and the Grand Canyon. No previous experience is needed, and all ages are accepted. Accommodation is in motels and cabins, and the cost is £1,500, which includes all expenses such as air fare, transport, and accommodation.

Explore Worldwide, Dept AH, 7 High Street, Aldershot, Hants GU11 1BH (0252 319448). A company that runs two- and three-week trips to countries such as Morocco, Algeria, Turkey, Egypt, India, Mexico, Russia, Peru and Bolivia using vehicles that vary from small buses to four-wheel drive trucks. Accommodation is either camping or in small hotels, and prices vary from £300 to £900. The minimum age is 18.

French Government Tourist Office, 178 Piccadilly, London W1V 0AL (01-499 6911). If you are planning a trip to France for a group of young people write to the address above for a list of and information on youth centres specialising in adventure pursuits (canoeing, skiing, mountaineering, sailing, and water sports).

Guerba Expeditions Ltd, Westfield House, Westbury, Wiltshire BA13 3EP (0380 830476). Overland expeditions to Africa using four-wheel drive trucks. Each trip includes a crew of three: a leader/driver, a second driver and a cook, and all camping equipment is included. The expeditions can last from two weeks to 40 weeks. Minimum age is 17.

Long Haul Expeditions, Tamar Travel Agents Ltd, 56 Bohun Grove, East Barnet, Herts EN4 8UB (01-440 1582). Long Haul trips last five months, and start in October, November or January. The route covers most of Africa: Tunisia, Algeria, Niger, Upper Volta, Togo, Nigeria, Zaïre, Ruanda, Tanzania and Kenya – 14,000 miles in all. During the journey there will be stops for two-day canoeing trips, climbing Mount Kilimanjaro, snorkelling off the beaches of Kenya and visiting game parks. This would really be the trip of a lifetime. Travellers camp, and use their own sleeping bags – all other equipment is provided. They take turns cooking and help with daily chores. It costs £900 plus extra costs of about £250 to include return flight, insurance, visas and food. Minimum age is 18.

Trailfinders, 42–48 Earl's Court Road, London W8 6EJ (01-937 9631). Trailfinders arrange three-week trips to various parts of Asia: one includes Japan, South Korea, Taiwan and Hong Kong, another covers Thailand, and a third begins in Bangkok and goes through Malaysia, Singapore, Indonesia and Bali. Transport is by air and overland, mostly by public transport. Costs vary from £200 to £600, but this does not include the return flight to Asia, which Trailfinders can also arrange for you.

Wexas International, 45 Brompton Road, Knightsbridge, London SW3 1DE (for general inquiries: 01-589 3315). If you or your family are planning to do a lot of travelling abroad, it would be worth your while to join Wexas. Membership costs £17.58 for an individual or £21.45 for a family. Membership benefits include the lowest possible price on scheduled airways, a wide range of world-wide trips, special travel insurance plus a subscription to *Traveller* magazine and a free copy of the 864-page *Traveller's Handbook*, with everything you need to know about long-haul travel.

Wexas claim that they provide trips for 'unpackaged people' and are currently offering 46 different holidays to 48 countries. These include an Indian Railway Tour, a Himalayan adventure, a trek to the Peruvian Andes or Little Tibet, a Botswana or Serengeti Safari, a Nile Valley Explorer and many others. Costs are kept as low as possible, depending partly on the accommodation on the various trips, which varies from comfortable hotels to camping in tents. No trip requires specialist skills, but most of them involve a lot of walking (in places where cars can't reach) so a good standard of physical fitness is required, plus a willingness to fit in with other members of the group. But Wexas emphasise that although you travel in a group, to take full advantage of cheap rates, you retain your own freedom to a great degree and combine the advantages of being with other people and keeping your own independence.

Cheap Travel

Cheap air fares are a constantly changing scene and it is impossible to lay down any strict guidelines or give an accurate price guide. It is perfectly possible, however, with a little research, to find fares that are half the price or less of scheduled air fares, whether your destination is Europe or further afield. For up-to-date information the best course is to get hold of copies of the magazines *Time Out*, *City Limits* or *Executive Travel*. These are all available from newsagents, although you might have to order them if you live outside London. At the back of the magazines are advertisements for cut-price fares to anywhere that you can think of (plus a few more): Rome, Naples, Madrid, Hong Kong, Bangkok, Calcutta, New York and so on. In addition, if you live in London, get hold of a free handout magazine written by Australians in London, called *Lam*, which lists cheap travel firms. Alternatively take a walk down the Earl's Court Road, where you will be spoilt for choice as every second shop is a travel agent.

   This is only a very short selection of travel agents or firms who specialise in various kinds of cheap air travel around the world, but as we have said, there are plenty more and don't forget that names and prices are changing all the time:

Apex Travel, 245 Oxford Street, London W1 (01-437 9561/2/3).

CTS London, 33 Windmill Street, London W1 (01-636 5915/6).

Discount Ticket Centre, 71 Praed Street, London W2 1NT (01-262 2616).

Discount Travel Centre, 216 Earl's Court Road, London SW5 (01-370 1146).

London Student Travel, 52 Grosvenor Gardens, London SW1 (01-730 9476/8111/3402).

STA Travel, 74 Old Brompton Road, London SW7 3LQ, *and* 117 Euston Road, London NW1 2SX (European Bookings – 01-581 8233; Intercontinental Bookings – 01-581 1022).

Trailfinders Travel Centre, 42–48 Earl's Court Road, London W8 6EJ (01-937 5400).

World Wide Flights, 401 Radnor House, 93 Regent Street, London W1 (01-439 6561).

Job Experience

Finding a job is no longer the automatically easy process it once was, and one of the best ways of being a successful applicant for a particular job is being able to offer your possible future employer some examples of previous job experience. You might have got a job in the holidays during your sixth-form year, or you might choose to take a few weeks or months after leaving school to earn some money and gain valuable experience at the same time. Even temporary jobs such as doing a paper round or being a Saturday girl/boy in a shop or supermarket can teach you a lot (if only about human nature!), but what we discuss here is more the idea of job experience which will lead you eventually to a permanent career of your own choosing, rather than one you may have just fallen into, which may possibly be uncongenial to you.

Some schools have organised a system in which parents are invited to take part to provide work experience for the sixth form during their holidays. This is how it works: all the parents are sent a form asking them if their place of work or profession can offer any job opportunities for 16-, 17- or 18-year-olds for one week or possibly two months. For instance, a farmer might want help over the harvest or a pair of extra hands for feeding the animals, or a local newspaper writer or journalist might be able to offer some kind of cub reporting. Other ideas are working in the offices of a solicitor, an architect, an estate agent, and so on, or in a hospital, seeing nursing and medicine at first hand.

The sixth formers who have had the work experience are then expected to submit their reports, some of which will find their way into the school magazine. The reports are a valuable guide to the school as to the usefulness of the scheme, and are indeed part of the work experience. Parents who can offer some kind of job are asked to make sure that it involves real work, and doesn't leave the young person involved merely standing around as a useless observer.

If your school does not have such a work experience scheme operating already, why not bring it to their notice and see if you can get one started?

You might find, after a short stint in a particular job, that you like it and would like to follow it up. In that case the Index Scheme (see page 242), under which 'gap' year students are paid the going rate for the job that they do, will be very useful to you.

If you are going on to further education in a university or polytechnic, then you might choose work experience which will be related to the course you will be taking. An obvious example is foreign languages, even if you only want to back up your O and A level with practical experience. The only way to learn to speak a language is to live in the country, not with other English people and if possible to work while you are there. Have a look at our Exchange section on pages 212–217 for information about language courses, or think about *au pair* work living with a family, or hotel work, grape picking and so on. There are several organisations which may help you, especially *Jobs in the Alps*, *Canvas Holidays* and *Concordia* (see pages 227 and 240–1).

Living abroad can also be combined with a language or cultural course. The Sorbonne and the Alliance Française in Paris, for instance, offer French courses to foreign students, as do organisations such as the British Institute in Florence (in Italian, obviously!).

Work Abroad

There are lots of books to help you on this subject (see page 247). *Working Holidays* (published by the Central Bureau) is especially useful on ideas for grape picking, farmwork, working on a kibbutz or as an *au pair*. Many of the activity holiday centres listed in Chapter 7 require help in the summer time for young volunteers, either school leavers or students. You need to offer some kind of qualification or experience to be taken on as an instructor in the various activities (canoeing, sailing, pony trekking, judo, fencing and so on) but there are also opportunities for unskilled work. You will receive food and accommodation and a small wage. If you enjoy working with children, as well as the outdoor life, you will find it stimulating and rewarding. Below are the addresses of two of the organisations who specially welcome volunteer helpers, but see pages 226–232 for the addresses of many others.

Canvas Holidays Ltd, Bull Plain, Hertford, Hertfordshire SG14 1DY (0992 59933). Canvas Holidays is an organisation which provides complete camping facilities on sites in Europe, mostly in France, but also in Germany, Spain, Italy, Switzerland and Austria. The facilities include fully equipped tents, which campers do not even have to put up themselves (this can be quite a bonus for the weary traveller!).

Vacancies exist on the camp sites for young workers from April until the end of July. The job includes putting up the tents (this can be very hard work), looking after the equipment and coping with day-to-day problems of the campers. On some sites there is a job as children's courier, concerned specifically with looking after the children of the holidaymakers. Accommodation (in tents), fares and insurance are paid for, and a wage of approximately £50 per week is paid. Interviews start in November and can be arranged around the country – obviously it is a great advantage to be able to speak the language of the country.

Grape Picking: Concordia (Youth Service Volunteers) Ltd, 8 Brunswick Place, Hove BN3 1ET (0723 772086). If you would like to go grape picking in France or Germany, Concordia will help to arrange it for you. The grape harvest starts at the end of September and lasts for two or three weeks. It is very hard work (you will need some sturdy rubber gloves!) with long hours and very simple living conditions, but plenty of free wine. Workers receive about £10 a day plus free board and lodging, but are expected to pay their own travelling expenses.

Concordia also runs fruit picking camps in the UK. Workers receive piece-rate wages as laid down by the Agricultural Wages Board, but have to pay a fee towards food and accommodation (which is usually basic). Write to the address above for more details.

Jobs in the Alps, PO Box 388, London SW1X 8LX. This is a private agency which sends boys and girls to work in Alpine resorts in

Switzerland. Most jobs are for the three to four months of the winter season (December to April), or the three months of the summer season (June to September). Most of the work is in hotels, with jobs such as waiters and waitresses, chambermaids, hall porters. There are also a few jobs available in sports shops, swimming pools or mountain restaurants. The work is hard – up to 50 hours a week – and the agency stresses that they are not amateur holiday jobs, and not a chance to take a free skiing holiday. A knowledge of a foreign language, especially German, would be a bonus, and would give you a chance of a more interesting job. Board and lodging are provided and pay is around £75 a week. Some jobs also earn good tips and most of them allow you reduced rates on ski lifts. Interviews for winter jobs are held by the end of September and for summer jobs by the end of April.

Jobs in the Alps will also arrange *au pair* postings in Switzerland. Write to them for more details.

PGL Young Adventure Limited, 2–5 Market Place, Ross on Wye, Herefordshire HR9 7AH (0989 65556). PGL runs holiday centres (residential and day camps) in sites throughout the UK, France and Holland. They provide a large range of activities and sports and have a very high ratio of helpers/holidaymakers. They provide helpers with board and lodging, and a basic wage which rises after six and then ten weeks' service.

Work in this Country

• The Index Scheme

Index Office, Robert Hyde House, 48 Bryanston Square, London W1H 7LN

The Index scheme was set up by a group of industrialists and careers staff at various schools. It enables boys and girls who are going on to university to find jobs in major industrial and commercial companies for six months during their 'gap' year. There are about a 100 places available each year, so obviously there is a lot of competition for each place. Schools recommend suitable sixth formers to the organisers of Index, who then put forward two or three candidates for each company to select the one or ones that they want. The successful candidate is expected to do a full job of work and earn his/her place. It is not simply work experience, but more of a concentrated training scheme as well as an opportunity to find out how industry works, what skills are required in management, and what variety of jobs are available. There should be plenty of opportunity to see a wide range of the company's activities. Pay is adequate but not excessive – usually at the trainee rate.

Applications should be sent in not later than the beginning of May, and the jobs begin either in October or January for a six-month period.

• YMCA National Centres
1. Fairthorne Manor, Curdridge, Southampton SO3 2GH (04892 5228)
2. Lakeside, Ulverston, Cumbria LA12 8BD (0448 31758)

The YMCA uses these centres to run residential courses on education and youth training, as well as adventure holidays and activity camps. During the summer they require volunteer helpers (school leavers and students), for a minimum of three to six weeks, to act as group leaders with the young campers, and to help instruct them in canoeing, sailing, swimming, climbing and so on. The YMCA will help pay train fares, and will provide full board and lodging, together with a little pocket money.

The following is a list of some useful addresses for those looking for job experience in banks, insurance, computers, industry, etc in the UK. Have a look at *Jobs in the Gap Year* (full details on page 245) which gives more useful addresses.

Barclays Bank Ltd, Fleetway House, 25 Farringdon Street, London EC4A 4LP (01-248 1234). The bank may be willing to offer you employment on general duties in a branch near your home if you are willing to work for at least one month and have a genuine interest in banking.

The Boots Company Ltd, Employment Manager, Nottingham NG2 3AA. Boots is prepared to offer jobs to school leavers with A levels in chemistry, physics or biology, especially those interested in laboratory work or pharmacy. They would like you to be able to spend up to twelve months working for them to make it worth their while employing you.

British Broadcasting Corporation, Engineering Recruitment Officer, Broadcasting House, London W1A 1AA (01-580 4468). Applicants must be going on to take a degree with a high electronics content. The BBC can offer such an applicant a year's training in the Research Department or in engineering design.

IBM United Kingdom Ltd, Graduate Recruitment Department, PO Box 41, North Harbour, Portsmouth PO6 3AU. IBM has a small number of vacancies for school leavers going on to higher education. The minimum work period is five months, and involves programming, computer operating, marketing and other administrative duties. If you are interested in computers or planning to make a career in them, this would be of great relevance to you.

Imperial Chemical Industries plc, Group Personnel Department (Recruitment Section), PO Box 6, Bessemer Road, Welwyn Garden City, Hertfordshire AL7 1HD. ICI has openings for pre-university school leavers in laboratory work or engineering in several of its departments. Candidates should have three relevant A levels and be prepared to work for six months to a year.

ICI Mond Division (Imperial Chemical Industries plc, Personnel Department, Mond Division, PO Box 13, The Heath, Runcorn, Cheshire WA7 4QF), is willing to offer several places each year to school leavers with good A levels who are waiting to go on to higher education. They will expect you to work for between six to twelve months, mainly in commercial and information technology departments.

Provident Life Association Ltd, Provident Way, Basingstoke, Hampshire RG21 2SZ (0256 470707). This insurance company will sometimes offer temporary jobs to pre-university students, but the jobs will obviously vary a great deal. Contact the address above for details.

Unilever UK Holdings, Personnel Officer, Lever Brothers Ltd, Lever House, 3 St James Road, Kingston upon Thames, Surrey KT1 2BA (01-549 1422). Unilever has companies throughout the country, so might be able to offer you something near where you live.

Useful Reading

If you are keen to take a break in your Gap year, but are not quite sure what sort of scheme or project you are looking for, then your best bet would be to get hold of some of the publications we list below and study them. As you will see, they cover volunteer work, working holidays, jobs abroad or in this country, as well as adventure holidays. Your school or library may have copies of these books already, if not, persuade them to invest in at least some of them. In particular, there are two publishing firms that specialise in this area:

Vacation Work, 9 Park End Street, Oxford (0865 241978), offers the most comprehensive list of travel and work guides, and we have included many of their books below.

The Lonely Planet firm of publishers operates from Australia, but all their books are readily available from good book shops over here. They specialise in cheap worldwide guides, especially in Asia and other far-flung places.

NB   In the following list, when we mention more than one book by the same publishing firm, the address will only be given in the first instance.

General books for the Gap year
Start off with the one that is free, which is a booklet of useful notes from the Information Department, National Council for Voluntary Organisations, 26 Bedford Square, London WC1 (01-636 4055).

A Year Off . . . A Year On?, published by CRAC (Cambridge Research and Advisory Centre) Publications, Hobsons, Bateman Street, Cambridge. Details of voluntary service in UK and abroad, adventure holidays, language courses, *au pair* and paying guest agencies and so on.

Gap Activity Projects Brochure, published by Gap Ltd, 7 Kings Road, Reading, Berks RG1 3AA (0734 594914/5). A wide variety of schemes are run (see also page 229).

Jobs in the Gap Year, published by the Independent Schools Careers Organisation, 12a–18a Princess Way, Camberley, Surrey GU15 3SP. Gives the full range of activities available to those thinking of a Gap year: voluntary work, study courses, office work, pre-university work in engineering/science, attachment to the armed forces, expeditions, work in holiday centres, the Index and Gap schemes, plus some student reports on their Gap-year experience.

Time Between, CRAC publications, address as above. What to do in a Gap year.

Voluntary Work
The International Directory of Voluntary Work by Gillian Nineham and David Woodworth, Vacation Work, 9 Park End Street, Oxford, £6.50.

The following two booklets list organisations and addresses for both voluntary work or jobs which will help you find a particular project to interest you:
Jobs Before Oxbridge, published by Oxford University Careers Service.
Jobs Before Cambridge, published by Cambridge University Careers Service.

Project Trust, published by Project Trust, Breacachadh Castle, Isle of Coll, Argyll PA78 6TB. A guide to voluntary projects offered by this organisation, see also page 231.

Sparetime, Sharetime: a guide to voluntary youth opportunities (free, but send postage), published by the National Youth Bureau, 17–23 Albion Street, Leicester LE1 6GD (0533 554775). Details on a wide range of projects for young people. Describes the projects and gives information on food, accommodation, age limits and so on.

The following two books deal specifically with volunteer jobs abroad:
Kibbutz Volunteer, Vacation Work, £3.95. Describes work available on a kibbutz (a commune for working and living) all year round for periods of 5 weeks upwards.
Volunteer Work Abroad, compiled by Hilary Sewell, published by the Central Bureau, Seymour Mews House, London W1H 9PE (01-486 5101), £3. Details of more than 100 organisations which run community service schemes in over 150 countries.

Jobs
In Britain:
The 'Index' Scheme, published by Index Office, Robert Hyde House, 48 Bryanston Square, London W1H 7LN. A booklet describing this scheme, which provides work-experience jobs in industry, commerce and business (see also page 242).

Summer Jobs in Britain, Vacation Work, £3.95. Details of 30,000

jobs in Britain, arranged by countries, together with notes on applying for a job. Also includes a section on voluntary work.

Abroad:
Camp America, Department GP, Camp America, 37 Queen's
Gate, London SW7 5HR. Helping in summer camps in the States:
the jobs run from late June to September (see page 226 for more
details).

Canvas Holidays Brochure, Canvas Holidays Ltd, Bull Plain,
Hertford, Hertfordshire SG14 1DY. Tells you all about the job
opportunities in the camp sites that this firm runs.

Jobs in the Alps Brochure, published by Southern Publishing Co,
Argus House, 50 North Street, Brighton BN1 1RX.

Summer Employment Directory of the United States, Vacation
Work, £5.95. Details of 50,000 summer jobs, arranged in States,
plus how to apply for a job in the USA (with sample letter).

Summer Jobs Abroad, Vacation Work, £3.95. Details of 30,000
vacancies worldwide with notes on applying for a job, work permit
regulations and cheap travel facilities.

Working Holidays, published by the Central Bureau (address
above), offers jobs abroad as far afield as Australia, Canada, Fin-
land and the Faroes, £4. Gives details of useful addresses, travel
concessions, domestic work, farmwork, community work, work
camps, etc.

Working in Ski Resorts – Europe, Vacation Work, £4.95. Describes
how to find jobs such as chalet girl, disc-jockey, ski technician, snow
clearer and so on. Tells you either how to get work in advance or
find it on the spot.

Travel and Adventure Holidays

If you go to any good book shop you will find shelves full of advice
on budget travel worldwide, where to go, how to get there, where to
stay, cheap fares and so on. We list here some of the titles aimed
particularly at students, but there are masses more, and new titles
are being published all the time.

ABC Guide to International Travel, published by ABC Travel
Guides. A magazine issued quarterly containing invaluable information on travel requirements to every country in the world. Visas,
injections, currency, climate, public holidays, customs, addresses of

consulates – you will find this and much more, all of it regularly up-dated.

Adventure Holidays, Vacation Work. Lists thousands of adventure and activity holidays in Britain and 100 countries throughout the world, including canoeing, climbing, cycling, flying (parachuting, gliding, ballooning), overland trekking, sailing, scuba-diving, safari, windsurfing, land yachting, etc.

Cycle Touring in France, £4.95, published by Muller Blond and White. All you need to know about travelling around France on a bike, including cheap places to stay.

Europe: A Manual for Hitch Hikers, Vacation Work, £3.95. Provides a very detailed guide on hitch-hiking in each western European country.

Europe by Rail, £6.95, published by Michael Müller Publications. A guide to European countries, and how to get there by train.

North East Asia on a Shoestring, The Lonely Planet, £5.95, covering China, Hong Kong, Japan, etc.

A Travel Survival Kit to Burma, The Lonely Planet, £4.95.
The Lonely Planet have also published travel survival kits to Canada, China, India, Mexico, New Zealand, Pakistan, Tibet and other countries.

South America on a Shoestring, The Lonely Planet, £6.95.

South East Asia on a Shoestring, The Lonely Planet, £5.95, covering Burma, Indonesia, Thailand, the Philippines, etc.

Travellers' Survival Kit, Vacation Work, £5.95. A country-by-country guide to each European country, including travel, hitch-hiking, accommodation, etc.

Travellers' Survival Kit to the East, Vacation Work, £4.95. A similar guide to countries east of Turkey.

Raising Money
Directory of Grant Producing Trusts. This is a very large volume, so go to a public reference library to consult it. It gives details of organisations prepared to give grants to people wanting to take part in worthwhile projects.

NOTES FOR
WORKING MOTHERS

Working mothers have always had a hard time during school holidays in getting their children looked after and kept occupied during the day. Things are now beginning to change, although very slowly, as more people realise that it is essential to provide childcare during the holidays and after school as well, and not to allow children to roam the streets on their own. There are two organisations which should be able to help you:

The National Out of School Alliance, Oxford House, Derbyshire Street, Bethnal Green Road, London E2 6HG (01-739 4787). An organisation set up in 1981 to help tackle the problem of latchkey children, as well as children whose mothers have to work during the holidays. Their aim is to provide schemes whereby children are picked up from school and taken to a safe play area or play centre where they stay until collected by their parents. During the holidays the children can spend all day at the centre where they are fed, cared for, and kept occupied and amused until the evening.

The Alliance is very keen for new members (membership for individuals is £5) to help in setting up out-of-school schemes on their own, and will give all the help and information needed. Two of their books include *Starting from Scratch*, which describes how to go about setting up such a scheme and *Finding the Money*, which tells you how to find it. A third publication, *Out of School in London*, is a very detailed directory of out-of-school groups in the Greater London area. Coverage around the country is still a bit patchy, but most major cities now have schemes, and new ones are constantly being set up. Contact the address above for news of groups near you.

The Alliance also provides an information service on childcare schemes in different areas, it carries out research into the quality of childcare and holiday schemes, runs conferences and training events to increase people's knowledge of the needs of school-age children and how to cater for them.

The Working Mothers' Association, 7 Spencer Walk, London SW15 1PL (01-228 3757 – Mon to Weds). The Association aims to provide a network of support groups for working parents throughout the country in which they can exchange information, meet other families and which will help them find good quality childcare in their area. There are now about 60 groups around the country in places such as Bath, Birmingham, Guildford and Glasgow, and new ones are springing up all the time – in fact the Association says that it has been nearly overwhelmed by the flood of inquiries and interest that it has received since starting up in 1985. They publish a booklet (£2 direct from the address above) called *The Working Mothers' Handbook* which is an invaluable guide to finding good childcare, as well as a leaflet *Setting up a Working Mothers' Group*. Membership of the Association costs £3 a year, which if you are a working parent is money very well spent. You will receive a quarterly newsletter, and be put in touch either with an existing group or with other working mothers in your area, perhaps with the idea of setting up a group of your own.

The Association can also provide you with details of other childcare organisations – of which we list a few below:

National Childcare Campaign, Wesley House, 70 Great Queen Street, London WC2B 5AY (01-405 5617). A campaign to provide comprehensive free childcare facilities funded by the State.

National Council of Voluntary Child Care Organisations, 8 Wakely Street, London EC1 (01-833 3319). Co-ordinates funding for childcare groups.

National Childminding Association, 13 London Road, Bromley, Kent BR1 1PQ (01-464 6164). Promotes the interests of childminders and tries to improve the quality of childcare by increasing resources and providing training schemes.

INDEX